From Widows
to Warriors

From Widows to Warriors

Women's Stories from the Old Testament

Lynn Japinga

WJK WESTMINSTER
JOHN KNOX PRESS
LOUISVILLE · KENTUCKY

First edition
Published by Westminster John Knox Press
Louisville, Kentucky

20 21 22 23 24 25 26 27 28 29—10 9 8 7 6 5 4 3 2 1

Book design by Drew Stevens
Cover design by Barbara LeVan Fisher, www.levanfisherdesign.com
Cover art: Zoe de la Mer, 1993 (oil on paper), Hugo, Marie (Contemporary Artist) / Private Collection / Bridgeman Images

Library of Congress Cataloging-in-Publication Data
Names: Japinga, Lynn, 1960- author.
Title: From widows to warriors : women's stories from the Old Testament / Lynn Japinga.
Description: First edition. | Louisville, Kentucky : WJK, Westminster John Knox Press, 2020. | Includes index. | Summary: "In this first of two volumes, Lynn Japinga acquaints us with the women of the Old Testament. This Bible study introduces and retells every female character who contributes to one or more Old Testament stories, diving deeply into what each woman's story means for us today with questions for reflection and discussion"-- Provided by publisher.
Identifiers: LCCN 2020024005 (print) | LCCN 2020024006 (ebook) | ISBN 9780664265694 (paperback) | ISBN 9781611649772 (ebook)
Subjects: LCSH: Women in the Bible. | Bible. Old Testament--Biography.
Classification: LCC BS575 .J375 2020 (print) | LCC BS575 (ebook) | DDC 221.9/22082--dc23
LC record available at https://lccn.loc.gov/2020024005
LC ebook record available at https://lccn.loc.gov/2020024006

Contents

Introduction

It is All Saints' Day at a Roman Catholic elementary school. The students are dressed as saints and biblical characters. The boys dress as the twelve apostles, Joseph, Jesus, and Pontius Pilate. No two boys wear the same costume, because they have learned about so many male religious figures. The girls are all dressed as either Eve or Mary, because these are the only two female religious figures they know. The student who described this event wondered why she had not learned about more women in the Bible who could be role models or examples for her faith.[1]

After reading the story of Deborah, another student wondered why she did not learn about her in Sunday school. "It would have made me and other girls grow up so much more determined and powerful." She had been taught that women were either sinful like Eve or pure like Mary. She wondered why neither society nor religion could find a more realistic view, which acknowledged that women could be both virtuous and sinful.[2]

More than a century earlier, Elizabeth Cady Stanton also wondered why preachers did not talk about Deborah. "We never hear sermons pointing women to the heroic virtues of Deborah as worthy of their imitation. Nothing is said in the pulpit to rouse them from the apathy of ages, to inspire them to do and dare great things. Oh, no! The lessons doled out to women, from the canon law, the Bible, the prayer-books and the catechisms, are meekness and self-abnegation; ever with covered heads (a badge of servitude) to do some humble service for man."[3]

1

Every semester in my Christian Feminism course, my students and I spend several class periods talking about women in the Bible. The students are surprised to find stories of rape, incest, prostitution, and murder. They are equally surprised to find positive stories about strong, talented, and faithful women. Some have regularly attended church and Sunday school or religious schools, and they wonder why they have never heard these stories before.

The obvious answer is that the stories are not being told. A quick scan of more than two hundred sermons by twentieth-century preachers found only five that featured a biblical woman.[4] Why don't preachers preach and teachers teach more about biblical women?

Lectionary preachers might claim that women rarely appear in the lectionary. It is true that many stories about women are either omitted or truncated; but it is also true that approximately twenty texts about women are used in the three-year cycle of Old Testament lessons. There are also occasions when the prescribed text could easily be expanded to include a woman's story.

Sometimes we bypass the stories about women because we think men will not be interested in them. Ironically, we assume that the women who make up two-thirds of most congregations are endlessly fascinated with yet another sermon on Abraham or Moses. If women can learn from the lives of men, why can't men learn from the lives of women?

People who are unfamiliar with these stories often assume that they are uninteresting and not worth preaching. They might think that all biblical women do is have babies, whine, and manipulate men. My experience with these stories has been just the opposite. Students and parishioners find them fascinating. The stories may be strange and difficult, but they are also surprisingly relevant to contemporary issues of warfare, poverty, and justice. They provide a welcome alternative to yet another sermon on the Prodigal Son or the Good Shepherd.

Another reason for caution is that many of the biblical stories that include women are about sex, violence, or sex *and* violence. Some texts might not be suitable for Sunday morning, but there are other opportunities to present them, particularly in educational settings where conversation can occur. The rape of Tamar might not be appropriate for first-graders, but it is certainly relevant for everyone older than thirteen. Students of Scripture might ask themselves why they are so reluctant to deal with sex and violence in the Bible. Our culture is permeated with sex and violence, and many of us are eager for some kind of biblical perspective on these issues. If the Bible can talk about sex and violence, perhaps we should be willing to do so as well.

Those who choose to explore these texts face some significant challenges. First, people know very little about women in the Old Testament, and what they think they know is often wrong. The first step in studying them, then, is to reexamine what people think they know about the text, particularly the stories about Eve, Bathsheba, Delilah, and Jezebel.

Second, teachers and commentators throughout history and down to today have read their own assumptions (and, often, their own prejudices) into the text. For example, in his commentary on the story of Sarah and Hagar, John Calvin describes Hagar as a stubborn, rebellious slave girl who did not appreciate the privilege of being pregnant with Abraham's child. Naughty Hagar ran away when she did not get her way. She was the sinner in the story. Yet Old Testament scholar Phyllis Trible finds in the same text a very different story about a young woman who was forced into a sexual relationship with a man old enough to be her grandfather. She ran away because Sarah abused her. Trible recognizes that Hagar was not the sinner but the sinned against.[5]

How do two authors draw such different conclusions from the same text? In part, interpretation is based on the author's social context. Calvin wrote in a time when slaves and women were supposed to know their place in the world and accept it without questioning. When Trible wrote four centuries later, she was acutely aware of those who were oppressed because of their race, class, and gender. Preachers and commentators try to interpret the text in a way that makes sense in their own contexts.

We humans constantly seek to explain the mysteries and uncertainties in our lives.[6] Biblical interpreters (commentators, teachers, preachers, readers) encounter texts that are strange, mysterious, offensive, contradictory, and weird. Jephthah killed his daughter, but he is named as a hero of the faith in Hebrews 11. God tolerated Lot's slow and reluctant departure from Sodom but turned Lot's wife into a pillar of salt when she looked back on her burning city. David forced Bathsheba into a sexual relationship and then had her husband killed to cover up her pregnancy, but David is considered the best Israelite king. These texts beg for more explanation, but the text itself does not explain, so commentators look for a way to resolve the tensions: Jephthah's daughter died willingly. Lot's wife disobeyed. Bathsheba seduced David.

Sometimes the Bible praises a character whose behavior is heinous, and then commentators tell a story that justifies their actions. Samson was an angry man who did not live up to his potential, but commentators blame Delilah for bringing down this "good" man. At times even God's strange behavior seems to need justification. Why did God tell Abraham to send Hagar away? She must have been a bad woman. Interpreters often want to tell a story in which God's actions always make sense and biblical characters do not commit heinous acts. They want the Bible to correspond with their vision of morality and justice. They want to believe that the biblical heroes are indeed heroes. They want to believe that bad people are punished and good people are rewarded. So if Rachel had no children, it is because God had closed her womb. If Dinah was sexually assaulted, it was her fault. Unfortunately, the Bible's vision of morality and justice does not always correspond with ours.

Many of the stories we tell ourselves in order to make life less mysterious and threatening turn out not to be true—and thus wind up being destructive. The same is true of the way preachers approach biblical stories. When interpreters misread the story of Eve and blame women for sin, they contribute to centuries of sexism, leading society to view women as inferior and dangerous. When commentators criticize a biblical woman like Miriam for speaking out or taking initiative, their words have a chilling effect on contemporary women readers. The stories we tell ourselves about the Bible have extraordinary power, but they are not always correct.

In this book I explore the stories that have been told about the women in the Old Testament. In preparing it, I read a number of commentaries[7] and often found helpful explanations and wise insights. A few commentators, however, told stories that said more about their own agendas and anxieties than about the texts themselves. They blamed women for men's sins. They made sweeping generalizations about female nature based on one woman's behavior. They filled in the gaps of the stories with elaborate imaginative description. Most of these emphasized women's weakness and sinfulness.

I am not without my own biases in my interpretation of these texts, and the stories I tell are also shaped by my own concerns. In the interest of transparency, here are some of the lenses through which I view the texts.

— People in the Bible are rarely entirely good or entirely sinful. They have mixed motives. The heroes of faith demonstrate tragic flaws; the sinful, messy people demonstrate moments of grace and goodness. Even the people who seem profoundly bad (Delilah and Jezebel) might be honored as heroes by their own people.

—There are examples of sin and grace in these stories, but not always where we expect to find them. Rahab has often been dismissed as a sinful prostitute, but she was the vehicle of grace. Tamar (Gen. 38) has been labeled as a naughty woman who seduced her father-in-law, but she was actually the righteous one. Interpreters have often focused on the sin of sexual impropriety, while the text itself is more concerned with injustice.

—There are signs of strength and courage in these stories, but they are not always immediately obvious. In the cultural context of the Old Testament, women were not educated and often not permitted to learn the Torah. They had few resources and little formal power or authority. Simply to take initiative or to speak up demonstrated a great deal of courage, even though it seems a minimal effort to modern readers. When Rizpah sat with dead bodies, it was a powerful example of courage.

Reading Stories of Old Testament Women Today

Some who read these stories try to make sense of them by discerning the moral lesson they teach. The story then becomes either an example of good behavior or a warning to avoid bad behavior. This strategy usually oversimplifies the story and underestimates the vast cultural difference between the Bible's time and ours.

It is more helpful to focus on discerning God's action in these stories. How is God being gracious? How is God bringing about shalom? How does God redeem human brokenness? How does God work through human beings to bring about God's purposes?

Some texts about women are so ugly and devoid of good news that they are difficult to read and interpret. Some feminist critics have even said these stories should not be proclaimed as the word of the Lord. Perhaps the better approach is to ask where we find the word of the Lord in such stories of human brokenness and sin.

At my church, following the reading of the Old Testament lesson, the reader says, "The word of the Lord," and the congregation responds, "Thanks be to God." When I have preached on a difficult text, I'm sure that my intonation added a verbal question mark. "The word of the Lord?" Can it be the word of the Lord if it seems to approve of Jephthah killing his daughter or Hosea beating Gomer?

What does it mean to say that the text is the word of the Lord? Some people claim that all parts of Scripture are inspired and infallible, but some biblical stories are horrible examples of human sinfulness. The "word of the Lord" in this case is "Do not do it this way!" These stories are not meant to be imitated but rather challenged and critiqued. I believe that all the stories of the Bible, even the ugliest, should be taken seriously. They deserve our attention, our conversation, and our criticism. We can challenge and critique the stories without fear, because we care about the texts and respect them, even if we cannot agree with or affirm them. Wrestling with the texts shows that we trust them and God enough to talk back.

One way to approach the most difficult stories is to ask how we might write a new ending for them. One of my students played the role of Martha in Lillian Hellman's play *The Children's Hour*. Her character shot herself out of despair at the end of the play. In a panel discussion after the play, I asked her how she dealt with the unremitting sadness and lack of hope and redemption. She said that she tried to write a new ending to the play. How might things have been different? Who could have intervened to change the course of action? Where might grace have been found?[8]

Those are wise words for difficult biblical stories as well. In the story of the rape of Tamar, for example, what might the characters have done differently? Rebekah tricked Isaac to get the blessing for her favorite son, Jacob, but then Jacob left home and she never saw him again. How might that story have been changed?

The biblical stories function as a mirror to say something true about human experience, both in the ancient world and in the twenty-first century. They can be horrifying and depressing. People dominate, hurt, and abuse each other, both then and now. The stories also show people being courageous and graceful and resisting evil.

A final word on how to read and use this book: Every section on one of the women of the Bible begins by briefly telling her story. Sometimes I will toss in something that a famous commentator has said—often to highlight how we have gotten these women's stories wrong. Then I will suggest ways to "dive deeper" into the character's story, and ways that story might connect to our own. These are certainly not exhaustive, and I invite readers to find many other ways to apply the text. It is my hope that both individual readers and Bible study groups will find resources here to enrich their encounter with Scripture.

1

The Matriarchs

EVE
(Genesis 2–3)

Eve is second only to Mary the mother of Jesus as the most written-about woman in the Bible, but authors come to radically different conclusions about her. She is described as both the culmination of creation and an afterthought. She is portrayed as a flawed, stupid woman easily tricked by the serpent; as a seductive, conniving woman who tricked her innocent husband; and as an intelligent woman in search of wisdom. The story of Eve is simple enough to be told in a children's picture Bible but complicated enough to mystify commentators and theologians. The simple story sounds like this: God created the first man, Adam, out of the dust. Adam was lonely, even after God created the animals for him, so God took one of Adam's ribs and made a woman to be his helper. They lived happily until the serpent convinced her to eat the forbidden fruit and she tricked Adam into sharing it. God drove them out of the garden of Eden and cursed Adam with hard work and Eve with painful childbirth and subordination to Adam.

This version of the story has several errors, but it has still been used to define the roles of men and women in life, marriage, and the church. The author of 1 Timothy wrote: "I permit no woman to teach or to have authority over a man; she is to keep silent. For Adam was formed first, then Eve; and Adam was not deceived, but the woman was

deceived and became a transgressor" (1 Tim. 2:12–14). Other interpreters conclude that because Eve was second to be created and first to
sin, all women are intellectually and spiritually inferior to men. Some
feminists have told the story in the same literal way and concluded that
the Bible cannot be a good book for women if it teaches that they are
the "second sex."

The story is actually more complex and nuanced. Genesis 1–3 is not
intended to be a science textbook or a verbatim transcript of what actually occurred at the beginning of time. It is a story or poem that people
recited to explain the origins of the world and humanity. In fact, Genesis 1–3 contains two different and conflicting creation stories. They
should not be read as literally true in all their details.[1] Still, the details
of the text should not be dismissed as irrelevant, because the stories are
embedded in our culture. Even people who do not read the Bible are
vaguely aware of Adam and Eve and the apple.[2]

In a groundbreaking essay first published in 1973, Old Testament
scholar Phyllis Trible offered a detailed retelling of the Genesis 2–3
story. She focused on the nuances of the Hebrew text itself, without
the influence of the interpretations that said women were secondary
and sinful. She saw that God created a human being (*adam*) out of
dust (*adamah*). Later, after deciding that the "earth-creature" needed a
partner, God put the *adam* to sleep, took out a rib, and built another
human being. Both were made in God's image. The woman was not
fragile or weak or less intelligent than the *adam*. She was the culmination of creation, not an afterthought.[3]

Trible also noted that the relationship between the two was an equal
partnership, not that of a leader and a follower or a master and a servant. The Hebrew word for help, *ezer*, usually refers to God's strength
and power, as in "Our help is in the name of the LORD, who made
heaven and earth" (Ps. 124:8). If God was the help that was stronger
than the *adam*, and animals were the help that was weaker, the woman
was a help equal to him. She was not there to do his chores or raise his
children, but to be an intimate partner who saved him from loneliness.
She was his equal, with the same mind, rationality, soul, spiritual sensitivity, and connection with the creator.[4]

The man delighted in the woman, and they were naked and not
ashamed. They had a relationship of trust, openness, and mutuality.
Whether Adam and Eve were real people or not, the author says that
in the beginning, human bodies and sexuality were good and valued.

Unfortunately, this openness and mutuality did not last. A serpent, one of God's own creatures, suddenly appeared and engaged in a conversation about the tree of the knowledge of good and evil. The woman said they would die if they ate from the tree. The serpent assured her that they would not die, but the tree would make them wise. She wanted to be wise, and the fruit was appealing; so she ate it and gave some to the man.

Some commentators conclude that Eve was gullible, stupid, naive, and easily seduced by the serpent. Ironically, they also say that she was smart enough to trick Adam into eating the fruit, since he was not present for the conversation with the serpent. Perhaps he was pulling weeds somewhere else in the garden. If he had been there, he would have nipped that conversation in the bud and saved Eve from a major mistake.

This is a popular interpretation, but it is not supported by the text. Eve gave the fruit to her husband *who was with her* (Gen. 3:6). If Adam was intellectually and spiritually superior to Eve, why didn't he challenge the serpent? Why didn't he refuse to eat the fruit? Phyllis Trible pointed out that the man does not appear to be very intelligent or spiritually discerning in this story.[5] The woman was thinking, questioning, and wrestling with the meaning of God's command. Adam said nothing, and when she gave him the fruit, he ate it without question.

Why was this so sinful? Were they disobedient? Arrogant? Proud? Or were they more like toddlers who were irresistibly drawn to touch the forbidden object? Was God an angry tyrant who set them up for failure?

These questions have intrigued readers for millennia, but the Bible does not answer them. The point of the story is that everything changed. Adam and Eve obtained knowledge, but it was not what they expected. The first thing they knew was that the nakedness that once delighted them now made them ashamed. They feared the judgment of God and each other, so they sewed fig leaves together in a pitiful and itchy attempt to cover themselves.

Their fear of exposure involved more than their bodies. They no longer felt comfortable encountering God in an easy, familiar way, so they hid. God came looking for them, saw their fear and shame, and asked if they had eaten from the tree. The man blamed the woman and indirectly the God who had given her to him. She was no longer a partner; rather, she was the source of his downfall. The woman blamed the serpent.

The consequences were devastating. To the woman, God said, "I will greatly increase your pangs in childbearing; in pain you shall bring forth children, yet your desire shall be for your husband, and he shall rule over you" (3:16). This verse has been used to justify male dominance, privilege, and even violence toward women. It has been used to exclude women from leadership in church and government, because they must be subordinate to all men, not just their husbands. Women have been denied the right to vote, to speak, and to be educated because of this verse.

Again, it is important to read the text carefully. The "curse of Eve" has been used to describe menstrual pain, labor pains, and the subordination of women, but God does not actually curse her. Still, life for women will change. They will experience painful labor, multiple pregnancies, and death in childbirth, but instead of refusing the sexual contact that produces pregnancy, they will desire men. This desire will cause emotional pain as well as physical. How often does a woman love a man who does not love her in return or is abusive to her?

The man experienced consequences in his vocation. The ground was cursed (though not the man), so the gardening that was originally pleasurable would be compromised by drought, tornadoes, and insects. Work would be hard.

Both shared equally in the most damaging effect of the fall. They lost the mutuality they shared in the beginning. All their relationships were distorted: with God, with their work, with their bodies, and with each other.

The creation that was so good in the beginning was now compromised by sin and brokenness. The two humans did not die immediately, but their lives were different and difficult. Adam and Eve experienced pain and loss. Their son Abel would be murdered by his brother Cain, who was then banished. They would never know the same kind of intimacy with God or each other as they had known in the garden. But there would be children, work, and a future of sorts. God would not abandon them. Life would continue in a different way.

Diving Deeper

Liberating Eve. Despite what many people have heard all their lives, this text does not say that women are secondary, inferior, or the cause of sin. Other ways to tell the story are better rooted in what the Bible actually says and not so influenced by an irrational fear of the power of women. How would you go about telling this story differently?[6]

Very good and very broken. This story illustrates the reality that the world and human beings were created to be very good. A new telling of it might explore what it means to be created in God's image and whether that image is the same for men and women. Glimpses of that original goodness still exist, but all of creation has been bent or damaged.

Ah, the humanity. We are limited, and much is beyond our control. We live with fear and doubt. We are lonely, sometimes in the midst of relationships. We have deep longings, for intimacy, for achievement, for clarity, for belonging. We want to make a difference. We want to be valued and appreciated. We want to be remembered. As we age, we realize our humanity and mortality in different ways. We get sick. We lose some of our abilities. We feel life closing in rather than opening up.[7] The realities of fear, loneliness, and loss are often labeled as sinful attitudes that religious people must rise above, but they are not sinful so much as they are part of being human.

"Flesh of my flesh." The story demonstrates the power of intimate relationships rooted in commitment, trust, and vulnerability. We experience such joy when we find a person with whom we can be fully ourselves. To be naked with a partner and confident of being loved, admired, and respected is all too rare in a society that often shames people both for being sexual and for their imperfect and inadequate bodies. Marriage and family can be a place to celebrate the goodness of love and relationships.

Marriage can also be the place where human brokenness is most profoundly evident. Intimate relationships are hard work, and they require a high degree of vulnerability and trust. It can be terrifying to be so close to another person, in part because our own fears and flaws become so evident. The story of Eve and Adam might help us to talk honestly about the joys and struggles of marriage. This passage does not give advice about specific gender roles, but it raises broader questions of how flawed people live together. What are realistic expectations of marriage?

Adam and Steve. As people you know debate the issue of same-sex marriage, it might be helpful to turn to this text. This story speaks of a man and a woman, but the dynamics of relationship are also true for two men or two women. It is human nature to long for a person with whom we can have a relationship of trust and intimacy, and yet we also struggle with our own insecurities. We waver between our desires for independence and for connection. This Scripture tells a story about

what it means to be a human being in a relationship, with all its potential for brokenness and healing, sadness and joy.

The world was created to be very good, but we all know that the
world is now a broken place. It is not the way it was meant to be. We
live in a world with glimpses of goodness and overwhelming signs of
evil. And yet, it is still God's world, and God is still creating, still gracious, still inviting human beings into relationship.

Questions for Reflection and Discussion

Thinking back over what you've heard about Eve in church and
elsewhere, was it more negative or positive? In what you heard,
did she bear more responsibility in the story than Adam, or less?

How would you tell the story of Eve differently than what you
have usually heard?

SARAH AND HAGAR
(Genesis 16–18; 21)

The story of the Israelites began when God made a covenant with
Abraham (Gen. 12). God promised to bless Abraham with land and
children if Abraham would trust God and move to a different place.
Abraham did so and became known as a heroic figure with strong faith
in God. No matter how faithful he is, a man cannot father a great
nation alone. Without Abraham's wife Sarah and the other matriarchs
who followed her, the nation of Israel would not exist.

God repeatedly appeared to Abraham (Gen. 12; 13; 15) and promised to give him land and offspring, but God did not address Sarah.
It is possible that Sarah knew nothing about the divine promise that
depended on her fertility. She did know that she had failed at the
most essential task of womanhood in her culture: she had no children.
Infertility was devastating, but it was even more painful because Sarah
believed that God had prevented her from having children (16:2).
Sarah had a plan. She took Hagar, her Egyptian slave girl, and gave her
to Abraham. In that culture a woman could give a slave to her husband
to impregnate and then raise the child as her own.[8] Abraham agreed

without hesitation, but Hagar was not asked whether she wanted to spend the night with a man old enough to be her grandfather. Her desires did not matter.[9]

Hagar conceived but then "looked with contempt on her mistress" (16:4). She was not respectful and subservient.[10] She might have resented being forced into an unwanted sexual relationship, but she took pride in the fact that she was pregnant while her old barren mistress was not. Sarah resented Hagar and her fertility even though she had initiated the process. Sarah blamed Abraham for her troubles with Hagar,[11] but Abraham abdicated all responsibility to Sarah, who "dealt harshly"[12] with Hagar until she fled into the wilderness (v. 6).

Hagar had been forced into a sexual relationship and physically abused, but she found the self-respect to stand up for herself. She refused to accept mistreatment. She ran away from domestic danger but found that the wilderness was also dangerous for a young pregnant woman with no resources.

An angel of the Lord found her and called her by name, unlike Abraham and Sarah, who repeatedly referred to her as a "slave-girl." The angel instructed her to return and submit to Sarah. This is not the recommended solution to domestic violence, but it might have been the only realistic and safe choice. Perhaps to soften this heartless command, the angel offered the good news that Hagar would have many offspring. The angel told Hagar to name her son Ishmael, which means "God hears." The child would live a conflicted life, but both he and Hagar would have a future. This was a rare and remarkable divine promise to a slave woman who did not belong to the chosen people.

Hagar's response is equally extraordinary. She gave God a name, "El-roi," or "God of seeing," because she had seen God and remained alive. Usually God names God's self, because the one doing the naming has a kind of power over the one who is named. Hagar is the only person in the Bible who named God.

More than a decade later, God again appeared to Abraham with the promise of land and offspring (Gen. 17). God explicitly promised that Sarah would give birth to a son. When Abraham heard that his elderly wife would conceive, he "fell on his face and laughed" (v. 17).[13] Abraham wondered whether God was referring to Hagar's son and said, "O that Ishmael might live in your sight!" (v. 18). God promised to bless Ishmael, but insisted that Sarah's son would have the special relationship with God.

In Genesis 18, God and two divine messengers appeared to Abraham and said that Sarah would have a son. Sarah was listening in on this conversation from her tent, and, like Abraham, she laughed. The men asked Abraham why she laughed. Finally, the Lord spoke to her directly. "Oh yes, you did laugh." Was that said in a shaming tone that suggested she was a doubting, faithless woman? Or was it said matter-of-factly, recognizing the shock and the strangeness of the announcement? Did God understand that she might be a little stunned by this? Maybe God laughed with her.[14]

Finally after all the years of waiting, Sarah conceived and bore a son. She was elated and announced, "God has brought laughter for me" (21:6). Sarah had given up hope, and yet as an old woman, she nursed a baby named Isaac, which means "laughter."

A few years later, when Isaac was weaned, Sarah's joy had turned to suspicion, competition, and anger. Sarah saw Ishmael playing with Isaac. We are not sure whether this was innocent play or if Ishmael was mocking or harming Isaac. Sarah told Abraham to fix the problem. Abraham hesitated, but God told Abraham to do whatever Sarah said.[15] God again promised that Ishmael would also become a great nation.

Abraham sent Hagar and Ishmael into the wilderness with only bread and water.[16] He did not provide a camel, tent, servant, or supplies, even though he was a wealthy man. Their meager provisions were soon gone. Hagar could not bear to watch Ishmael die, so she laid him under a bush and wept. Once again, Hagar was cared for by an angel, who showed her a well of water. This sad story had a happy ending. Ishmael married an Egyptian wife and had many sons (25:13–15). God was present with them, and Hagar and Ishmael prospered.

The Bible says no more about Sarah except that she died at the age of 127. When Abraham died at the age of 175, Isaac and Ishmael buried him with Sarah. The two sons with competing mothers shared their grief over the loss of their father.

Diving Deeper

A long and winding road. This story is often told as an uplifting one about the faith of God's chosen people. Abraham and Sarah trusted God through a long period of infertility until God intervened and provided a son.[17] The story is much more complicated. Twice Abraham put Sarah at risk by saying that she was his sister and allowing a ruler to claim her (Gen. 12 and 20). They waited decades for the promised baby, only to hear that Abraham should sacrifice him (Gen. 22).

Abraham and Sarah were flawed and inconsistently faithful. They did not immediately understand the nuances of their call, and they made mistakes, but God continued to speak to them. Their uncertainties make them more human and relatable.

Blaming the women. Sarah has been criticized as impatient, jealous, and manipulative because she did not trust God and because her attempt to "help" God endangered her family.[18] Her actions are actually understandable in light of cultural expectations. She was desperate to have a baby, not because she had a character flaw or a pathological desire for motherhood, but because she was nothing without a son. Sarah's real sin was that she mistreated Hagar. She took Hagar and gave her to Abraham. Then, when Hagar conceived, Sarah was angry and abusive. She used Hagar when it suited her purpose and then sent her away.

It is easy to criticize Sarah, but she treated Hagar as she had been treated. They were both trapped in a patriarchal culture. Neither woman had much autonomy, although Sarah had more freedom than Hagar. If they had worked together and cared for each other, both of their lives might have been better.[19] Instead, they competed with and undermined each other. Sarah was the victim of oppression, but she was also the oppressor. She took and gave Hagar in the same way that she had been taken and given by Abraham. Hagar is not the sinner in this story but the sinned against.[20]

One of the painful realities of the feminist movement has been that while middle-class white women recognized their own oppression, they did not always recognize the ways they oppressed women of other classes or ethnic groups. White women in the South mistreated the slave women who worked for them. Middle-class women hired African American or Hispanic women as domestics, at times without providing adequate pay or respect.[21] Readers might consider the ways that white privilege shapes relationships and assumptions. What is a responsible and just way to deal with power and privilege? How can women be in solidarity with one another?

A way out of no way. Hagar had a difficult life, but in the end God provided the resources she needed to survive and to make a way out of no way.[22] Many women in the world identify with Hagar and her experience of poverty, oppression, violence, and homelessness. African American women in particular have been drawn to her experience of both suffering and God's presence in her life. This story can be good news for people who are struggling and feel that they have been abandoned.

Creative baby making. The ancient story of Sarah and Hagar might help us think about modern-day reproductive technologies. In what ways are these technologies helpful and gracious ways to assist infertile or same-sex couples in having children? In what ways might those technologies be harmful? If a couple is infertile, should they simply accept that as God's will for their lives? Is conception in a petri dish contrary to "nature"? How much money should they spend trying to conceive? The story of Sarah and Hagar does not provide direct answers to these questions but offers a way to discuss them.

One family, three faiths. This story sheds light on the relationship between the three Abrahamic faiths: Judaism, Christianity, and Islam. There have always been tensions between these groups, particularly during the Crusades in the Middle Ages. Each faith has claimed that God blesses only them and that they alone deserve power and privilege in the world.[23]

God chose Abraham and Sarah and the Israelites not because of their worth and not because God loved only them; God chose to bless the rest of the world through the Israelites. The full story of Abraham, Sarah, and Hagar shows clearly that God did not reject or punish Ishmael. In Genesis 16, God told Hagar that Ishmael would be a great nation. In Genesis 17, God told Abraham that although Isaac was the promised child, God would bless Ishmael and make him a great nation too. God chose to have a particular relationship with the Israelites, but God did not reject the rest of the world. Rather, the Israelites would be the means by which God would finally redeem the whole world.

This has not been easy for contemporary religious people to understand or to live out. At their worst, Judaism, Christianity, and Islam have claimed an exclusive relationship with God. Each has attempted to give the other faiths a secondary status or no status at all. Extremists in each group have terrorized the others. The story of Abraham, Sarah, Isaac, Hagar, and Ishmael suggests a different reality. Divine blessing of one nation does not require divine cursing of others. God has enough grace and goodness for all.

Questions for Reflection and Discussion

Do you agree that Sarah was treated differently than Abraham when each of them laughed at the idea of having a child in their old age? If so, why do you think that was?

How do you think you would have reacted to Hagar, had you been in Sarah's place?

LOT'S WIFE AND DAUGHTERS
(Genesis 19)

The story of Lot and his daughters is often cited as evidence that homosexual behavior is sinful, but the moral of the story is not so obvious. Lot had accompanied his uncle Abraham to the land of Canaan and chose to live in the fertile area around Sodom and Gomorrah. Unfortunately, the inhabitants were particularly evil.[24] Two divine messengers came to Sodom to visit Lot and spent the night at his home. That evening, all the men of the city surrounded the house and asked Lot to bring out the strangers. The NRSV says the local men wanted to "know" the strangers (Gen. 19:5), but this did not mean making their acquaintance over pizza and a beer. The local men resented having strangers in their midst, so they wanted to rape the strangers, put them in their place, and show them who was boss. This was an act of dominance and aggression.

According to the rules of hospitality at the time, since Lot had offered shelter to the visitors, he was responsible for their welfare and safety. Lot tried to divert the attention of the mob by offering his two virgin daughters to do with as they pleased. Lot would have sacrificed his daughters to preserve the dignity of two strangers. The text reports this horrifying detail matter-of-factly, but the women must have felt both terrified and completely betrayed by their father who showed no desire to protect them. He was not a role model for biblical family values.

The men of Sodom were not interested in raping virgin women. The divine messengers pulled Lot into the house away from the mob and struck the men with blindness. The messengers then informed Lot that Sodom and Gomorrah would be destroyed because of their wickedness. They ordered Lot to leave the city, but he lingered until the messengers took Lot and his wife and daughters by the hand and brought them out of the city. On the way out, the angels told Lot to flee to the hills and not look back. Was this command addressed to all four of them? In Hebrew the advice is in the masculine singular form, which suggests that the angels spoke only to Lot. If so, did he pass along the instructions to his wife and daughters?

Once they had escaped from Sodom, fire and sulfur rained down, and the cities and their inhabitants were destroyed. Lot's wife looked back to the city, and she was transformed into a pillar of salt. That seems like a harsh punishment, especially given the angels' tolerance of Lot's reluctant departure.

After losing their home and watching the destruction of the city, the death of their neighbors, and Mrs. Lot turned into a pillar of salt, Lot and his daughters moved into a cave in the hills. Here the story takes an even more bizarre turn. The daughters saw no possibility for marriage and children in their current circumstances. They seemed to think that the destruction had been so widespread that they were the only ones left alive. They wanted children, but they did not know where they would find men to help conceive those children. They knew of only one living man.

The daughters plied their father with wine until he was drunk, and the older daughter went to lie with him. The second night they repeated the process and the second daughter slept with him. The women became pregnant and gave birth to sons named Moab and Ben-ammi, whose descendants became the despised foreign nations of Moab and Ammon.[25] Some commentators believe that this strange incest story was used both to insult the Moabites and Ammonites and to justify the Israelites' hatred of them. Ironically, the story also demonstrates that in hating the Moabites and Ammonites, the Israelites hated their own flesh and blood. Several centuries later, the Israelites were shocked when something good came out of Moab. Ruth was a Moabite, a stranger and an alien, and yet she became the grandmother of King David and an ancestor of Jesus.

This story is troubling in so many ways, and commentators have expended a great deal of effort to explain the odd and offensive actions and redeem the story with a moral lesson. The first problem is that Lot's behavior was inexcusable, and yet the author of 2 Peter 2:7 referred to him as righteous. Faced with this incongruity, some commentators attempted to justify Lot's horrifying actions.

The second problem in this story is that God appears to be angry and capricious in punishing Lot's wife so harshly for a relatively minor sin. Many commentators cannot interpret a story in a way that implies that God is capricious, so they justify her punishment by insisting that she disobeyed a clear divine order. A few commentators are more compassionate. They point out that she was grieving the loss of her home and possibly other children who lived in the city. She looked back to memories of her family, her friends, her life. She mourned the people she loved who were being destroyed.

The third problem in this story is the incest between Lot and his daughters. Each time, the text reports that Lot "did not know when she lay down or when she rose" (Gen. 19:33, 35). Some readers wonder how that was possible. Could a man, even when old and inebriated, not know that he was having sex? Martin Luther explained that Lot knew at the time what was happening, but his mind was so disturbed because of grief and loss that he did not *remember* what had happened.[26]

Diving Deeper

The story of Lot's wife and daughters is horrifying to modern readers. There is so much brokenness and so little redemption. Still, this strange story is worth telling, in part because it illustrates the difficulty of interpreting Scripture when there are such vast cultural differences between the biblical world and ours.

What is the sin? The common understanding is that the sin in this story is homosexuality, but that is not accurate. It is likely that the men who wanted to rape the divine messengers were not homosexual men driven by sexual desire, but heterosexual men driven by the desire to dominate and humiliate the strangers. Their sin was violence. Lot also displayed an appalling form of parental brokenness. He misused his power as a father to offer his daughters to the violent mob. The daughters, in turn, manipulated their father into having sex with them, out of anger, revenge, or desperation. The real sin in each situation was the misuse of power in a way that damaged another person.

Perhaps we should pose this question of sin not to judge these biblical characters for their flaws but to tell a powerful and relevant story of human brokenness. The townsmen desire to violently humiliate the stranger. The sins of the father are visited upon the next generation. Neither the community nor the family is a place of safety and grace.

Proof-texting. The story of Sodom and Gomorrah is one of the seven passages in Scripture that are frequently used to condemn homosexual behavior, but the story says nothing about loving mutual relationships between two men. God was indeed angry with the men of Sodom, not because of their sexual orientation, but because of their desire to violate and abuse the strangers.

Family values? Lot was rightly appalled by the idea that his male guests were threatened with sexual violence, but his alternative would have subjected his daughters to sexual violence. He might have believed he was choosing the lesser of two evils, but this was an epic parenting failure.[27]

He broke trust with his daughters, and later his daughters broke trust with him. This story illustrates the ambiguity of biblical morality and "family values." Should we adopt hard-and-fast rules about (homo)sexuality from a culture where giving daughters over to be raped was more acceptable than allowing strangers to be raped? Perhaps we cannot draw eternal moral lessons from every ancient biblical story.

Pillar of salt. Why was the simple act of looking back so disastrous for Lot's wife?[28] Sometimes we look back because the past seems so much better. We were younger, happier, and more attractive. We might be overwhelmed with the noise and the chaos of our current lives and look back longingly at what seemed to be a simpler and happier time.

It is also possible to look back on the past and be paralyzed by it. We let ourselves be defined by a broken relationship, a failure, an addiction. We cannot move on. We cannot see how God might be working in a new way. We cannot see how God might bring grace and healing. We cannot allow ourselves to hope. We are locked into the past and we cannot move, just as Lot's wife could not move after she became a pillar of salt.[29]

New life. The strange and somewhat unsettling good news in this story is that Lot's daughters had sons. In the midst of absolute chaos and uncertainty, they wanted to have children. They took a risk and broke a taboo because their hope for the future superseded the traditional moral code against incest.[30] Contemporary readers are not called to imitate them, but to see that new life can grow out of despair and destruction. God took that dysfunctional family and made their descendant, Ruth the Moabite, an ancestor of Jesus. The future was born in that cave.

Questions for Reflection and Discussion

When Lot's wife was turned into a pillar of salt, did the punishment fit the crime? Why, or why not?

Had you heard the story of Lot's daughters before this study? How did you react when you heard it?

REBEKAH
(Genesis 24–28)

Rebekah was an intensely focused woman who put a great deal of energy into her role as the mother of Jacob and Esau. She might be described in contemporary terms as a helicopter parent or a tiger mother. She is both admired and criticized for her maternal devotion and preference for one son over the other.

Isaac, the son of Sarah and Abraham, was forty years old and a bachelor. Abraham sent a servant to his hometown of Haran to find a woman who would marry Isaac. The servant was anxious about the responsibility and asked God to help him find the right woman. The servant told God that he would ask a woman at the local well for a drink of water, and if she offered to water his camels as well, he would know that she was the one God had "appointed" for Isaac (Gen. 24:14). The first woman he asked graciously offered to water his camels. Her name was Rebekah, and she was related to Abraham. After hearing the servant's story about how she had been the answer to his prayer, she courageously agreed to travel five hundred miles to marry a stranger. The text does not say whether they had any form of courtship; it simply reports that Isaac took her into his mother's tent, loved her, and was comforted in his grief over the loss of his mother. The text does not say whether she loved him.

Rebekah had difficulty conceiving, but she displayed no angst over her infertility. After twenty years without children, Isaac prayed for his wife,[31] and Rebekah conceived (25:21). She had a difficult pregnancy, and she complained to God: "If it is to be this way, why do I live?" (v. 22). God responded that two nations were in her womb, and the older child would serve the younger, contrary to the usual pattern, which privileged the firstborn. Later, she gave birth first to Esau, and then to Jacob. When the boys grew older, each parent had a particular connection with one son. Isaac loved Esau because he liked to eat the game that Esau brought home, and Rebekah loved Jacob, for reasons that are not given.[32]

When the sons were about forty years old, the blind, elderly Isaac asked Esau to hunt game and prepare a meal for him. Isaac would then give Esau the blessing due the firstborn son. Rebekah overheard this and quickly developed an alternative plan. Based on the word she received from God when she was pregnant, she advised Jacob to pretend to be Esau so that he could receive the blessing. She told Jacob to kill two goats so that she could fix Isaac's favorite food. Jacob protested that his skin was smooth, and Isaac would know by touch that he was not Esau. Rebekah solved that problem by placing the goat skins on Jacob's hands and neck.

Dressed in Esau's clothes and the goat hair, Jacob entered his father's tent and claimed to be Esau. Isaac was puzzled by hearing Jacob's voice coming from Esau's body, but finally gave Jacob the blessing due to the firstborn, promising him wealth, success, and the service of his brother.

Jacob had barely left the tent when Esau returned home and Isaac realized his mistake. The frail old man was angry that he had been tricked, and sad that his beloved Esau had been cheated. Esau was furious with his brother and resented the paltry blessing left for him. Twice Esau pleaded, "Bless me, me also, father!" (27:34, 38). Modern readers might wonder why Isaac could not simply take back the words of blessing, but words had power. Once a blessing was given, it could not be taken away. Jacob had stolen the blessing, and Rebekah had helped, although it is not clear whether Isaac and Esau knew of her involvement.

Esau was so angry that he threatened to kill Jacob, so Rebekah advised Jacob to go to her brother Laban's home until Esau cooled off. To make it seem like Isaac's idea, she complained about the foreign (Hittite) women that Esau had married, so Isaac sent Jacob off to search for an acceptable wife (28:1–5). Jacob did not return for at least two decades, and there is no evidence that Rebekah ever saw him again. She had helped her favorite son obtain the blessing but lost his presence in her life.

Some commentators disapprove of Rebekah and think she deserved to lose Jacob. They criticize her for being deceptive, scheming, and controlling. Others acknowledge that she had received a divine oracle expressing preference for Jacob but criticize her response. If she had told Isaac about the oracle, he would have blessed the right son without being tricked. Some simply fail to mention Rebekah's story or dismiss her as insignificant.

Yet Rebekah was not simply a helicopter mother with an intense and inappropriate preference for one son over the other. She preferred Jacob at least in part because God preferred him. She was not a selfish, scheming woman concerned for her own well-being. She was attuned to the will of God for her children.

Rebekah had few options. If she had told Isaac about the oracle, he might not have believed her, or he might have resented the fact that she received the word from God rather than him.[33] Rightly or wrongly, she did not think that she could be honest about the reason she took Jacob's side. Her actions appear secretive or manipulative, but she had to work behind the scenes. She did not have the power to give the blessing to the son God had designated. Only Isaac could do that, and Isaac was following both the law of primogeniture and his own preference for Esau. Rebekah deceived Isaac because that was her only option in a culture where the opinions and faith of women were not highly regarded.

What if the roles had been reversed? What if Isaac had received the oracle and blessed Jacob instead of Esau? Would he have been criticized? If he had deceived his wife, would anyone have noticed? As a father, he would not have needed to manipulate. He could have simply blessed the son he had chosen.[34]

Diving Deeper

Rebekah loved Jacob. This story illustrates the tensions that result when children are not equally valued and loved. One child may be the favorite who can do no wrong. Another is never good enough to gain parental approval. Favoritism can lead to serious conflict within families, in part because the less-favored child may act out in order to obtain attention and concern. The athletic parent has a natural affinity with the athletic daughter but struggles to connect with the musical son. The scientific parent connects easily with the academically gifted child but is impatient with the child who has difficulty learning. How is it possible to treasure children equally when we may have more in common with one than another?

Favoritism causes problems within a family, and yet God often plays favorites. God acts in surprising ways, favoring the weak over the strong and the second child over the firstborn. Even more puzzling is that the people God chooses to bless usually do not deserve God's favor. God did not choose Jacob because he was or would be an exemplary human being, but to show that God does not operate according to human rules and patterns.

Bless you. How do parents bless their children, not simply with an inheritance but with their words, actions, and unconditional affirmation? Some of the most impoverished families genuinely bless their children, while some of the wealthiest families leave their children feeling cursed rather than blessed. To bless is to affirm, to value, to love unconditionally, to pass on wisdom, to delight in. To bless is to seek the best for another.[35]

If she waters my camels. The story raises a timeless and challenging question: how do people discern the right marriage partner? Since most of us generally lack a servant, camels, and a water jar, what tools do we use to make difficult life decisions? How do we discern whether a person is a potential spouse? How do we know which college to attend or which job to take?

Reconciliation. Rebekah's story is particularly poignant because it ends so sadly. Her favorite son, Jacob, had to leave home, and she probably never saw him again. She might have wondered if getting him the blessing was worth it. What happened to Rebekah after Isaac died and she was left alone? She would be expected to live with her son, but she had said openly that she did not approve of Esau or his wives. Did she live alone, or did she reconcile with Esau and grow to appreciate his wives and love their children? The Bible does not provide these details, but it still might help us better understand Rebekah to ask these questions. What would have to happen for healing to occur between Rebekah and Esau and his wives? What might she need to say to him? What might he need to say to her? How do family members forge a new relationship when they have hurt one another in the past?[36]

Rebekah was a strong, courageous woman who demonstrated a powerful love for her son Jacob. We can admire that love and respect her courage while recognizing that her family was wounded by the favoritism she and Isaac demonstrated to their sons. In the end, Jacob and Esau reconciled. God had blessing enough for both of them.

Questions for Reflection and Discussion

Jacob was Rebekah's favorite, which is why she wanted him to receive Isaac's blessing. Was God playing favorites when God chose

Jacob, rather than Esau, as the one through whom God would fulfill the promise to make Abraham's bloodline a great nation?

Did you find Rebekah to be a manipulative person? Why, or why not?

RACHEL AND LEAH
(Genesis 29–30)

The story of Rachel and Leah sounds a bit like an episode of *Big Love* or *Sister Wives*. Two sisters married to the same man compete for his attention so that they can give birth to sons. They are often portrayed as shallow and jealous minor characters, and yet without them and their children, the twelve tribes of Israel would not exist.

Jacob had tricked his father, Isaac, into giving him his brother Esau's blessing[37] and then left home to escape Esau's wrath and find a wife. He went to Haran, his mother's hometown, and stopped at a well, where he met his beautiful cousin Rachel. Her father, Laban, welcomed him eagerly, and Jacob promised to work for seven years in order to marry Rachel. She had an older sister named Leah. The Hebrew text notes that Leah's eyes were *rakk*, which can mean weak, tender, delicate, or soft. The NRSV translates, "Leah's eyes were lovely," implying that she had one good feature but she could not compete with Rachel, who was "graceful and beautiful" (Gen. 29:17). The Revised Standard Version and New International Version (and several others) translate *rakk* as "weak eyes," as if Leah were cross-eyed.

After seven years, Jacob arranged the wedding, but at some point in the festivities, he switched Leah for Rachel, and Jacob spent the night with the wrong woman. "When morning came, it was Leah!" (29:25). The wedding night did not occur in the bridal suite at the local Hilton Hotel, but in a dark tent with a heavily veiled bride.[38] Jacob was furious with Laban for deceiving him, but Laban claimed that it was not customary for the younger sister to marry before the older. Jacob had little choice but to work seven more years in order to marry Rachel too, although the second wedding occurred just a week after the first.

The complications of polygamy were exacerbated when God intervened. "When the LORD saw that Leah was unloved, he opened her womb; but Rachel was barren" (29:31). Leah gave birth to four sons and gave each one a name with theological and personal significance. Three times she chose a name that expressed her hope that Jacob would love her. Each time she was disappointed. Each name reflected her diminishing expectations. Finally, when the fourth son, Judah, was born, she chose a name that meant she would praise God.

While Leah produced one boy after another, Rachel was barren. She envied her sister, and she took it out on Jacob: "Give me children, or I shall die!" (30:1). Jacob retorted that the infertility was not his fault, but hers, because God was withholding children from her. Rachel then decided to use a surrogate, as Jacob's grandmother Sarah had done. Rachel offered her maid Bilhah to Jacob, and Bilhah had two sons.

The competition continued. Leah had stopped having children, perhaps because Jacob was not sleeping in her tent. She gave her maid Zilpah to Jacob, and Zilpah had two sons. Rachel felt she was losing ground in this race, and when Leah's oldest son Reuben found some mandrakes, which were thought to aid fertility, she asked Leah to share them. Leah responded angrily, perhaps reflecting years of frustration, "Is it a small matter that you have taken away my husband? Would you take away my son's mandrakes also?" (30:15). Rachel offered her a deal: Jacob could sleep with Leah for a night if Rachel could have some of the mandrakes, which she hoped would make her fertile.[39]

Leah went to meet Jacob and announced, "You must come in to me; for I have hired you with my son's mandrakes" (30:16).[40] The night was successful, "God heeded Leah" (v. 17), and she had a son. Jacob must have returned to her tent on at least two more occasions, because she had a sixth son and a daughter.

Finally, after years of waiting, "God remembered Rachel, . . . and opened her womb" (30:22). She had a son named Joseph. Later she had another son, Benjamin, but she died in childbirth (35:16–20). Did one woman "win" the competition in the end?[41] Rachel was the mother of Jacob's favorite son, Joseph, but King David, Moses, and the most influential tribes of Israel descended from Leah's sons Judah and Levi. Leah's children were in the end more influential and powerful. The real winners in this contest were Jacob and the nation of Israel.

Diving Deeper

People have usually approached these stories in one of two ways. One approach emphasizes Jacob's heroic, spiritual qualities. Yes, he had flaws, but they led to profound encounters with God. He stole Esau's birthright and ran away but had a powerful dream about God. Later, when he was afraid to meet Esau, he wrestled with an angel. These stories seem more spiritually uplifting than his messy personal life, and they usually ignore his wives altogether.[42] The second approach does pay attention to Rachel and Leah, but often by referring to their bad behavior as examples of what not to do. These authors describe the wives of Jacob as weak, silly, sinful women who do not need to be taken seriously. But perhaps there's a third way to read these stories, one that can provide a more nuanced and complete view of both Jacob and the women.

"Give me children, or I shall die!" In this cultural context, women's lives were defined by bearing children. Rachel did not long for children because she was an immature, silly woman but because her culture said she was nothing if she did not have them. We might dismiss her "Give me children, or I shall die" comment as hysterical and manipulative, but to her, the lack of children was tantamount to death. Similarly, Leah is sometimes mocked for her desperate yearning for Jacob's love, but she was trapped in a marriage she might not have wanted, without any other options for intimacy. Who can blame her for wanting some measure of love and respect from Jacob?

Likewise, we might be tempted to say impatiently to Rachel and Leah, "Get a life and stop waiting for love or children." But this was their life. These women should not be trivialized or dismissed by labeling them petty, catty, or conniving. There are many women like them who want to have children. They may not need children for economic security, but they have reasons of their own. This desire should not be ridiculed.

"Surely now my husband will love me." It is important to understand the cultural context of these stories, but it is also important to realize that the longing for love and children is still a part of human life in the twenty-first century. Unfortunately, some relationships are marred by unrequited desire and prolonged pain. A man loves a woman more than she loves him. A woman loves another woman but is afraid to say so. One partner loves another who is emotionally abusive. It hurts to long for something we do not have, whether children, love, or fulfilling work. Even having a mostly good life does not spare us from grieving what is missing. One of my students noted that Leah had children and wanted love, and Rachel had love and wanted children.[43] By naming and acknowledging these deep human needs, we can recognize them and take them seriously. We desperately want relationships, even though we recognize that they are fragile.

God opened her womb. The text claims that God made Leah fertile because she was unloved, and Jacob insisted that God had closed Rachel's womb. This raises troubling questions for women who are wrestling with infertility. If women get pregnant, is it because God wants them to? If they don't, is God punishing them? Does God use fertility as a reward? Is birth control problematic because it limits the rewards God can provide? To what degree should these beliefs about God and fertility shape current discussion?

Biblical marriage. In some religious circles, a "biblical view of marriage" is a basis for defining twenty-first-century marriage, but this example of biblical marriage is particularly problematic. Laban sold his daughters to Jacob and tricked him into marrying Leah. The two women offered Jacob their maids when they could not conceive. The heroic Jacob became the father of the twelve tribes of the Israelites by sleeping with four different women. In this culture, polygamy and surrogacy might not have been conducive to healthy marriages, but they were acceptable ways to build a nation. We might question the wisdom and justice of women giving their handmaids to their husbands, but at the time it was a legitimate way for an infertile woman to have children. Still, life in this family was often tense and competitive. The family values in this text are not intended to be imitated.

Spirituality and motherhood. The church has often defined spirituality in male terms of transcendence and separation. To be spiritual is to wrestle alone with God. To be spiritual is not to need human relationships. How might women define spirituality differently based on their experience of giving birth? Why is the desire for children so powerful? The process of pregnancy and birth allows women to be cocreators with God. They nurture new life within their own bodies. They nurture children to adulthood. They find that God is not only present in the big dreams and dramatic wrestling that Jacob experiences. God is also present in the desire for love and the desire for children. God is present in the relationships and the connections, the marriages and the births. God is present in ordinary, messy lives.

Questions for Reflection and Discussion

Have you ever wanted something the way Rachel wanted to be a mother?

This story's understanding of marriage seems so different from how we understand it in our culture. Why do you think that is, and what does it mean for how we read the Bible?

DINAH
(Genesis 34)

Dinah was the daughter of Jacob and Leah. After Jacob and his family left Laban's home, they settled in a Canaanite town named Shechem. They thought of Canaan as the land God had promised to them, but the Canaanites still lived there and the two groups did not live happily together.

Dinah was probably a teenager when the family settled in the area. The NRSV says that she went out to visit the women of the region, but a more literal translation says that she went out to "see." The text reports that she was seen by a man named Shechem, who "seized her and lay with her by force" (Gen. 34:2). This violent act was oddly followed by affection: "His soul was drawn to Dinah . . . ; he loved the girl, and spoke tenderly to her" (v. 3). Then he ordered his father to get her as his wife.

This puzzling sequence of events raises a number of questions. If Shechem was a stranger who raped Dinah, it seems odd that he later wanted to marry her and that she was willing to do so. It is possible that they knew each other and Shechem took advantage of her and forced her into sex (what we might call date rape). Once she had lost her virginity, she had no choice except to marry him. It is also possible that they had developed a mutual relationship and she willingly engaged in sexual activity. Each of these interpretations can be supported by the ambiguous language of the text. The author of Genesis uses three verbs to describe Shechem's actions. The first is "he took her," which is used frequently for a man taking a woman to marry or to bed. The NRSV translates it as "seized," which is a harsher connotation than is usually given to this word. Other translations say he took her. The second verb is "he lay with her," which was a common word for sexual contact. The third verb could indicate physical force or moral defilement. The Jerusalem Bible translates the phrases as "raped and so defiled." The King James Version says he "humbled" her.

Some commentators insist that Shechem violently raped Dinah and was simply trying to make himself appear less heinous when he spoke kindly to her. They insist that she was not able to consent. Others argue that the language of taking and laying with suggests a typical sexual relationship, which was complicated by the fact that she was a virgin acting without permission and was therefore "defiled" in the eyes of her family.

What if Dinah had met Shechem on one of her forays into the town? Perhaps they grew to care about each other and wanted to marry, but she knew her family would not approve because he was an outsider. They had a mutual sexual relationship, which her brothers labeled as rape because a young woman did not have the right to consent to a relationship. Her virginity belonged to her father, and he had not given consent.[44] She was now "damaged goods" and had no value as a virgin. She might have loved Shechem and wanted to marry him, but her opinion did not matter. Her brothers thought he was an unclean outsider who had raped their sister. This interpretation makes the most sense given the language of the story. It explains why he wanted to marry her and why she agreed, but it also explains why her family used the language of rape.[45]

Commentators use this text to denounce not only Dinah, but also women in general, for curiosity, initiative, and independence. They frequently point out that Dinah went out to see, and curiosity was the beginning of her downfall. Women belong in the private sphere, safe in their homes under the protection of father or husband. They have no good reason to go out in public, and danger results when they do.

It is possible that Dinah was a flighty, needy, bored young woman, but the text does not say. The commentators develop an elaborate story from the brief statement that she went out to see the women of the town. The story they tell justifies the blaming of Dinah. If she had not been needy, neurotic, and lonely, she would not have gone out. If she had not been superficial and interested in the clothes and jewels the women were wearing, she would not have gone out. If she had not been so curious, she would not have gone out. Female independence makes some commentators very nervous.

These interpretations raise questions about consent and illustrate the complexities of distinguishing between sexual assault and seduction. According to contemporary definitions of sexual assault, if Shechem took Dinah to his palace and sexually assaulted her, that was clearly rape. If he invited her to the palace, gave her dinner and wine, and then demanded sex as "payment," that was rape. If he invited her to the palace, gave her food and wine, and she willingly kissed him but said no when he demanded sex, that was rape. If the encounter was entirely based on mutual attraction and she was a willing partner, it was not a rape, although Dinah's brothers would have disagreed. It is impossible to say definitively what happened and to what degree Shechem forced Dinah and to what degree she consented. There is not enough evidence to blame Dinah for her behavior.

When Jacob heard what happened to his daughter, he did nothing at first.[46] His sons were furious, but less because their sister had been harmed and more because they believed Dinah had been polluted and the family had been shamed by outsiders.

Shechem's father, Hamor, asked Jacob if Dinah could marry Shechem. The sons of Jacob agreed to the marriage, but only if all the men of the town were circumcised. Hamor and Shechem assented to this bizarre request and persuaded the rest of the townsmen to agree as well, perhaps by exaggerating the benefits they could expect. "Will not their livestock, their property, and all their animals be ours?" (34:23)

The men of the town were circumcised, and while they were incapacitated, Simeon and Levi slipped into the town, killed all the men, and took Dinah back home. Was Dinah relieved to be free or did she mourn the loss of Shechem? The men did not ask her opinion. The brothers plundered the city of its livestock, possessions, women, and children. This violent (over)reaction seems completely out of proportion. Ironically, although the brothers considered sex between Dinah and Shechem disgraceful, they were willing to capture and rape (or at least force into marriage) the women of the town. The brothers did not care as much about protecting their sister or preserving ethnic purity as they did about avenging their family's honor and making a profit.

After all this destruction, Jacob expressed his fear that the vengeance had made him look bad among the neighbors, who were now more likely to attack him. The brothers were unrepentant. "Should our sister be treated like a whore?" (34:31)

This incident demonstrates the failure of the chosen people to be the blessing to the nations that God intended. Instead, Jacob's sons deceived Shechem and Hamor and destroyed their town. Deceit was a recurring genetic flaw in this family.[47]

Diving Deeper

Sexual ethics: consent. This story deals with issues of date rape and consent that are painfully relevant to teens and college students in particular. What does consent mean in a sexual relationship, espe-cially when alcohol might be involved? One partner might label a sexual encounter a rape, while the other assumed there was consent. In these cases, it is one person's word against another's. The conflicts that result from these scenarios have been extremely difficult for the students involved, and colleges and universities have struggled to find fair ways to handle these incidents in the absence of clear proof of what occurred.

Honor and violence: "Should our sister be treated like a whore?" In some cultures, family members might kill a man who dishonors a woman, or they might kill the woman herself.[48] A similar reaction also occurs on a broader scale. When a nation has been insulted or attacked, it is easy to overreact in defense of its honor. Leaders are tempted to take quick military action so that they do not appear weak and passive.

How might we as Christians offer a thoughtful, measured response when emotions are high and people are prone to overreaction? When people feel shamed, violated, or invaded,[49] the immediate urge is for vengeance. How can the "enemy" be punished? How can a sense of honor and superiority be restored?[50] The challenge of the gospel is to find alternatives to vengeance and violence.

Questions for Reflection and Discussion

Why do you think earlier commentators were anxious to blame Dinah for what happened to her?

This story has a violent ending that brings no glory to God. What might Jacob and his sons have done differently to change that ending?

TAMAR
(Genesis 38)

When a woman's security depends on producing children, to what lengths should she go in order to have them? If a woman had no hus-band, could she use any means necessary to conceive a child?

That was Tamar's dilemma.

Judah was the fourth son of Jacob and Leah. Judah married a

Canaanite woman, and they had three sons. Er, the first son, married Tamar. Before they had children, Er died suddenly, and the text explains that God killed him because he was wicked. Judah told his second son, Onan, to "perform the duty of a brother-in-law" (Gen. 38:8), which meant getting Tamar pregnant.[51]

Onan did not want to comply. He might have resented being told to impregnate a woman he had not chosen. He might have refused because a son for his brother reduced his share of the inheritance. Onan pretended to do his duty, but "he spilled his semen on the ground whenever he went in to his brother's wife" (38:9). Unless Tamar reported his actions, she would appear to be infertile.

The text reports that God was displeased with Onan and killed him also. Judah was understandably upset and did not want to lose his last son to this dangerous woman, so Judah sent her back to live in her father's house and promised that she could marry the third son, Shelah, when he was older.

After some years, Shelah had grown but Judah had not arranged a marriage. Tamar was living in her father's house, where she might have been a financial burden. She had no way to earn a living. She was still controlled by her father-in-law and could not marry anyone else. She was trapped in a life with a precarious future.

Tamar heard that Judah's wife had died and that Judah was on his way to a sheepshearing, so she removed her widow's clothes, dressed in a way that both hid her face and signaled her sexual availability, and sat in a spot along the road where Judah would pass by. Their meeting was abrupt and devoid of any social niceties. He immediately asked her for sex. She asked for payment, and he offered to send a goat. She asked for collateral, and he gave her several pieces of identification and then "went in to her" (38:18). She then returned to her widow's clothes and life. She had taken an enormous risk.

Judah sent a messenger with the goat to pay her, but she was nowhere to be found. Three months later, Judah learned that Tamar was pregnant because she had "played the whore." Judah did not hesitate to judge and punish her even though she was living in her father's home. "Let her be burned," he said (38:24). Perhaps he was glad to be rid of her and the threat she posed to his last surviving child.

Tamar must have been terrified, but she had a trump card. She brought out the items that Judah had given her. To his credit, Judah acknowledged his property, and then added that "she is more in the right [or, 'more righteous'] than I, since I did not give her to my son Shelah" (38:26).

Diving Deeper

The problem of patience, or "why we can't wait." Some who have commented on this passage say that Tamar should have been patient and waited for God to bring her justice. In a similar way, during the civil rights movement in the 1950s and 1960s, African Americans were told that if they were patient, polite, and hardworking, eventually they would be given the right to cast a vote and eat at a lunch counter. In the meantime, they should wait. In response, Martin Luther King Jr. described the typical experience of African Americans, which included lynch mobs, hate-filled policemen, poverty, exclusion, and humiliation. He concluded, "When you are harried by day and haunted by night by the fact that you are a Negro, living constantly at tiptoe stance never quite knowing what to expect next, and plagued with inner fears and outer resentments; when you are forever fighting a degenerating sense of 'nobodiness'; then you will understand why we find it difficult to wait."[52]

Tamar and King had very different experiences, but they shared the sense that they could no longer wait for the people in power to grant them freedom. They did what they needed to do to seek justice. They were not selfish but righteous.

Do the right thing. Judah quickly acknowledged that he was the father of Tamar's child and that she was more righteous than he. It must have been an awkward and embarrassing moment for him, but he spoke the truth. In this story, justice was more important than sexual propriety. Tamar was not chastised but praised.

This is not the only morally complex situation in which justice proves to be more important than strict obedience to the rules. Two senior citizens choose not to marry because it would threaten their financial security. A man whose wife no longer recognizes him because of Alzheimer's disease continues to visit and care for her but develops a close relationship with another woman. These choices may be "more righteous" even though they seem to challenge conventional morality.[53]

The blessing of Tamar. At the end of the story of Ruth (another widowed woman who takes unorthodox but courageous action to have a child), the people in the community offered a blessing to Ruth's new husband, Boaz: "May your house be like the house of Perez, whom Tamar bore to Judah" (Ruth 4:12). Tamar was cited as an example of fertility and goodwill. She was clearly not a shameful pariah or a bad girl but a respected and admired woman of the past.

Tamar also appears in the genealogy of Jesus in Matthew 1, with Ruth, Rahab, and Bathsheba. It proves that the good news of the gospel insists that Christ's lineage is indeed interwoven with the messy history of humanity. It should not be shocking, but comforting. Tamar is a model of grace and courage in the midst of family dysfunction.

Questions for Reflection and Discussion

Was Tamar right to have confronted Judah? Have you ever had to stand up to a family member or authority figure?

Were you surprised that Tamar is listed as one of Jesus' ancestors? Why do you think that Matthew considered it necessary to mention her?

POTIPHAR'S WIFE
(Genesis 39)

Like the story of Dinah in a previous section, the story of Potiphar's wife raises questions about lust, desire, power, and sexual behavior.

This time, however, the initiator was a woman.

Joseph, the target of her desire, was the son of Rachel and Jacob. His brothers sold Joseph into slavery because they resented the preferential treatment he received from their father. Joseph was taken to Egypt, where he was bought by Potiphar, an officer in Pharaoh's court. Joseph was given a great deal of responsibility in Potiphar's household and proved to be honest, reliable, and hardworking.

Joseph faced an uncomfortable challenge every day when he went to work. The boss's wife, Mrs. Potiphar, took a liking to Joseph because he was handsome and repeatedly asked him to lie with her. He refused, not only because he would not betray his master's trust but also because it would be a sin against God. She continued to pressure him, and one day when they were alone, she grabbed his robe and tried to force him. He escaped but left his outer robe behind. She told the servants and then her husband that Joseph had tried to rape her but ran away when she protested. Potiphar was furious and put Joseph in prison.

It was a blow to be imprisoned for a crime he did not commit, but

Joseph worked hard and earned the respect of the people in charge. Two of the prisoners had strange dreams, which Joseph interpreted. Later, one of them remembered Joseph when Pharaoh had a mysterious dream. Joseph's interpretation of Pharaoh's dream was his ticket out of prison and into agricultural management for Egypt. Later he reunited with his brothers and assured them he bore no grudges, because God had used him to save the whole family from starvation.

This story reads like a morality tale in which the characters represent common archetypes. Joseph is the hero: a wise, hardworking, virtuous young man. He was sold into slavery and then falsely accused of rape, but each time his effort and morality helped him rise above his difficult circumstances. Potiphar's wife is the dangerous woman who tempts the virtuous man to enjoy pleasure with her.[54] She is a foil who creates tension and conflict so that Joseph can prove his worth. Commentators typically praise the faith and virtue of Joseph and criticize Mrs. Potiphar both for her sexual assertiveness and for her false accusation of rape.

This story points at the double standard in the definition of sinful behavior. In both the Bible and contemporary culture, men are encouraged to take the initiative in relationships, even to pursue a woman who seems reluctant at first. If she initially says no, he might win her over with his charm and persistence. If a woman pursues a man, she is deemed aggressive and unladylike.

A similar double standard exists regarding age. An older man who dates or marries a much younger woman is assumed to be virile and powerful. An older woman who pursues a younger man is dismissively labeled as a "cougar" and considered somewhat pathetic.

Women have often been blamed for inciting male lust. They are criticized for leading men on or for provoking catcalls, whistles, and even rape because of what they wear or where they go. By that logic, perhaps Joseph had invited Mrs. Potiphar's interest in him and was at fault for being handsome. Why has it been so easy for men to claim that women ask for attention and are at fault when they receive it?

Diving Deeper

"Come, lie with me." The story raises significant contemporary concerns about sexuality, power, fear, and anxiety. The Christian tradition has often viewed women either as dangerous sexual temptresses or

as passive, asexual beings concerned only about having children, but surely there's more to it than that. Women are sexual beings just as men are. Women are not sinful or flawed because they express sexual desire. It is natural and appropriate when women find other people attractive. Men and women may express sexual desire in different ways and with different intensity, but they are equally sexual beings. Both men and women can be too aggressive or too passive in their relationships. Both men and women can experience lust when their own desires take precedence over the welfare and well-being of the other person. The power, joys, limits, and dangers of sexuality should be owned, acknowledged, and valued in both men and women so that sexuality can be a positive, life-giving part of identity rather than something that must always be feared and tightly controlled.

A more helpful and relevant approach to this story would focus not on the sin of sexual desire but on the misuse of power. The sin or brokenness in this story is not that Mrs. Potiphar experienced sexual desire for Joseph but that she misused her power over him. In contemporary language, she committed sexual harassment. She tried to force Joseph into a sexual relationship, and when he refused, she punished him. To simply chastise Mrs. Potiphar for sexual desire and praise Joseph because he said no, even at great cost, is to miss the point of the story.

As we think more about issues of power and sexuality, we need to give one another space to speak honestly about our experiences. Because men have traditionally had more positions of power in our society, they have more often been the perpetrators of sexual harassment and abuse. As women increasingly move into positions of power, they may also be tempted to abuse their power. How can we help one another think through these issues? How can we learn how to mentor and encourage while maintaining clear boundaries? How do we seek the welfare of those "below" us? How can we use our power responsibly?

Personal integrity. Joseph might have benefited in some way from having a sexual relationship with the boss's wife, but he would not use her invitation to improve his status. Joseph might have found Mrs. Potiphar attractive, but he refused to accept her invitation. He knew that it was not wise or healthy to engage in a relationship in which one person had so much power, so he stood up for himself. He preserved his integrity. He honored his commitments to his employer and to God even though he paid a price for them.

How do we make decisions based more on personal integrity than on blind obedience to the rules? One way is to make decisions based on a sense of our own worth and integrity. Doing right just because it is what we think others expect of us becomes hard to sustain.

Questions for Reflection and Discussion

Is the cost of preserving integrity ever too high? People sometimes choose to stay silent when they fear losing their job or status or relationships. When might that be a wiser response?

Many of these stories speak of women's sexuality in one-dimensional terms: they see women either as sexual aggressors or as the victims of male sexual aggression. Can you think of other places in the Bible where we find more balanced, healthy pictures of female sexuality?

2

Women of the Exodus

THE WOMEN WHO KEPT MOSES ALIVE
(Exodus 1–2)

The midwives. Jacob and his sons and their families had moved to Egypt in search of food. Jacob's son Joseph[1] had saved Egypt from starvation, but several centuries later, Pharaoh did not remember Joseph, and he feared the Israelites' physical and numerical strength. He tried first to exhaust them with brutally hard work, but the Israelites made even more babies, so the pharaoh turned to murder. He ordered the Hebrew midwives[2] to kill the male Israelite babies at birth. He might have intended that the midwives quickly smother the boys and tell the mothers they were stillborn. The midwives refused to obey this command because they feared God. Fear did not mean cowering in terror before an angry God but having a healthy sense of respect for God's ways. They answered to a higher authority than the king of Egypt. They were in the business of life, not death.[3]

When the king learned that the Israelite women still gave birth to boys, he asked why the midwives had defied his orders. They said, "Because the Hebrew women are not like the Egyptian women; for they are vigorous [full of life] and give birth before the midwife comes to them" (Exod. 1:19).[4] Whether they were lying or telling the truth, their response was an act of creative resistance that kept the babies alive. In the face of such violence, saving lives was more important than always telling the truth.

Because of the resistance of the midwives, the Israelites continued to multiply. The frustrated king developed a new plan and told the Egyptian people that every Hebrew baby boy should be thrown into the Nile River. The daughters could live. What threat could they be? One of the great ironies in this story is that the king wanted to eliminate the boys, who might rebel when they became adults, but the girls and women undermined his plans. The king assumed that women were weak and harmless, but wise, resourceful women brought down his kingdom.

Moses' two mothers. The command to throw the infant Hebrew boys into the Nile must have had a chilling effect on potential parents. Amram and Jochebed[5] had a baby but defied the order. His mother hid him at home for three months, then waterproofed a basket so it would float.[6] She put the child in the basket and the basket in the reeds next to the riverbank. His sister stood nearby to keep watch. She is not named here but likely was Miriam.[7]

The story in Exodus 2:1–10 does not say how long the basket was in the river. Perhaps Jochebed placed it in the river just before she knew someone would come. Still, she took a big risk. As she hoped, someone found the basket, and the rescuer was not an ordinary Egyptian but the daughter of Pharaoh. She opened the basket, found the crying baby, and took pity on him. She realized immediately that it must be one of the Hebrew children. The baby's sister then left her hiding place, approached Pharaoh's daughter, and offered to call a nurse from the Hebrew women to feed the child. Pharaoh's daughter agreed, so the sister fetched their mother, and Pharaoh's daughter paid her to nurse the baby until he was weaned. Then Jochebed brought him back to Pharaoh's daughter, who raised him as her own son and named him Moses.

Moses' birth mother and sister were clever, courageous, and quick-thinking. There is no evidence that Moses' father participated in any of these subversive activities.[8]

Pharaoh's daughter took an even greater risk. She defied her own father to save another woman's child. She could have drowned Moses with a quick flip of the basket, but she chose to be compassionate.[9] Perhaps she realized that her father's policies were futile and immoral.

These stories demonstrate that although Moses is the hero of the book of Exodus, without the midwives and Moses' mother, sister, and foster mother, there would have been no adult Moses. He and countless other baby boys were kept alive by the civil disobedience of the midwives. Moses lived to adulthood because women risked their lives to save him.

Diving Deeper

Ruthless. Although the story has a happy ending, it begins with an indictment of powerful people who ruthlessly oppressed the powerless. The Egyptians had all the power, yet they still tyrannized the Israelite slaves with brutal labor and infanticide. Slave owners know deep down that the system is built on injustice, and they constantly fear rebellion.

During the period of American slavery, the southern states enacted restrictive pass laws to prevent slaves from leaving the plantation without permission. The states feared that the slaves might organize and kill their owners in the night. The owners did not ask why the slaves might be angry enough to revolt. They only asked how the slaves could be controlled and further dehumanized so they would be too demoralized to plan a rebellion.

People and institutions with power often expend a great deal of energy to maintain their power against the threat of rebellion, rather than ask what injustice is sparking the rebellion. Some wealthy business owners resist the organization of labor unions or an increase in the minimum wage because they do not want to lose profits. Some white people resist discussion of white privilege and resent the phrase "black lives matter" because they do not want to acknowledge their own racism. Those in power will often do anything they can to keep those below them in their place. If they began to let go of their fear, however, they might find they could live more easily and creatively. How does the gospel enable people to let go of the power that they hold so tightly?

"They did not do as the king commanded." Resistance to oppression often begins in small actions. The enslaved Israelites did not have the power to defeat Pharaoh, but the midwives could save the boys and the mothers could save Moses. It is easy to be intimidated by slavery, apartheid, and segregation because these systems are so large and tenacious. They effectively demoralize and disempower people until they believe they are powerless, but sometimes when one person challenges the system, other people also refuse to be passive in the face of evil.

During World War II in Europe, the members of the resistance movement also refused to be passive. No individual could overthrow Hitler or dismantle the concentration camps, but Oskar Schindler found jobs for Jews that kept them out of the gas chamber. Corrie and Betsie ten Boom hid Jews in a cupboard in their house. Miep Gies and other helpers smuggled food to Anne Frank and her family when they were in hiding. Many others defied the Nazis in order to provide food or shelter or false documents. They could not end the oppression, but they could do something that made a difference.[10]

Like the midwives, members of the resistance sometimes had to lie in order to forge identity cards or help Allied pilots to escape. A lie seemed like a minor matter in the face of a demonic system. What does it mean to speak the truth when the truth means death and a lie means life? Does God demand a legalistic truth-telling when lives are at stake? Or does God care more about justice, compassion, and saving lives?

Call the midwife. This story reminds us that the midwife can be a powerful image of God. Midwives at their best are knowledgeable, supportive, calm, and relaxed. They coach the mother through the birth process, but they cannot do the work for the mother or take her pain away. They can be present, and they can make the delivery more comfortable and less frightening. So it is with God, who does not promise to take pain away or do the hard work for us but is present, active, supportive, and encouraging in the midst of struggle and pain.[11]

The helpers. Fred Rogers, of *Mr. Rogers' Neighborhood,* said that when he was a boy and saw scary stories and pictures on the news, his mother would say to him, "Look for the helpers. You will always find people who are helping."[12] He encouraged the children who watched his show to do the same.

Who was a supportive, encouraging friend who kept you going when you wanted to quit? Who was a wise person who gave you good advice? Who stood up for herself or others and taught you to do the same?

When you were a child or a teenager, was there someone who went out of their way to watch over you and keep you out of trouble? Who was the friend in junior high who stuck with you even though you were sort of an odd kid? Who was the teacher who saw potential in you when no one else did?

We can probably think of a dozen or more people who have helped us to survive and have made our lives what they are today. Identifying the helpers in our lives is a way to identify examples of grace and care and compassion. It enables us to see the ways that God is working in our lives in surprising ways through surprising people.

Questions for Reflection and Discussion

The Hebrew midwives engaged in a form of civil disobedience, choosing to follow the laws of God rather than those of flawed human rulers like Pharaoh. Can you think of situations in our society that would lead you to consider similar small acts of disobedience?

The author challenges us to identify the helpers (like these midwives) in times of trouble or difficulty. Are there times when someone looking for the helpers would have seen you?

MIRIAM
(Exodus 2; 15; Numbers 12)

Miriam is identified as a prophet (Exod. 15:20), which raises the hope that perhaps women can be valued for their leadership role in the Israelite community. Unfortunately, the Bible says little about Miriam except that she led the Israelite women in a song and was punished once for bad behavior. The text leaves a number of questions unanswered.

Miriam is one of a cadre of strong women who appear at the beginning of the book of Exodus.[13] She was the older sister of Moses who watched over him when his mother put him in a basket in the Nile.[14]

When Pharaoh's daughter found Moses, Miriam offered to find a Hebrew woman (their mother!) to nurse the child. Miriam has only one line of dialogue and one explicit action in this story, but she was clearly smart, quick-thinking, and courageous. Her mother might have coached her on what to say to Pharaoh's daughter, but her timing must have been just right to appear helpful without being intrusive and without raising suspicion that she was the baby's sister.

Nothing more is said of Miriam until eighty years had passed. Her brother Moses grew up in Pharaoh's household, encountered the God of Israel in a burning bush, and was sent to Egypt, along with his brother Aaron, to free the Israelites from slavery (Exod. 2–14). The reluctant Pharaoh finally let the people go, but almost immediately changed his mind and pursued them. The Israelites were trapped by the Red Sea until God parted the water, and they walked through on dry ground. When the Egyptian soldiers followed, they all drowned. Moses and the Israelites celebrated their victory with a song that began, "I will sing to the LORD, for he has triumphed gloriously; horse and rider he has thrown into the sea" (15:1). The song praised the God who delivered the Israelites from Egypt, brought them safely into the promised land, and defeated the enemy nations who had occupied their land.[15]

After the song ends at verse 18, the text says again that the Egyptians drowned in the sea after the Israelites walked through on dry ground. Another round of song follows, with different singers. "The prophet Miriam, Aaron's sister, took a tambourine in her hand; and all the women went out after her with tambourines and with dancing. And Miriam sang to them: 'Sing to the LORD, for he has triumphed gloriously; horse and rider he has thrown into the sea'" (vv. 20–21). Did the men sing the song first and then the women repeated it? Was this an antiphonal song in which the men sang all the verses listed in 15:1–18 and the women sang the "chorus" in 15:21? Was Moses like Gladys Knight, and Miriam and the women were the Pips who provided the backup?

These details may seem trivial, but they raise an important question. Women in this culture more often served as singers and drummers, so the song was likely first sung by Miriam and the women. Did a later editor of the text assume that Moses must have composed the song and directed the singing, since he was the leader of the Israelites? Was Miriam's leadership role possibly minimized by someone uncomfortable with her influence?[16]

The fact that Miriam is mentioned as song leader suggests that she had a significant role among the people. If she created the song, she demonstrated a remarkable ability to put words to music and capture the sense of celebration and gratitude among the people. If she was the song leader, she demonstrated an ability to get people singing together, which is no easy task, as any choir director or minister of music knows.

Miriam appears again in Numbers 12, but her story there cannot be understood without the larger context. In Numbers 11, Moses angrily vented to God about the Israelites' constant whining. He had reached the end of his patience. God offered Moses a plan for shared leadership, and seventy men received some of the spirit or power that Moses possessed. After a discussion about who could receive this power, Moses said, "Would that all the LORD's people were prophets, and that the LORD would put his spirit on them" (11:29). This incident suggests that both God and Moses thought it would be wise to share the leadership of the Israelite community, since Moses seemed ready to crack under the strain.

Sometime later, Miriam and Aaron raised some questions about Moses and his leadership (12:1–2). First, they criticized his marriage to a Cushite woman. Some commentators argue that "Cush" was another name for Midian, so the Cushite woman was Zipporah, the woman Moses married in Exodus 2. Other commentators say that Cush was a region near Ethiopia, so the Cushite woman must have been a second wife. If so, Miriam might have been angry because she cared about Zipporah and did not like the way Moses had treated her.[17] It is also possible that Miriam saw herself as Moses' confidante and disliked losing her position to the new wife.

A number of commentators suggest that Miriam and Aaron resented the Cushite wife because Israelites were not supposed to marry foreign women. Miriam and Aaron asked what they considered a legitimate question. Should a leader of the Israelites be breaking the rules and setting a bad example?

The two also posed a second question, "Has the LORD spoken only through Moses? Has he not spoken through us also?" (12:2). Perhaps they felt that they had worked as hard as Moses at leading the cranky Israelites but did not get the respect and recognition they deserved. Perhaps they were jealous of Moses and his authority. Perhaps they had tried to ease Moses' load by sharing in the leadership but he insisted on doing it all himself and then complained about being overworked. If the spirit could be shared with seventy others, why could it not be shared with them?

God took greater offense at their questions than Moses did. God appeared in a pillar of cloud to address Aaron and Miriam directly. God gave a stirring defense of Moses, reminding them that other prophets might receive dreams and visions, but God spoke to Moses face-to-face. Aaron and Miriam should not have presumed to criticize Moses. God then punished Miriam with a form of leprosy. Aaron shared equally in the complaint but was not punished. Why was Miriam punished so harshly? Did she instigate the complaints while Aaron only reluctantly agreed?[18] Or was Aaron spared because leprosy would make him unclean and unable to fulfill his priestly role?

Aaron appealed to Moses on her behalf, addressing him as "my lord," which must have been particularly humiliating given that he had just challenged Moses' leadership. Moses prayed that God would heal Miriam, which God did, but she was sent to isolation outside the camp, as the diagnosis of leprosy required. This "time-out" may seem innocuous, but imagine a woman living alone outside the camp without shelter or protection from predators and the elements. Did anyone sit with her or bring food and water? The people did not leave without her, but waited until she returned before continuing their journey, a sign that she was respected and valued.[19]

Miriam was a strong, feisty woman much appreciated by her peers. Did her success and popularity pose a threat to her brothers?[20] Did they, perhaps with God's help, conspire to take her down a peg? Were strong women leaders simply not welcome in this culture? Or was she really a jealous, competitive woman?

Diving Deeper

Silenced. In the process of writing this book, I was often surprised to discover women whose names and stories I had never heard before. Miriam was different. I knew she was a prophet and a leader, and I expected the Bible to contain multiple stories of her work among the Israelites. Instead, I found silence. Miriam cared for baby Moses, led some singing, and was punished for being uppity. Where were the stories about her life, her work, her contributions? And why is the "bad" Miriam of Numbers 12 remembered more than the strong woman in Exodus?

Carol Lakey Hess describes a Sunday school lesson for young teens that portrayed Miriam as a jealous woman who resented Moses' leadership. She was a good choir director but she overreached when she tried to exercise spiritual leadership. The author of the curriculum compared Miriam to a girl in a high school youth group who helped plan the youth Sunday service but was angry when she was asked to sing rather than to preach. The moral of the story was that the readers should be content to exercise the gifts they had been given and avoid overreaching and thinking more highly of themselves than they ought to think.[21]

Unfortunately, some women in American culture are also punished for speaking up. Sheryl Sandberg in her book *Lean In* provides multiple examples of women who kept quiet because they were afraid of being ignored, misunderstood, criticized, or punished for expressing their opinion. Women report that in meetings they have frequently presented an idea that was ignored until a man presented the same idea a few minutes later.[22]

For women who have been silenced, the good news of the gospel comes to them in the form of people and institutions that are willing to listen. It is not enough simply to say that God hears the voices of the marginalized. The church, society, corporate world, and other institutions and structures need to be more intentional about listening to women, not just upper-middle-class women with MBAs, but all women. What they say may not be easy to hear, because many women will tell a painful story of exclusion. But there will be truth and gospel when those in power choose to lean in and listen.

There is so much silence about Miriam, and what the text does say can be disconcerting. When women leaders are so rare, it is difficult to acknowledge their imperfections, but preachers do not do the women in the Bible any favors by downplaying their flaws. Like the male characters, they are human. They make mistakes. They should not be more harshly criticized when they fail, and they should not be excused.[23]

Miriam, Aaron, Moses, and the rest of us are flawed and complex people. Sometimes we sing joyfully, and then we get testy with each other. Sometimes we are courageous. Sometimes we don't want to be leaders anymore. Sometimes we are confident, and then we are terrified. Sometimes we demonstrate great spiritual maturity and insight, and then we don't. But the amazing thing is that God uses Miriam and Aaron and Moses with all their gifts and all their flaws. And God uses us, with all our gifts and all our flaws, for the good of the kingdom.

Questions for Reflection and Discussion

What were Miriam's strengths? What were her flaws? How do you see the relationship between the two?

Had you been Miriam, what would you have said to God when you were struck with leprosy?

ZIPPORAH
(Exodus 2–4)

Moses lived in Egypt after being raised by Pharaoh's daughter. There are no details about this period of his life, except that he killed an Egyptian who was beating an Israelite (Exod. 2:11–12). Moses then fled to Midian and was sitting at a well when the seven daughters of Jethro (or Reuel), the high priest of Midian, came to water their sheep. They were harassed by some shepherds, and Moses gallantly fended them off and drew water for the sheep. When the daughters arrived home, they told their father about the "Egyptian" stranger who helped them. Moses was invited to dinner and welcomed into the family. Later Jethro gave his daughter Zipporah to Moses. The Bible does not say whether she wanted to marry him.[24]

Moses kept busy tending his father-in-law's sheep, but God had a larger vocation planned for him. One day Moses heard the voice of God speaking to him from a burning bush. God told a terrified Moses to go to Pharaoh and bring the Israelites out of Egypt. That was a daunting task, and Moses began to make excuses. "What if they don't listen to me?" "I am not eloquent." "Please send someone else." God was remarkably patient with this litany of excuses, but eventually became irritated, and sent Moses' brother Aaron along to serve as a spokesperson.

Moses is often criticized for his reluctance, but he had reasons for caution. Going to Egypt meant confronting his adoptive family. There is no evidence that Moses identified with the Israelites or their faith. Moses may not have known God, but God knew Moses. God made an offer that Moses could not refuse, and Moses reluctantly agreed to go, but his heart was not in it.

Moses took Zipporah and their sons and started to Egypt. On the way, they had a bizarre and frightening encounter with God. They stopped to rest for the night, and the text reports that "the LORD met him and tried to kill him" (4:24). The text does not identify the antecedents to the pronouns. Did God want to kill Moses or one of the sons? God had recently gone to some trouble to convince a reluctant Moses to go to Egypt to free the Israelites. Why would God now want to kill him? Was this a test? The Bible does not say whether God appeared in a physical form or as a voice, but Moses was paralyzed with fear and did not defend himself or his son. Zipporah somehow discerned what God wanted, and she took a flint (a piece of stone used for starting fires) and circumcised her son.

The text does not say why she did this. Commentators speculate that God was angry because either Moses or one or both sons had not yet been circumcised. Zipporah might have refused to allow her sons to be circumcised at birth because she was not an Israelite. Perhaps Moses had not circumcised his sons because he had been raised as an Egyptian and did not identify with the Israelites or their religious practices.

Whatever the reason for her action, Zipporah was a gutsy woman with nerves of steel who could perform emergency surgery on her son without losing her lunch. When she finished the circumcision, she took the bloody foreskin and touched "his" feet with it. Again the Hebrew does not specify the antecedent. Did she touch Moses or the son? And what exactly did she touch with the foreskin? The Hebrew word for "feet" is often a euphemism for "genitals." Some commentators suggest that she touched Moses' genitals with the son's foreskin, which symbolically meant that Moses was circumcised too. Others say that putting the blood on Moses foreshadowed the later command that the Israelites put lamb's blood on their doors so that the angel of death would "pass over" them. Zipporah served as a mediator between God and Moses just as Moses would serve as a mediator between God and the Israelites. God's mysterious anger subsided when Zipporah circumcised the child.

Zipporah twice referred to Moses as a "bridegroom of blood" (4:25, 26). It is hard to say whether she was angry, frustrated, terrified, or relieved. She might have been relieved that she had saved her husband's life but annoyed to be left with blood on her hands. She might have been angry that Moses was being pursued by an angry God. She might have resented Moses for making their marriage complicated and difficult.[25]

The Bible does not say why this incident occurred. Perhaps it was a reminder to Moses that he was about to begin a life-and-death struggle with the Egyptians. If Pharaoh did not let the Israelites go, Moses would have to announce that God would kill the firstborn sons of all the Egyptians. In this strange encounter with God, Moses learned how it felt to have God threaten his life and the life of his son. This was what the Egyptians would feel as well.[26]

This encounter might have served as an awakening for the reluctant Moses. Perhaps he was still second-guessing his abilities and making excuses. The emphasis on circumcision might have forced Moses to identify with the people of Israel. If he was going to lead them, he would have to participate in their religious practices, including circumcision. Zipporah understood that and acted quickly to save Moses and/or the child.[27]

Diving Deeper

The Bible gives us little information about Zipporah. It is clear, however, that she was a bold, courageous woman who would not sit by passively while God killed her husband and/or son. She did not back down from this terrifying God. Although she was not an Israelite, she was spiritually perceptive enough to realize what might appease God.[28] As an infant, Moses' life had been saved by the midwives, his mother

Jochebed, his sister Miriam, and his adoptive mother, Pharaoh's daughter. In adulthood, his wife Zipporah saved his life.

The vagaries of vocation. Moses did not have a clear sense of vocation for much of his life. He was probably in his seventies when he encountered God in the burning bush. God called him to a new vocation, but Moses was reluctant. Then God tried to kill him. Vocation for Moses was definitely a process of growth and development. This perspective on Moses is less heroic, but more human and relatable.

In the hands of an angry God. What are we to make of the "visceral, untamed, and hostile" image of God presented in this text?[29] The Israelites cheered the angry God who acted on their behalf and killed the Egyptian children and drowned the Egyptian soldiers. Divine anger was far more offensive and mysterious when directed at God's own people. Perhaps this event was a means for Moses to encounter this demanding and dangerous side of God.

In C. S. Lewis's *The Lion, the Witch, and the Wardrobe,* the characters discuss Aslan the lion, who is the God-figure. Someone asks nervously, "Is he [the lion] quite safe?" A resident of Narnia with more experience responds, "Course he isn't safe. But he's good."[30] Perhaps the point of a story like this one is not that we be terrified of God, or that we feel pressured to shape up, but that we recognize the mystery, freedom, holiness, and transcendence of God.

Questions for Reflection and Discussion

How did Zipporah know that circumcising her son was the solution to the strange situation in which she and her family found themselves in this story?

Why is it easier to think about divine violence when it is directed against the firstborn of the Egyptians than when Moses, Zipporah, and their family are threatened?

THE DAUGHTERS OF ZELOPHEHAD
(Numbers 27; 36)

Which of these statements is more true of religious faith? (1) Rules are rules. A community is shaped by its laws and traditions, and they should not be changed. (2) Rules are made to be broken. Laws are made for particular circumstances and contexts, but those particulars change over the course of time, and laws need to change with them.

The book of Numbers describes the forty-year period during which the Israelites wandered in the wilderness. None of the adults who were freed from Egypt were allowed to enter Canaan. Only their children could do that. Still, all of the Israelite men who had been freed from Egypt were promised a share of the new land, even if they would not be able to live in it.

The rule in Israel was that only sons could inherit their father's property. If a man died without sons, his property was given to other male members of his family. The five daughters of Zelophehad thought the rule was unjust. Their father had no sons, but his daughters did not want their father's name and right to property to be lost. The daughters wanted to preserve his name and memory by preserving his land for their descendants. They knew the tradition that only sons inherited property. They knew the rules, but in this case the rules seemed unjust, so the daughters approached Moses to plead their case.

The Bible reports that "the daughters of Zelophehad came forward" (Num. 27:1). This is an understated summary of an action that took a great deal of courage. Many people in the book of Numbers came forward, with unhappy results. The Israelites complained that they had no meat, and God struck them with a plague (Num. 11). Miriam and Aaron asked whether God spoke only through Moses, and Miriam was punished with leprosy (Num. 12). Korah, Dathan, and Abiram expressed doubts about Moses' leadership, and they and their families were swallowed up by the ground (Num. 16). Coming forward to make a request was not a casual or safe action. Questioning authority could be dangerous.

The women did not quietly and apologetically sidle up to Moses in private and beg for a favor. They came to the entrance of the tent of meeting, where the people worshiped. The daughters made their case before Moses, Eleazar the priest, the leaders, and the people. "Our father died in the wilderness," they said. "Why should the name of our father be taken away from his clan because he had no son? Give to us a possession among our father's brothers" (27:4).[31]

This does not seem like a radical request to contemporary readers who assume that men and women have an equal right to inherit property, but Israelite culture was patrilinear, meaning that men passed their property to their sons, or to other male family members if they had no sons. Daughters received a dowry but lived on their husband's land with his family. The request for women to receive land was a significant departure from the traditional pattern.[32]

Moses was not prepared to answer their question and asked God for advice. God's answer was understated, surprising, and powerful: "The daughters of Zelophehad are right in what they are saying" (27:7). God acknowledged the validity of their request and told Moses to give them their father's portion of the land. This was not merely an exception to the rule. God made it clear that the rules were changed to allow all daughters to inherit land if there were no sons.

Modern readers might ask why daughters did not inherit equally along with their brothers. The practice arose out of the Israelites' precise system of land distribution. Once the land had been apportioned, and each family received a roughly equal section, it was important to keep the land in the family. If a woman inherited land, and then married a man from another tribe, her land would belong to him and his tribe, and one tribe could then acquire more than its fair share. This problem could be avoided if women did not inherit land.

In Numbers 36, members of Zelophehad's tribe asked what would happen if the daughters married outside the tribe. Moses acknowledged their concern and advised the women to marry men within their clan. The text reports that the daughters did as they were told. They married their cousins, and their inheritance remained in the tribe.

The skeptical reader might conclude that, once again, women did as they were told. They won justice for their father at the cost of their freedom to marry any man in Israel. The women were indeed willing to compromise, but they had actually been given a radical freedom. Moses told the women to marry "whom they think best" (36:6), which allowed them an unusual amount of choice in a culture where women were usually given and taken without regard to their preferences. Because they owned land, they were highly desirable candidates for marriage. Moses trusted their ability to choose their spouses from among the many men who might want to marry them. These women with the courage to come forward were rewarded with both their father's land and a high degree of freedom.

Diving Deeper

They came forward. The daughters might have been dismissed as selfish and greedy, or criticized for not knowing their place as women, or even punished for challenging authority. It would have been safer for them to hold back, keep quiet, and tell themselves that they would keep their father's memory alive even if his land was lost. But they came forward. They were polite but direct.

It still takes courage to come forward in search of justice. In the early nineteenth century in the United States, married women could not own property. A single woman could inherit property from her father, but once she married, it belonged to her husband. He owned her wages as well. In 1836, some women came forward to the New York state legislature to ask that the laws be changed. The legislature needed twelve years and repeated requests to decide that the women were "right in what they are saying" and pass the Married Women's Property Act in 1848. It took another seventy-two years and many more acts of coming forward before women received the right to vote in 1920.

Women and members of ethnic minority groups find that they still need to come forward in the church, in business, in education, and in politics to seek justice, respect, and equal opportunities. Coming forward is risky, because they may be labeled selfish, greedy, or impatient. They may be accused of challenging the institution to change before people are ready. It can be especially difficult to come forward in the church, when the rules and traditions have become sacrosanct and resistant to change.

Recently, African Americans have had many painful reasons to come forward in search of justice. They have protested and marched and gathered in Ferguson, Baltimore, Charleston, and many other places. The protesters have often been criticized, treated harshly, or arrested. They speak a truth that is painful to hear: racism is alive and well in America. What are some of the ways that those coming forward might be encouraged and supported? What laws and practices need to be changed in order to make the world a just and safe place for everyone?

Equal opportunity? The Israelites believed that every man was entitled to a piece of land, which provided a family with food and security. The rules ensured that everyone had land and no one benefited from the misfortune of others.

American culture has been shaped by a myth that says everyone can succeed if they work hard enough. Unlike the Israelite rule of relative equality, however, people do not start with the same resources. Consider a child who is born in a wealthy suburb of a large city. Her parents provide her with nourishing organic food, excellent schools, medical care, and many opportunities in music and sports. She lives in a safe neighborhood with parks, a library, and a community pool. Consider another child who is born the same day in a rundown and economically depressed urban neighborhood. Her parents work hard at their minimum-wage jobs but there is never enough money. The neighborhood is dangerous. There is a crack house on the next block, and there have been drive-by shootings. There are no parks or libraries. The school system is ranked the lowest in the state, and while the teachers do their best, they are overwhelmed with the desperate needs of the students, which preclude their learning. Do these two children have an equal opportunity to succeed?

Imagine a bicycle race in which one person is riding a top-quality bike like those used in the Tour de France. The other is riding a heavy, ancient, beat-up, single-speed bike. It probably does not matter who is more skilled or fit. The person on the expensive bike has a distinct advantage.[33]

It does not feel like good news for privileged people to be reminded that they are riding a very expensive bicycle or that they benefit from the color of their skin. They have been taught that God has given them their privileges. This story might help people explore a radically different economic system in which the goal is the equitable distribution of resources.

Tradition and change. When should a community's laws and social practices be preserved and when should they be changed? How does a community decide? In the 1950s, Jim Crow laws seemed reasonable and necessary to many white southerners, but racist and demeaning to African Americans. These laws were finally changed, not because of majority public opinion, but because they were unjust. As social attitudes change over time, it becomes clear that some laws written for an earlier time are no longer relevant. Even the US Constitution was changed when it became clear that slavery was wrong or that women should have the right to vote. Still, this process causes a great deal of uncertainty and conflict.

The story of the daughters of Zelophehad might serve as a model for LGBTQ people and their allies who seek change in the church. They have been coming forward now for many years, asking for the rules to be changed so they can be fully included. They know that there are seven passages of Scripture that have been used to exclude them, but they appeal to the deeper biblical values of justice, equity, and grace. They believe that the assumptions and practices that exclude ought to be changed so that all of God's people are welcomed. Some churches have recognized that they are right in what they are asking and have begun to change the laws in order to be welcoming and inclusive.[34]

Questions for Reflection and Discussion

Have there been times when you have had to "come forward" on your own behalf or on behalf of others?

What situations in your community need someone to step forward and help?

3

Women of the Promised Land

RAHAB
(Joshua 2; 6)

The story of Rahab shows how difficult it can be to move beyond one's past. Rahab was a Canaanite woman who helped the Israelites and was protected when her city was destroyed. She was a woman of faith and courage, yet the Bible repeatedly refers to her as "Rahab the prostitute." Was she a particularly brazen and seductive woman who led men into temptation?

The story begins with a reconnaissance mission. Forty years after the exodus, the Israelites were trying the regain the land of Canaan. Two Israelite men went to spy out the city of Jericho before the Israelites attacked it. The men stopped first at a house built into the wall surrounding the city. The house belonged to a prostitute named Rahab.

Their visit quickly became public knowledge. The Jericho version of Homeland Security informed the king that spies had arrived in the city. The king ordered Rahab to turn the men in, but instead, she hid them on her roof. When the king's agents appeared at her house, she said that the men had been there earlier, but they had left through the gates of the city (Josh. 2:2–6).

After the agents left, Rahab demanded a deal with the spies. She had saved their lives, she said, and she asked the spies to save the lives of her family members in return. Rahab did not belong to the Israelite people, but she saw that they were more powerful and successful than their numbers would suggest. They appeared to have a mysterious divine force on their side that had freed them from slavery in Egypt. She recognized the power of the God of the Israelites and knew her town did not have a chance.

The spies promised to help if Rahab hung a red cord in the window of her house. Some months later, when the spies returned with the Israelite army, they kept their word, and "Rahab the prostitute" and her family were spared (6:25). She and her family were welcomed into the Israelite community because she had protected the spies.

Rahab is named three times in the New Testament. In the genealogy of Jesus in Matthew 1, she is identified as the mother of Boaz[1] and the wife of Salmon. The author of Hebrews 11:31 says of her, "By faith Rahab the prostitute did not perish with those who were disobedient, because she had received the spies in peace." In describing the need for good works in addition to faith, James 2:25 asks, "Was not Rahab the prostitute also justified by works when she welcomed the messengers and sent them out by another road?"

Rahab is the only person in the Hebrews 11 list of faithful people to be saddled with a negative label. King David is not called "David the murderer" or "David the adulterer." Samson is not identified as "the gullible guy tricked by Delilah." Jephthah sacrificed his daughter, but he is not labeled "Jephthah the incredibly stupid father." Men are described by their faithful actions.

Why is she repeatedly labeled as a prostitute? Even when she is praised for her faith or works, the praise is qualified by the label. The woman has a lot to live down. Rahab had a number of strikes against her. She was female and a foreigner. The most troubling issue, however, was her identity as a prostitute. The approval rating of that profession was no higher than it is now. Prostitutes gave men safe outlets for their sexual energy, but they were despised and marginalized. Prostitution was the last resort for desperate women, who had few ways to support themselves if they did not marry. Rahab's career "choice" came from her need to survive and support her family.

When the biblical authors so blithely called her a prostitute, they emphasized her gender and sexuality and made her appear immoral. Perhaps the name-calling was an attempt to discredit her or take her down a peg. Maybe the New Testament authors resented her influence and wanted to limit it. Mary Magdalene has been treated in a similar way by the Christian tradition. Many people think that she was a prostitute, even though there is absolutely no biblical evidence for this label. It is possible that as she grew more powerful and respected in the early church, some folks wanted to discredit her, and labeling her a prostitute was an effective way to do so.

Perhaps the idea of a prostitute as a role model seemed to offer a compelling example of grace in action. Some commentators put a positive spin on this name-calling and conclude that she was labeled as a prostitute to emphasize that God can forgive anyone, no matter how broken. That may be true, but why not label men's sinful behavior? The name-calling suggests that the church finds it more difficult to forgive and forget when somebody has a juicy piece of brokenness in their past. Rahab appears in the list of the faithful, but she can't live down her past. She made a new life for herself and her family in Israel, but the authors of James and Hebrews had to remind readers who she once was.

Perhaps the good news is that Rahab is *in* the list of the faithful. This "fallen," foreign woman was spiritually perceptive enough to recognize the power of God at work among the Israelites. She realized that they had not crossed the Red Sea or defeated their enemies on their own power. She saw that God was the source of their strength. Many of the Israelites were not so astute.

Maybe the label "prostitute" does not matter so much to God. The authors emphasized her sinfulness, but perhaps God saw a woman who did what she had to do to save herself and her family. God saw the courageous choices she made to help the spies. In God's vocabulary, maybe her name was not Rahab the prostitute, but Rahab the faithful, Rahab the courageous, Rahab the quick-thinking negotiator, or Rahab the wise.

Diving Deeper

Name-calling. Most people have been called an ugly name at some point in their lives: "fatso" or "stupid" or "clumsy" or maybe a name related to ethnicity or sexuality. We say "sticks and stones may break my bones, but words can never hurt me," but we know that is not true. Names like "loser," "failure," or "disappointment" can make us feel that we will never amount to anything. Names like "slut," "stoner," or "dumb jock" can define us long after high school is over. How do people shake off past indiscretions or failures if other people bring them up again and again?

The good news is that God does not call us by those names. God sees the pain those names cause. God knows that human beings are worth infinitely more than their negative labels. The good news is that God uses a new vocabulary and gives us new names. God calls people "beloved" or "God's own people" or "saint." God sees the gifts and graces in people and calls them by those names.

Hospitality. We would do better to focus on Rahab's gifts and strengths rather than her profession. One such gift was radical hospitality. The spies were strangers who intended to destroy her city and yet she "dealt kindly" with them (Josh. 2:12). She showed them steadfast love, or *hesed*, a word often used to describe God's actions. She took an incredible risk and put herself in danger in order to care for strangers. In what ways might Christians be called to radical hospitality and steadfast love in their own contexts? How might they care for refugees? The homeless? The poor? Those of another religious tradition?

"The LORD your God is indeed God." Rahab's story demonstrates that insight about faith, grace, and God can come from unusual quarters. She was not an Israelite, but she recognized the power of God. Other people melted in fear because of this power, but she aligned herself with it. Similarly, in contemporary culture there are people who do not identify with any particular religion and yet demonstrate perceptive insight about faith and grace.

"The prostitute." Once when I preached on the story of Rahab, a preteen girl wrote a note to her mother on the bulletin, "What's a prostitute?" The mother wrote an answer, and the girl quickly erased it! When we come together to study Scripture we should enter a safe place to deal with the mess and complications of life.

Prostitution is often glamorized, as in the movie *Pretty Woman*, where the beautiful and elegant Julia Roberts falls in love with a handsome, wealthy, generous client who eventually marries her. The movie bears little resemblance to reality. Prostitution is ugly, dangerous, brutal work, which women do mostly because they have no other choices.

Julia Roberts's character could leave prostitution when she chose to do so, but the victims of human trafficking cannot. They have been tricked or forced into the business, and they cannot get out. In some countries, prostitution has become a vital part of the tourism industry. Hotel guests can purchase sexual activity along with a room. This practice has been particularly pervasive in some third-world countries, but every year a significant amount of sex trafficking occurs in early February in the US city where the Super Bowl is being played. Religious people need to be aware of the devastation caused by human traffick-ing. The story of Rahab does not offer easy solutions to these contem-porary questions, but it does provide a powerful story of the grace of God working through the "fallen," the foreign, and the marginalized.

A conversion story? Some commentators claim that once she discovered the God of the Israelites, Rahab had no further desire to be a harlot. She turned her house into a bed and breakfast or she sold the flax that was drying on the roof. Unfortunately, this reading perpetuates the idea that prostitution is a choice made by a sinful woman rather than an economic necessity. It might be inspirational to claim that the "fallen" Rahab finds God and turns her life around, but the text does not say definitively that this happened. She certainly did not join "the church." It may be more comfortable to read this story as a conversion narrative that proclaims that even the worst people are redeemable. No one needs to be trapped and marked by the past. God's grace can forgive and transform even the worst sinner. But the more challenging option might be to consider that a woman might be at the same time a prostitute and a gracious, faithful, hospitable, and spiritually perceptive person.

Questions for Reflection and Discussion

Even though the label of "prostitute" has stuck with her, we remember Rahab for so much more. What do you want people to remember about you?

Rahab exercised a costly and dangerous form of hospitality when she welcomed the Hebrew spies. In what ways does following our faith today cost us?

ACHSAH
(Joshua 15; Judges 1)

The story of Achsah is brief and easily overlooked, given its location in the midst of battle scenes. The five verses, Joshua 15:15–19//Judges 1:11–15, show both the constraints on a woman who is the property of her father and the power of a woman's voice when she uses it to speak up for herself.

The books of Joshua and Judges describe the process by which the Israelites laid claim to the land that God had promised them. In this vignette, Caleb decided to attack the Canaanite city of Debir. To motivate his soldiers to bravery, he offered to give his daughter Achsah to the man who defeated the city. Othniel, a relative of Caleb's, won the battle, took the city, and received Achsah as a wife. She appeared to have no choice in the matter. She was a prize who was given and taken regardless of her wishes. She was her father's property, and he could use her as he chose. Love and affection were not required for marriage.

To her credit, Achsah did not simply fade into the background as a silent, docile, well-behaved woman. When she and Othniel began their marriage, she encouraged him to ask her father for a field. Had Caleb failed to provide an adequate dowry? Had he given them poor land?

The next obvious step in this process would be for Othniel to ask Caleb for land. Instead, the text reports that Achsah rode a donkey to her father's home.[2] The text does not say what transpired between her suggestion that Othniel ask for a field and her arrival at her father's. Did Othniel refuse to make the request because he was afraid to offend his father-in-law? Did Achsah get tired of waiting for Othniel to act and decide to make the request herself? Did they agree that the request should come from her? Or did Othniel ask for a field, but Caleb either refused or gave them dry land that Achsah found unacceptable?[3]

When Achsah arrived at her father's home, he immediately asked what she wanted, and she did not hesitate. "Give me a present," she said. She did not ask politely, but used the imperative. Some commentators criticize her for being greedy and failing to appreciate what she had already received. Others suggest that the couple had been given dry land in the Negeb region, and they needed water to make the crops grow. She asked specifically for the *Gulloth-mayim*, "springs of water." Her father gave her two springs.

The Tanakh, a Jewish translation, offers an interesting alternative interpretation. When Caleb asked why she had come, the Tanakh translates Achsah's response, "Give me a present, for you have given me away as Negeb-land" (Josh. 15:19). This implies that she was confronting her father about the fact that he offered her as a prize to a victorious soldier, and she was seeking compensation for being used in this way. If she had to live with this man she had not chosen, they at least needed some fertile land.

This story vividly illustrates women's status as property. Achsah's father gave her away as a prize to a victorious soldier. She could have passively resigned herself to her fate. She might have assumed that because she had no choice in marriage that she had no choice or voice at all. Instead, she took the initiative to ask for land, just as the daughters of Zelophehad did in Numbers 27. Achsah might not have been able to choose her own husband, but she refused to be passive about their life together. She did not simply accept the dry land she had been given. She told her father that she needed something better, and he recognized the validity of her request. She may have been taken and given, but she did not give up her voice.

Diving Deeper

Don't be afraid to ask. Many women in the world are still limited by the rules of their culture. Sometimes they may not vote, drive a car, own property, use birth control, or get an education. This story encourages women to use their voices in the ways that are open to them, ask for what they need, and stand up for themselves.

Malala Yousafzai spoke out about the importance of education for girls in Pakistan, even after she was shot in the head by someone who thought her advocacy was inappropriate. She won a Nobel Peace Prize.

After seeing dozens of women die from multiple pregnancies, Margaret Sanger tried to make birth control accessible to women in New York City. Her clinic was shut down because it was considered obscene to talk about birth control or send it through the mail. She persisted and later was a driving force in the development of birth control pills.

Nicholas Kristof and Sheryl WuDunn tell the story of Saima, a woman from Pakistan who was desperately poor, with an unemployed husband who regularly beat her. A microfinance organization gave her a loan of $65. She bought beads and cloth and began to embroider. She paid off her husband's debt, educated her children, renovated her house, employed other women, and put her husband to work. When she had access to even the most minimal resources, she was able to turn her life around.[4]

Achsah refused to be silent. She asked for what she needed. She used her springs in the desert to grow enough food for her family, just as Saima used her beads and cloth to make a living for herself and her family. These two women might have had limited choices, but they did not give up their voices.

Questions for Reflection and Discussion

How do you know when you are standing up for yourself, and when you are making a pest of yourself? Is finding the answer harder for women than for men? Is it harder for you?

Can you name times when you've felt like someone's property, or when someone saw you more as a means to an end than as a real person?

DEBORAH
(Judges 4–5)

Deborah is a woman leader who is respected and valued for her wisdom and intelligence. She is identified as a prophet and "a mother in Israel" (Judg. 4:4; 5:7).

The book of Judges describes a transitional time in the history of the Israelites. The twelve tribes did not yet function as a nation governed by a king, but were led by a series of judges. A pattern appears throughout the book: the Israelites "did what was evil in the sight of the LORD" (4:1), were oppressed by the Canaanites or Philistines, and begged God for relief. Each time, God appointed a judge to fight the oppressor and restore moral and spiritual order to the community.

On this occasion, the Israelites had been oppressed for twenty years by the king of Canaan. This time, the judge whom God raised up was a woman. Deborah is identified as a prophet, a person who could be trusted to convey God's words to the people. The NRSV also describes her as the "wife of Lappidoth" (4:4), but the word *lappidoth* can mean "torches" or "fire," so some scholars translate the phrase to mean a fiery or spirited woman.[5]

Deborah carried out her role as judge in an "office" under a tree in a high-traffic area, and people came to her for advice and guidance. She also served as a military adviser. She summoned Barak, the Israelite army commander, and gave him a word from the Lord. Barak needed to gather up his troops and go to battle against Sisera, the general of the Canaanite army. God promised victory over Sisera, but Barak was reluctant. The Canaanites had nine hundred iron chariots, and he was afraid that even with ten thousand troops, the Israelites would be defeated. He told Deborah that he would go to battle only if she went also. This strong, confident military man refused to go to battle without a woman! Deborah agreed to accompany him, but she also said that Barak would not receive the glory and acclaim for the victory. Instead, she said, a woman would receive all the glory.

Barak gathered his troops and waited for further instruction. Deborah determined the timetable for the attack. "Up!" she said to Barak. "For this is the day on which the LORD has given Sisera into your hand" (4:14). God threw Sisera and his chariots into a panic,[6] which enabled Barak and his troops to kill all of Sisera's soldiers. Sisera was humiliated and ran away to the tent of Jael, a woman who offered him food and shelter, and then killed him.[7]

Deborah and Barak celebrated the victory over the Canaanites with a song, recorded in Judges 5. Both Deborah and Barak are named, but the Hebrew verb for "sing" (5:1) is feminine singular rather than plural. This suggests that in an earlier version of the story, Deborah was the only singer, and Barak's name might have been added later. The song also makes it clear that the real hero of the story was Jael.

Some commentators have argued that Deborah was an exception to the rule that women did not lead and that God only chose her because there were no men available. Abraham Kuyper, perhaps because of his experience with Dutch queens, wrote that women leaders could be the source of "inspiring influences," which could "awaken the sleeping ones."[8] The Bible presents Deborah in a very positive light. She is respected for her wisdom, intelligence, initiative, and connection with God. Deborah confidently exercised leadership and made decisions. She told a military man what to do and when to do it. These were not ordinary roles for women in her time, but God spoke through her as God did through other prophets. The Israelites trusted her enough to seek her advice and judgment. Barak valued her direction and presence.

Diving Deeper

"Awaken the sleeping ones." Deborah's story reminds us of the stories of Elizabeth Cady Stanton, Alice Paul, Indira Gandhi, Golda Meir, Rosa Parks, Shirley Chisholm, and Barbara Jordan. What shaped these women? What gave them courage? How did they bring about change? How did their religious faith shape their leadership style? Women do not all lead in the same way. Like men, they choose different strategies

depending on their contexts and personalities. These women, and many others, have helped to "awaken the sleeping ones." How is God calling us to awaken the gifts and the courage of other people and inspire them to action?

Why is it that so many countries have thrived under the political leadership of gifted women, but when women run for office in the United States, the media focus on their hair, clothes, and ankles? Does the Christian tradition continue to reinforce gender stereotypes that suggest women are too emotional and irrational to be trusted with leadership? How might we challenge those assumptions by using the stories of strong women like Deborah?

Man up! Deborah serves as a coach or encourager for Barak. The text is not clear whether he was fearful or lacked self-confidence or failed to see the opportunity to engage Sisera in battle. Perhaps he wasn't sure he could trust God or Deborah. She was not resentful or angry about his hesitation. Instead, this fiery woman "lit a fire" under Barak. She encouraged him to take action, and she provided motivation and strategy and insight. She knew the right time to act. He, in turn, did not appear to resent her leadership or direction. He saw her as the embodiment of God's presence.

The phrase "man up" has become part of the lexicon of my college students over the last few years. It means get going, do the work, take responsibility. Deborah simply says "Up!" to Barak, but the meaning is the same. She tells him it is time to go, and he responds. What might happen in the world if a leader lit a fire in a person who did not know how gifted she was? How many tired, discouraged, hopeless people might find the energy to take action if they were encouraged? How many people do not realize how gifted they are until a Deborah figure points it out to them? Grace can come in the form of a leader who can identify the gifts of others, encourage their use, and stand alongside people in difficult situations.

The patron saint of caution. In attempting to celebrate the strength of Deborah in this story, a reader might be tempted to poke fun at Barak as weak and fearful, but he is better seen as the patron saint of caution. He did not leap into military action without weighing his options, counting the cost, and thinking it through. These are wise practices that should be emulated when leaders are tempted to use force out of a need to look tough or to get vengeance or to show the world who is boss. Barak sought advice to ensure that military action was the best strategy. His caution is something to imitate, not ridicule.

We're in this together. One of my students preached a sermon on this story that emphasized the cooperation between Barak and Deborah. She noted that they had a high degree of trust. They did not try to do each other's jobs. They did not second-guess each other. They did not try to protect their egos. They provide a model for men and women who work together.[9]

"Mother in Israel." Churches that celebrate Mother's Day might consider this story as an alternative to texts celebrating biological mothers. Deborah might not have had children, but she functioned in ways that mothers do: leading, encouraging, nurturing, teaching. Recalling her story would help us remember the women in our lives who have functioned in these ways. We have only one biological mother, but many other women care for us. This approach celebrates the gifts of women without exacerbating the pain of those for whom Mother's Day is more about loss and grief than celebration.

Questions for Reflection and Discussion

Do you think Deborah was a hero? Has she shown up in any lists of biblical heroes you've read or heard in a sermon?

Did you know the story of Deborah when you were a child? Would you have considered her a role model? Would you want your children to do so?

JAEL
(Judges 4–5)

The story of Jael confounds stereotypes and assumptions about women in the Bible. She was not a quiet nurturing woman in need of protection and guidance. Instead, she committed a violent act and was praised for it.

The previous section about Deborah provides essential background for Jael's story. Deborah was a judge who encouraged Barak, the Israelite general, to go to battle against Sisera, the general of the Canaanite army. When Barak refused to go to war without Deborah, she told him that a woman would defeat Sisera. Barak destroyed the army, but Sisera escaped.

Sisera was on the run, looking for shelter. He must have been exhausted from the battle and demoralized from the unexpected defeat. He had escaped with his life, but his army had been destroyed. He knew there were Canaanites living in the area, and he hoped he might find an ally who would take him in. He came upon the tent of Jael and assumed she would be sympathetic, because her husband was allied with the Canaanites.

Jael went out to meet Sisera and welcomed him graciously. She invited him into her tent and assured him that he had nothing to fear. She made him comfortable and anticipated his every need. She covered him with a blanket, recognizing that he might be cold and exhausted. He asked for a drink of water, but she went the extra mile and gave him milk. He wanted to take a nap, so he asked her to stand guard at the door of the tent and deny he was there if anyone asked. Finally, exhaustion, stress, and despair caught up with him, and he fell asleep. Then the kind, gracious Jael took a hammer and drove a tent peg into his head until it reached the ground, an act that required considerable strength of both arm and stomach. The text reports matter-of-factly: "and he died" (Judg. 4:21).

Barak, the Israelite general, was tracking Sisera, and Jael went to meet him. She brought him into her tent, and "there was Sisera lying dead, with the tent peg in his temple" (4:22). Barak did not get the credit for killing him.

This text has a slightly comic or farcical tone to it, despite its gruesome conclusion. Sisera thought he had found a safe house, so he let down his guard and allowed himself to be cared for after a hard day in battle. What threat could a woman be? Sisera escaped the Israelite army only to be "nailed" by a woman.

The Bible is not clear about her ethnicity or motivation. If she was an Israelite married to a Canaanite, she chose to be loyal to her own people rather than her husband's. If she was a Canaanite, she betrayed her own people. Did she, like Rahab, see the power of the Israelites' God and choose to align with them? Or was she a calculating opportunist who chose to side with the winners?

Whatever her motive, when Deborah and Barak celebrated their victory they sang, "Most blessed of women be Jael" (5:24).[10] Sisera was defeated by a woman. The Canaanites and all their chariots were defeated by the weaker Israelites.

Jael is a hero whose actions nonetheless make us profoundly uncomfortable. Killing an enemy in warfare is acceptable, but it seems underhanded and treacherous to offer hospitality and then kill a guest when he is vulnerable.

Jael did violate the rules of hospitality, but only after Sisera had broken several rules himself. He should not have asked her for hospitality, because it was improper for a woman to invite a strange man into her tent. A guest should not ask for anything, even water to quench his thirst, but should wait for the host to offer food and drink. Sisera also put Jael at risk by asking that she lie about his presence. His actions could be perceived as demanding and aggressive, so she was released from the obligations of hospitality.

Sisera was not a harmless traveler who asked for a glass of water. He was the general of an enemy army, in a time when women and children were routinely carried off to become slaves. He might have raped or killed her, so she was justifiably cautious. She was in a precarious position. If she did not provide hospitality, he might kill her, but if she cared for him, the Israelites would be angry with her.

Jael's action is disturbing in part because she confounded gender stereotypes. Women are supposed to be the kinder, gentler sex, but she was a killer. What is considered "normal" violence when done by a man seems more horrifying when done by a woman. Would a man have been criticized for doing what Jael did? Or would he have been praised for helping the Israelites?

Some interpreters have identified sexual overtones in the story. Jael invited Sisera to "turn aside" into her tent (4:18), a phrase that is sometimes used as a sexual invitation; perhaps her intent was to wear him out before dispatching him. This is an intriguing theory, but it is a bit demeaning to suggest that Jael could defeat Sisera only if she used sex, that because her wit and strength were not sufficient she had to use her womanly wiles to seduce him.[11] Rather than stretching the text for a logical explanation, perhaps we could simply acknowledge that Jael was a strong, courageous woman.

Diving Deeper

Jael was an admirable woman in many ways. She acted heroically to eliminate Sisera. If she had not killed him, Barak would have when he arrived at her home. She killed him by taking advantage of his vulnerability. That is unsettling, yet she is praised as the "most blessed of women."

A culture of violence. The Old Testament frequently advocates violence as the way for the Israelites to take and protect their promised land. Although the Canaanites had been there first, the Israelites believed that it was their calling to drive out the foreigners using murder, rape, plunder, and any other means necessary. Did God command this? If so, God appears to allow and encourage violence as a way to punish sin, fight oppression, and wipe out idolatry. Violence is affirmed, even praised, when it is used against the outsider in the service of God, truth, and justice.[12]

Some commentators suggest that God did not command the violence, but the Israelites assumed that violence was required in order to regain their land and live in relative peace. They claimed that God had commanded the killing to justify their own penchant for violence.

Throughout history people have claimed divine sanction to kill people who were in their way. European settlers destroyed indigenous peoples in North America, South America, and Central America, and native people in Africa. Christians and Muslims killed one another during the Crusades. Warfare continues in the Middle East. Read uncritically, the Bible appears to justify the use of violence to eliminate those who seem to be trespassing on "promised land," even if they have lived there for centuries.

The Old Testament, particularly Judges, is a violent book. It should not be surprising when deeply religious people turn to violence in the service of their God, because there is clear precedent in the Bible. Does this story demonstrate the character of God? Are there alternative biblical models to the mass destruction of people who appear to be a threat?

Are women naturally more peaceful? In light of the mass murder and destruction that occur in biblical texts, Jael's killing of Sisera seems relatively tame, and yet people find her offensive because nice women don't kill people with tent pegs. Why are violent acts more offensive when committed by a woman? Do we assume that women are naturally more peaceful and nonviolent? Women have traditionally been socialized to be loving, gentle, and nurturing. They are taught to use their words to resolve conflict, while men are allowed to use their fists. Still, women are quite capable of violence.

These assumptions shape debates about whether women should serve in the military, particularly in combat roles. Some people are horrified by the idea of women killing or being killed, but perhaps the more significant question to ask is whether violence is suitable for either sex. If being a soldier is not a good vocation for women, then it is not for men either.

A different ending? We can affirm Jael's courage while at the same time encouraging one another to seek out other ways of solving problems and responding to violence. In the midst of civil war in Liberia in the 1990s, thousands of Muslim and Christian women gathered to pray and protest against the violence and injustice. Their actions forced the president to engage in peace talks, and he was eventually replaced with Ellen Johnson Sirleaf, the first woman president of an African country.[13]

The glimmer of good news in the story is that God used a woman to bring down a general. The better news might be to consider creative ways to avoid violence and live at peace with our neighbors.

Questions for Reflection and Discussion

Has anyone ever underestimated you, the way Sisera failed to recognize Jael as a threat? Why was that the case?

Jael used violence as an act of war, and still we find this story shocking. What does that tell us about violence?

JEPHTHAH'S DAUGHTER
(Judges 11)

In this story, bad parenting, bad religion, and bad judgment come together in a perfect storm of violence. Jephthah committed a horrifying act of violence upon his daughter, and yet the book of Hebrews praises him as a man of heroic faith. Commentators have tried to find something redemptive to justify the New Testament's praise of Jephthah, but many of their efforts are as unsettling as the text itself.

Jephthah was a soldier who was asked to lead the Israelites in a battle against the Ammonites. He had a lot at stake because he had been promised a role in city politics if he won the battle. Jephthah did not seem to be particularly religious, but the text reports that "the spirit [*ruach*] of the LORD came upon Jephthah" (Judg. 11:29).[14] Jephthah had not asked or prayed for this spirit, and it is possible that he did not know it had come upon him.

Before the battle began, he made a vow. He promised that if God gave him victory over the Ammonites, he would offer as a burnt offering "whoever"[15] came out of the house to greet him when he arrived home after the battle. What was Jephthah thinking? Perhaps he assumed that he would see a goat wandering in the yard, but the custom of the time was that women and children often came to greet the returning hero. The nature of desperate vows is that they are not well thought out.

Should Jephthah have made a vow at all? Some commentators claim that since the spirit of the Lord had come upon him, the spirit had motivated the vow. Jephthah then obediently carried out the vow in gratitude for the victory, even at tremendous cost to himself. Phyllis Trible suggested instead that the vow demonstrated Jephthah's doubt and disbelief. If he had indeed received God's spirit, he should have trusted in the divine power and presence rather than manipulating God with this vow.[16]

Jephthah and his men routed the Ammonites, and the hero returned to his hometown. He was greeted by his daughter, his only child, dancing and singing his praises. He was stunned, and his first instinct was to blame her. "Alas, my daughter! You have brought me very low; you have become the cause of great trouble to me" (11:35). This mean-spirited and selfish comment is a classic example of blaming the victim. She did not force him to make the vow.

Jephthah indirectly blamed God for his own bad choices. He claimed that he had made a vow and could not take it back. Jephthah told himself a story that God was harsh and unyielding and preferred blind obedience and a dead daughter to a broken vow. The daughter responded obediently and gave her father permission to carry out the vow. Some commentators rationalize that the vow must have been appropriate because she willingly accepted her fate. She was a good girl who recognized the importance of keeping a vow and obeyed her father even at the cost of her life. She believed it was better for her to die than for Jephthah to break his vow. She modeled the virtue of submission, especially for daughters. Cheryl Exum sarcastically summarized the moral of the story these interpreters told: "Submit to paternal authority. You may have to sacrifice your autonomy; you may lose your life, and even your name, but your sacrifice will be remembered, indeed celebrated, for generations to come."[17] Elizabeth Cady Stanton was also appalled by this interpretation of the story. She wrote, "We often hear people laud the beautiful submission and the self-sacrifice of this nameless maiden. To me it is pitiful and painful." Stanton wished that the daughter would have demonstrated a "dignified whole-souled rebellion," and refused to give her father power over her life. She should have told him that her self-development was a "higher duty than self-sacrifice."[18]

Unfortunately, texts of terror are not so easily redeemed. To excuse Jephthah by portraying his daughter in saintly terms avoids the difficult questions that this story raises about the nature of vows, the nature of faith, and the nature of God.

Diving Deeper

Role model? This story makes us think about Jephthah's character. "How," we might ask, "could the author of Hebrews praise the faith of such a terrible father?"[19] Some commentators claim that the praise justified the murder of his daughter. This approach raises more questions than it answers. Did God demand that Jephthah fulfill his vow? What kind of God would see the death of an innocent girl as an act of worship?[20]

Nor should we consider Jephthah a role model, regardless of what the book of Hebrews says. His place on the list of faithful people should not be used to justify his bad parenting, bad judgment, and bad religion. All the people on that list were flawed in various ways, and the author of Hebrews was not endorsing their behavior. Jephthah might have been a man of faith, but he made a serious error regarding his daughter. Neither his vow nor his sacrifice of her should be labeled virtuous in order to maintain a consistent portrayal of him. We should acknowledge that faithful people make mistakes, rather than make the errors into virtues.

It may also be helpful to remind ourselves that people may inaccurately discern God's will. Jephthah claimed that his vow was irrevocable, but God did not say that, and Jephthah's actions were not consistent with the mercy of God.

"Whole-souled rebellion." We might also ask about Jephthah's daughter's decisions. Did her obedience redeem an ugly story? Are contemporary readers called to go and do likewise? Or should she have stood up for herself and refused to acquiesce to Jephthah's crazy scheme? Should she have demonstrated "whole-souled rebellion" instead of obeying?

In a way, Jephthah's daughter did value her own life. She chose to spend her last months with her friends, grieving over her lost future. That would have been a "whole-souled rebellion" in her time. The fact that her action was remembered by young women for generations means that she did make a difference. She did what she could.

We might reflect on when it is necessary to engage in a "whole-souled rebellion." A teenage girl refuses to tolerate her mother's emotional abuse of her, even though it means she can no longer live at home. Rosa Parks refused to leave her seat on the bus. Girls who have been disfigured by acid thrown in their faces refuse to hide away in shame. A woman in India stood up against a bully who was holding her daughter as a sex slave, and empowered her community to resist as well.[21] The good news of the gospel is often found in resistance and rebellion rather than blind obedience.

You promised! Some vows are made in a stressful moment, without a great deal of forethought. A soldier in a foxhole under enemy fire says, "God, if you get me through this, I will become a priest." A woman waiting to see whether her diagnosis is lung cancer says, "God, if this is just pneumonia, I promise I will never smoke again." It is generally understood that these vows are made in desperation and that God would not expect them to be carried out.

People make vows out of superstition, anxiety, and fear. They desperately want God to heal or fix or save, so they bargain. "God, if you do this for me, then I will do that for you." They try to convince God to act by promising something in return. Is this congruent with our beliefs about God as gracious and loving?

People also make vows to one another, and these can be difficult to keep. Couples enter into marriage with optimism, hope, and the promise to love forever. Unfortunately, the spouse who seemed so wonderful can turn out to be physically or emotionally abusive. What do vows mean in these situations? When keeping a vow means living in danger or despair or a dead marriage, does God expect that the vows must be kept at all costs?

A woman in her fifties promises her parents that she will not put them in a nursing home. The parents live well into their nineties, and the woman is seventy-five and no longer has the physical strength to care for her parents. As she researches nursing homes, her parents repeatedly remind her that she promised to care for them.

Sometimes people keep their vows at great cost to themselves or others. In Colleen McCullough's book *The Thorn Birds*, Father Ralph was a Roman Catholic priest who loved Meggie Cleary. Other than one week together, he did not allow himself to be in a relationship with her. He said he had to keep his vow to the church, but he also enjoyed the power of his position and wanted to ascend the church hierarchy. Was he virtuous because he kept the vow? Or did he sacrifice a meaningful relationship to his lust for power?

Some people argue that vows must be kept because God always keeps promises, but there are several biblical passages in which God changes. In Judges 10:13–14, God refused to free the willful Israelites from their oppressors, but in 10:16, God "could no longer bear to see Israel suffer" and decided to intervene. In Hosea, God promised to punish Israel as a parent would punish a rebellious son, but God could not do it and extended steadfast love instead. If God's mercy can supersede a vow that God has made, why can't Jephthah allow mercy to supersede his vow?

Questions for Reflection and Discussion

Jephthah is celebrated as a hero of faith in the book of Hebrews, yet his faith held only destructive consequences for his daughter. In what ways have you seen religious belief yield toxic fruit for people you know?

Jephthah's daughter practiced the virtue of obedience, when she should have reacted with "whole-souled rebellion." It seems easy to see why her father's rash vow called for that rebellion, but not every situation is so clear-cut. How do you decide when to accept authority, and when to challenge it?

SAMSON'S MOTHER / MANOAH'S WIFE
(Judges 13–14)

Tucked between the grim stories of Jephthah's daughter (Judg. 11) and the rape and murder of the concubine (Judg. 19) is a vignette about a strong woman who demonstrates faith in a quiet, unassuming way. The woman is not named; she is identified only by her relationships as the wife of Manoah and the mother of Samson. Her story is nearly lost in the drama of her famous son, which is unfortunate, because she has a calm, sensible presence, and a faith that is worth emulating.

Once again, the Israelites were behaving badly, but instead of naming a new judge, the text introduces a couple. Manoah had a wife who was barren. That sounds like a dead end, but when the Bible mentions a barren woman, she is usually not barren for long. An angel of the Lord appeared to the wife of Manoah and told her that she would give birth to a son. They should not cut his hair, and they should raise him as a Nazirite who was consecrated to the service of God.[22] One day this son would "begin to deliver" the Israelites from the Philistines (Judg. 13:5).[23]

The angel came to the woman when she was alone and spoke to her directly. She did not keep the information to herself, however, but told her husband, Manoah, that "a man of God" had come to her (13:6). His appearance was awe-inspiring, she said, but she had not asked his name or where he had come from.

Manoah was understandably skeptical. Why would a strange man tell his wife that she would become pregnant? Would a legitimate divine messenger bypass the husband and speak directly to the wife? Perhaps he was jealous of her experience. Manoah wanted to have a divine encounter of his own, so he prayed that God would again send the "man of God" to provide further instruction. The Bible reports that God listened, but instead of coming to Manoah, the angel appeared again to the woman when she was alone. Mrs. Manoah did not try to possess the experience for herself. She ran to get her husband, and he followed her back to the field where the angel was. Manoah asked the angel to clarify the rules for raising their son, but the angel deflected his questions. The woman should follow the instructions she had already been given. There was nothing more that Manoah needed to know.

Manoah felt left out and wanted some control over the situation, but the visitor felt no obligation to include him in the information loop. Manoah asked the angel to stay for dinner, but the angel refused and suggested Manoah make a burnt offering instead. When he did, the angel rose into the air along with the smoke. Finally Manoah realized he had been talking to an angel, not a human. He was overwhelmed by the magnitude of this encounter and had a bit of a meltdown. We just saw God, he said. We are going to die!

Mrs. Manoah calmly responded that if God had meant to kill them, God would not have accepted the burnt offering or said these things about their son. Essentially, she told Manoah to "chill out." She did not overreact. She was thoughtful and rational and demonstrated spiritual insight and maturity.

Usually in Scripture when a divine messenger announces that a barren woman will conceive, it is a sign that the child will play an important role in the life of the Israelites. Much was expected of such a child. Unfortunately, the child born to Manoah and his wife proved to be a great disappointment.

Their son Samson was a man with more brawn than brain. He had big biceps and a big ego. He could kill a lion with his bare hands. He could kill a thousand Philistines with the jawbone of an ass. Samson was strong, but he was flawed. He was distracted with wine and women, riddles and revenge. He was selfish and demanding and hot-tempered. He lacked emotional intelligence and spiritual sensitivity.

Given that his parents appeared to be relatively stable, faithful people, how did Samson turn out to be such a disaster? Samson had devoted parents who tried to instill in him a sense of vocation and faith, but he rebelled. When he wanted to marry a woman his parents disapproved of, he ordered his father, "Get her for me, because she pleases me" (14:3). This defiant behavior did not bode well for the future.

Some commentators blame the parents, especially his mother, for his failures. She must have coddled and indulged him because of his special birth, so he became a spoiled brat. They must have been overly involved parents who pushed him so hard that he rebelled. They failed to mold him into the leader he was supposed to be. The commentators want to tell a story that makes sense, but there is no evidence of parental failure in the text.

Samson did redeem himself many years later when he engineered a mass killing of Philistines at the cost of his own life. The author of the book of Hebrews includes Samson in the list of faithful people in Hebrews 11, along with Barak and Jephthah.

It is unfortunate that Mrs. Manoah did not make the list of faithful people, because she is the real hero of the story. She was a spiritually mature and sensitive woman, and the angel respected her enough to speak to her directly. One commentator wrote of her, "An unnamed woman bears the closest relationship to God and models the behavior that God wills for God's people throughout the book of Judges—attentiveness to God's word and a distinctive lifestyle that sets one apart from other nations and their destructive ways."[24]

Manoah, on the other hand, is portrayed as a man who sought answers and certainty. He needed a direct encounter with the angel. He wanted evidence, clarity, and clear directions for the future, but he and his wife were given only what they needed to know.

Diving Deeper

Different faith for different folks. Samson represents a flashy and heroic type of faith. He asked for God's help on a big project. He ended his life and the lives of many Philistines with a dramatic flourish. Manoah represents a more questioning style of faith. He wanted clarity, certainty, and control. Mrs. Manoah represents a type of faith that is steady and confident. Her faith does not get so much publicity and acclaim, which is unfortunate, because she is a solid rock of calm, and most of us could use more of her type of faith.

Few people have the dramatic vocation of Samson. We are not called to kill the Philistines with our superhuman strength. Most of us are called to quieter, less dramatic vocations. We teach students, care for people, create things, tend our children, make decisions. We may think something is lacking in us because we don't have the big dramatic faith and the big dramatic calling. We're not pulling down any pillars. But a quiet, solid faith is a gift. It is nothing to be ashamed of.

We may share with Manoah the desire that God would speak to us directly and give us clear guidance for the future. We would like an intimate, special relationship in which we feel God's presence and know God's name and God's plan for our lives. But sometimes, the more we try to find certainty about the future, the more it eludes us. God only provides guidance for the next step. The angel told Manoah: You have what you need. You have enough to work with.[25]

Will our children have faith? Many parents of millennials took their children to church and encouraged their attendance at Sunday school and youth group, but these young adults now show little interest in attending church. This is actually not a new phenomenon. Many baby boomers refused to attend church when they were young adults because church seemed old-fashioned and irrelevant. Even Puritan parents in the 1630s could not understand why their children did not have the same dramatic conversion experiences they had. What happens when parents make baptismal vows that they will raise their children in the faith, but once the children are free to make their own choices, they do not choose church? Are the parents flawed? The children? The church?

Problem child. This story raises questions that many parents ask when their children make poor life choices. Were we bad parents? How could our child who was raised with love turn out to be so angry and hurtful? What did we do wrong? Society is quick to blame the parents, especially when someone commits a particularly heinous and senseless crime. Parents are not the only influences in children's lives, however, and some children make poor choices even when they have been raised in love.

Readers might speculate on the relationship between Samson and his parents. What was Samson like as a young man? When did they start to see his rebellious qualities? How did they feel about his unfortunate marriage? What did they think of Delilah? Their story illustrates what most parents know too well. Parenting is hard work, and our children are their own people.

For those of us with "tiny control issues"[26] about parenting, vocation, and all the other challenges of life, it can be a word of grace to hear that we have what we need to know.

Questions for Reflection and Discussion

Not all of us are called to big, loud forms of service. What are some of the quiet, unflashy ways people have taken care of you? Have they received credit for doing so? Did they want it?

As the author says, people are quick to judge parents when children turn out differently than we hoped. What are some of the other influences on children, besides their parents? How are you in a position to be an influence for good in some child's life?

DELILAH
(Judges 16)

The name Delilah evokes images of seduction and womanly wiles. Even those unfamiliar with Scripture may know that Delilah is a bad girl of the Bible. Common knowledge says that she tricked Samson, lied to him, and used sex to get what she wanted. She embodies the evil temptress who endangers good men. Commentators support these assumptions by describing her as a vixen, seductress, tramp, tart, conniver, cheat, tease, slut, and whore.

Samson, the man who loved Delilah, was volatile, impulsive, and powerful. His birth was marked by a divine intervention and a calling to a distinctive lifestyle.[27] His vocation was to destroy the Philistines who tormented the Israelites, but he was repeatedly distracted by Philistine women, who should have been off-limits. He married a Philistine woman, against the advice of his parents, but the marriage lasted only a week and ended with the death of his wife, her father, and a thousand Philistines.[28]

He settled down and served as a leader and a judge in Israel. He continued to torment the Philistines, but they were unable to capture him because of his brute strength. They were desperate to learn the source of his strength and how he might be overpowered.

They saw that Samson had a weak spot. He was fond of women and did not always make wise choices about relationships. Samson fell in love with a woman named Delilah. She was from the valley of Sorek, which was probably somewhere between the territories of the Israelites and the Philistines. Her nationality is not stated, but she was likely either a Philistine or sympathetic to their cause. She is not identified as any man's wife, sister, or daughter, which meant that she had to provide for herself and make her own decisions. She had a house of her own, which signified financial independence. Since female independence was rare in this culture, some commentators assume that she must have been a prostitute, because there were so few ways for women to earn money. She is not identified as such by the Bible.[29]

The leaders of the Philistines asked her to use Samson's love for her to find out what made him so powerful. They promised her a great deal of money in exchange for information. The text does not say why she agreed. Was she a smart businesswoman who saw a lucrative deal that would secure her financial future? Was she a patriotic and loyal Philistine who wanted to help eliminate a man who had tormented her people? Perhaps Samson had killed one of her family members and she was driven by revenge.

Delilah accepted the challenge to discover the source of Samson's strength. Popular belief suggests that she tricked or seduced him, but the text shows no evidence of this. She asked him directly for the information she wanted: "Please tell me what makes your strength so great, and how you could be bound, so that one could subdue you" (Judg. 16:6). She could not be any more straightforward. Three times, Samson gave her a wrong answer. Three times she did what he said would weaken him. Each time he broke free. She did not lie or trick him, but Samson was definitely not very bright. Did he not realize that she might be trying to capture him? She actually had the Philistines lying in wait! How could he be so clueless and naive? Was this a man in love? A man who was gullible? Overconfident?

Delilah became frustrated by Samson's lack of honesty, although she was rather naive herself to assume he would volunteer information that could destroy him. After the first attempts to capture him had failed, she accused him of mocking and lying to her. Finally, after the third attempt, she cut to the heart of their relationship. "How can you say, 'I love you,' when your heart is not with me?" (16:15). She nagged him for several days until he was "tired to death" (v. 16). Delilah might have whined and manipulated to get what she wanted, but she did not lie to Samson. She did not trade sexual favors for information. She simply kept asking.

Finally he told her the truth: the secret to his strength was in his hair. She sensed that this was the real story, and again Philistines came to her home to wait. She took advantage of an intimate moment when Samson fell asleep "on her knees" or in her lap.[30] Then she called a man who cut Samson's hair. This time when she said, "The Philistines are upon you" (v. 20), Samson woke up and found that the spirit of the Lord, the source of his strength, had left him, and he was powerless. The Philistines easily captured him, gouged out his eyes, and put him in prison.

While he was in prison, Samson's hair began to grow back. The Philistines threw a party to celebrate their victory over Samson and brought him in to provide the entertainment. They enjoyed seeing that he was weak, blind, and humiliated. Despite his blindness, Samson saw an opportunity. He positioned himself between the two pillars that held up the roof, where many of the Philistines were standing. He prayed that God would give him strength to get revenge, and he pulled down the pillars. The house collapsed, and thousands of Philistines died. Samson killed more Philistines in one night than he had killed during his lifetime.

Samson ended his life with a flourish. He finally lived out his calling to destroy the Philistines, at the cost of his own life. He was not a smart or spiritually astute man. He did not honor his Nazirite vows. He showed little interest in God, and his destruction of the Philistines was motivated more by revenge than by vocation.

Despite this less than admirable record, Samson was treated as a hero. He was included in a list of faithful superstars in Hebrews 11. How could he be praised for faith he did not appear to have? How can he be lauded as a hero when he was a dangerous and troubled man? One way to resolve the contradiction is to shift the blame away from him and onto Delilah, who tricked him. She was a femme fatale, a deadly woman. She was a strumpet who took advantage of him. She was greedy. She had no conscience. Poor Samson could kill a lion with his bare hands, but he was no match for Delilah. Commentators claim that he only told her the secret of his strength because she pouted, and he loved her so much that he could not bear to see her unhappy. If Delilah had not led him astray, he would have been the kind of judge he was meant to be.

Diving Deeper

Many have told the story of Samson and Delilah as a particular kind of cautionary tale. Don't give your heart to a woman. Don't tell her your secrets. Don't let down your guard. Don't be vulnerable. Women cannot be trusted. It is certainly appropriate to recognize Delilah's role in Samson's downfall, but it is not appropriate to excuse Samson by portraying him as the helpless victim of a conniving woman.

What Delilah did not do. Delilah was a flawed woman, but Samson had problems of his own. Their story reminds us all to take responsibility for our own sinfulness rather than blaming others.[31]

What Delilah did. Delilah misused intimacy. She extracted Samson's secret and used his love for her to betray him. Samson should not have trusted her, but he was drawn into the web of sexual attraction and was not thinking clearly.

Samson was his own worst enemy. Samson was an arrogant and defiant man. His attraction to Philistine women was a way to thumb his nose at his parents, the Israelites, religion, and God. Perhaps Samson resented his calling and the Nazirite vows. Maybe he did not want to be a hero. He repeatedly acted out in foolish and risky ways. He was extremely confident in his strength and invincibility. How could a lowly woman outsmart him? He always got what he wanted.

Perhaps Samson lost sight of the fact that his strength came from God and began to believe that his strength was under his control. Perhaps he finally told Delilah about his hair because if the strength was not in his hair, it would not matter if she cut it off. He had not honored the Nazirite vows about avoiding alcohol and corpses, and he had never been punished. Samson might have stopped thinking about his vocation and the source of his strength.

There are many contemporary examples of this. A politician is elected to office in order to serve the people but is quickly enticed by the possibilities of power and influence. A pastor of a growing church thinks only about what tactics might bring more new people to worship. A gifted high school athlete thinks more about attracting college scholarships than about the success of the team. It is easy to think that success is all about us and forget both our vocation and the source of our strength.

A matter of perspective. The Israelites thought that Delilah was a very bad woman because she sold Samson out for money. Delilah would have had a different perspective. She needed money to survive in a culture where there were few ways for women to earn a living, and the deal with the Philistines ensured her future. The Philistines thought that Delilah was a hero. She sought the welfare of her country. She took down the powerful and previously untouchable Samson. No one in the Philistine army had been able to do that. She was a patriotic and loyal Philistine.

Questions for Reflection and Discussion

Why is it so easy to overlook Samson's faults and overstate Delilah's? Given Samson's obvious flaws, why do we think it necessary to excuse him at her expense?

Have you ever come to take God's blessings and grace for granted, as Samson did? What was the outcome for you?

THE LEVITE'S CONCUBINE
(Judges 19–21)

The story of the concubine begins with the rape and murder of one woman and ends with more than one hundred thousand deaths, the forced marriages of six hundred women, and the destruction of several towns. The moral fabric of society in Israel had almost completely unraveled. When the book of Judges begins, the Israelites were killing the Canaanites and Philistines. When it ends, the Israelites were killing each other. There was no king in Israel, the narrator says repeatedly, and everyone did what was right in their own eyes.

A Levite took a concubine, but she left him and returned to her father's house (Judg. 19:1–2). The New International Version, King James Version, and most other versions translate the Hebrew word that described her behavior (*zanah*) as "she played the harlot" (whore) or "she prostituted herself." Interpreters conclude that she engaged in an adulterous relationship, left the Levite, and returned to her father's house.

This interpretation raises a number of questions. Adultery was punishable by death (Deut. 22:22), so the Levite could have had her killed immediately. An adulterous woman would have brought shame on her family if she returned to her home. It is unlikely that a jilted husband would have tried so hard to get his wife back. The first-century scholars who translated the Hebrew text into Greek concluded that *zanah* was not the correct word. They suggested instead that the concubine left because she was angry (*anaph*) with the Levite, perhaps because he had mistreated her.

This reading resolves some of the problems in the text. Women could not initiate divorce or gain possession of the family home, so returning to her father's house might have been her only option if she chose to leave her husband. If she was angry with the Levite, it explains why he wanted to "speak tenderly to her and bring her back" (Judg. 19:3).

Her father welcomed his son-in-law, and they spent several days eating and drinking. The daughter did not participate in the male conviviality. Was she touched by the Levite's desire to win her back? Was she angry that he had come? Was she afraid of him? Did the father suspect that his daughter did not like the Levite? She was not consulted.

When they finally left late on the fifth day, they did not get far before dark. They went to Gibeah, a city in the tribe of Benjamin, and waited for someone to offer hospitality. An old man took pity on them and invited them to his home.

Their evening was interrupted by pounding on the door. A group of townsmen, "a perverse lot" (19:22), asked the owner of the house to send out the Levite so they could rape him. The host tried to divert the men by offering his virgin daughter and the Levite's concubine, with the advice to "ravish them and do whatever you want to them; but against this man do not do such a vile thing" (v. 24). The men did not listen and continued to demand the Levite, who finally "seized" his concubine and shoved her out the door to the mob. They raped and abused her all night, and in the morning they let her go. She made her way to the door of the house and collapsed. No one noticed.[32]

The Levite did not express concern, go out to look for her, or wait up to see if she returned. In the morning, when he stepped outside to leave, his concubine was lying at the door. He said, "Get up, we are going" (19:28). There was no answer. She might have been unconscious. She might have been dead. He put her on the donkey, and when he arrived home he cut her up into twelve pieces and sent one body part to each of the tribes of Israel as a call to military action against the tribe of Benjamin. Something terrible had happened to his property, and something must be done.

This story is horrifying and offensive in so many ways. The host was justifiably frightened, but how could he blithely offer his daughter to a gang of rapists? The Levite's actions are even more disturbing. He pursued the concubine, but once she was under his control, he did not care enough to protect her. He expressed no grief or sadness. His callous words, "Get up, we are going," are some of the most unfeeling, insensitive words in Scripture.

The woman's story is profoundly sad. She was "given" and "taken," regardless of her wishes. She had no voice, until finally her body parts were allowed to "speak" about her death. Even then, they told the Levite's story, not hers.

The story raises many difficult questions. Why did the men so easily offer up women to be raped? Why was it more important to protect the men than the women? Why was the Levite so callous? The commentators' attempts to answer these questions and justify the men's behavior can be as horrifying as the actions themselves.

Commentators note that when men offered women to the rapists, it was not mere self-protection, but an attempt to avoid the sin of "unnatural sex." It was more horrific for men to be raped, in part because women simply had less value, but also because when women were raped, the sex was "natural." This fear and loathing of unnatural sex made their actions understandable, though not excusable.[33]

Some commentators argue that although the woman was treated badly, the gang rape was an appropriate punishment for her adulterous behavior. The penalty for adultery was death, and although she had escaped punishment at the time, now she was paying the price. This approach tries to mitigate the horror of the story by claiming that the victim deserved it.

Other commentators suggest that she died of shame. It is disturbing to realize how pervasive and long-standing is the idea that women should feel it is their fault that they have been raped.[34] The Levite threw her out to the mob, but *she* was the one who died of shame!

For many years when I taught this story I ended here, not realizing that the murder and mayhem had just begun. After the Israelites received the body parts in the mail, four hundred thousand soldiers gathered in support of the Levite. They asked what had happened, and he said, "The lords of Gibeah rose up against me, and surrounded the house at night. They intended to kill me, and they raped my concubine until she died" (20:5).

The Levite had edited the story. He suggested that respected community leaders (the "lords of Gibeah") had attacked them, while the narrator called them a "perverse lot," a group of ruffians. They were probably angry, marginalized men who wanted to show these strangers who was boss. Second, the Levite said that the men wanted to murder him, which was not necessarily their intent. He might have been too embarrassed to mention the intent to rape him. Finally, he said that the men raped the woman until she died, which was not true, since she managed to make her way back to the house. The Levite did not admit that he threw her out to the mob or that he did not seem to care what happened to her.

The story made the Israelite soldiers furious, and they "united as one" (Judg. 20:11). They asked the tribe of Benjamin to hand over the "scoundrels" who committed the crime, but the Benjaminites refused and raised up an army of twenty-six thousand men (vv. 13–15).

The Israelite soldiers asked God which of their tribes should be the first to fight against the Benjaminites. They did not ask God *whether* they should start a civil war but assumed God's approval. The Israelites were soundly defeated on the first two days of battle, despite outnumbering the Benjaminites by a ratio of sixteen to one. Finally, on the third day, the narrator reports that "the LORD defeated Benjamin" (20:35). All the Benjaminite soldiers died except for six hundred who escaped. The Israelites destroyed the rest of the tribe and set the towns on fire.

Then, in a bizarre twist to the story, the Israelites realized the magnitude of the damage they had done to their own people. They wept bitterly, and asked God why one tribe was "lacking in Israel" (21:3). The obvious divine answer would have been, "Because you just killed them all in a fit of overzealous rage!" The Israelites were incapable of such self-awareness. It was easier to blame God for the destruction of the Benjaminites.

The Israelites' newfound compassion inspired them to help the remnant of the tribe rebuild itself. The six hundred men who escaped needed wives, but the Israelite soldiers had vowed that they would never give their daughters in marriage to any of the Benjaminite men (21:1). Creative problem solving was required.

The Israelites had also vowed that anyone who did not participate in the punishment of the tribe of Benjamin would be killed (21:5). The men of the city of Jabesh-gilead had declined to participate, so the Israelites killed all the inhabitants, except for four hundred virgins who were given as wives to the Benjaminites.

Again the story says that the Israelites had compassion for the two hundred wifeless men, because "the LORD had made a breach in the tribes of Israel" (21:15).[35] The concern was admirable but the rationale was disingenuous. How convenient to blame this murder and mayhem on God! The Israelites learned of a festival in the town of Shiloh, where young women would be dancing in a public, accessible space, and advised the still-single men of Benjamin to each abduct a woman to take for a wife. The women, of course, had no choice. These innocent women, along with those from Jabesh-gilead, were forced into marriages and sexual relationships that they did not choose, all as a result of the rape of the concubine.

The story concludes in an oddly happy way. The Benjaminites rebuilt their towns, and the Israelites returned to their homes. But the narrator has the last word: "In those days there was no king in Israel; all the people did what was right in their own eyes" (21:25).

Diving Deeper

What are we to make of this brutal and disheartening story? There is no good news amid the murder and mayhem. And yet, the story mirrors some contemporary practices of international relations and warfare. One act of terrorism can lead to massive reprisals. People and nations are edgy and quick to react to any threat. Complete loyalty is demanded, and those who question the legitimacy of a violent response are often dismissed as cowardly and unpatriotic.

God, why did you do this? The Israelites consulted God when it seemed convenient, but they did not ask the right question. They asked who should go first into battle and not whether they should go at all. The Israelites also failed to take responsibility for their actions, preferring to blame God for the loss of the Benjaminites. Perhaps the most powerful and relevant aspect of this story is that it so vividly exposes both the futility of violence and the ways in which people try to justify their actions by claiming they were doing God's work.

Women and children? Thousands of innocent women and children were killed in this story. Similarly, in the past century, innocent people have been increasingly at risk in warfare. In World War II, millions of civilians were killed by starvation, in concentration camps, or when their cities were bombed. Recent "civil" warfare in some countries has actually encouraged the rape and murder of women and children as a way to terrify and dehumanize. When a nation is willing to inflict or permit violence toward the least powerful, it shows a blatant disregard for human life. Similar events continue to occur. Compare, for example, the abduction of the two hundred girls in Nigeria with the abduction of the girls from the festival. It is often difficult to know how to respond when violence happens in another part of the world. A religious community might not be able to solve or prevent these problems on the other side of the world, but its members can at least be informed about the problems. Perhaps their response can be nothing more than indignation, empathy, lament, and prayer, but these actions are better than silence and ignorance.

This text is an ugly story of human evil masquerading as righteous indignation and even compassion. It speaks painful truth about humans behaving badly, seeking revenge, and using brutality to terrorize. After reading this story, one of my students wrote that she wished that there had been a great big "and the Lord was displeased" evaluation at the end of it. She wanted to see that God explicitly disapproved of the bad behavior displayed here. Unfortunately, God's displeasure is not explicit. Still, the narrator at least made it clear that this kind of ridiculous violence was no way for a community to live. Everyone did what was right in their own eyes, but their moral vision had been completely compromised.

Questions for Reflection and Discussion

This is among the most difficult stories in the Old Testament. Can this story still function as the word of God for you? If so, in what way do you hear God speaking in this story?

Are there ways that we, too, pursue the "devices and desires of our own hearts" (as the Book of Common Prayer puts it) and then try to pin the blame on God when the results go predictably awry?

RUTH AND NAOMI
(Ruth 1–4)

The book of Ruth is often thought to be a sweet, tender story with a romantic ending. Ruth is a nice young woman who cares for her mother-in-law, finds a man, and lives happily ever after. The story is actually far more complex, interesting, and relevant.

The story begins with a family in crisis. Elimelech, his wife Naomi, and their sons, Mahlon and Chilion, left their home in Bethlehem because of a famine and moved to Moab, where there was food.[36] Elimelech died, and the sons married Moabite women. Soon the sons died as well, and Naomi was alone. In a culture where there were no social security or pension checks, and no way for older women to support themselves, sons were the only source of economic stability. Her daughters-in-law, Orpah and Ruth, had also lost their husbands and their financial support, but they were young and could marry again. Naomi was bereft.

Naomi decided to return home to Bethlehem. The young women wanted to go with her, but she told them to leave, because she could not have more sons who might become husbands to them.[37] Naomi felt like a dried-up old woman without promise or possibility. Naomi believed that God had turned against her. She was drowning in depression, grief, and anger. Ruth and Orpah would be better off without her.

Orpah did what Naomi asked and returned to her family. Why stay with someone who did not want her around? Orpah decided that home was in Moab, with her own family.

Ruth chose to make her home with Naomi. In a culture where husbands were the key to survival and success, a poor, powerless young woman promised her life to a poor, powerless older woman. Ruth adopted Naomi's people and even her God. In response, Naomi was silent and sullen. She did not thank Ruth or acknowledge her commitment. Did she resent Ruth's insistence on accompanying her? Was she embarrassed to return to Bethlehem with a Moabite woman in tow?

When they arrived in Bethlehem, Naomi announced that she was changing her name from Naomi, which means "pleasant," to Mara, which means "bitter." She blamed God for her reversal of fortune. "The Almighty has dealt bitterly with me. I went away full, but the LORD has brought me back empty; why call me Naomi when the LORD has dealt harshly with me, and the Almighty has brought calamity upon me?" (Ruth 1:20–21).

Naomi's words were raw and honest. She had lost everything. She was lonely, weary, hopeless, and utterly discouraged. She did not see the gift her daughter-in-law had given her, but Ruth was there, and it was the beginning of the barley harvest.

The women settled into Bethlehem, and Ruth took one of the few opportunities available to women other than prostitution. She went into the fields after the reapers had harvested the barley and picked up the scraps that were left behind. Ruth chose a field apparently at random, but the narrator notes: "As it happened, she came to the part of the field belonging to Boaz, who was of the family of Elimelech." Was her choice of Boaz's field simply coincidence? Or did God guide her there?

Boaz came to the field, saw Ruth working, and asked whom she belonged to. Boaz recognized that she had no one to protect her, so he gave her extra food and encouraged her to continue to work in his fields. Ruth asked why he was so gracious to her, and he responded that he knew she had been kind to Naomi. He offered a blessing to her: "May you have a full reward from the LORD, the God of Israel, under whose wings you have come for refuge!" (2:12).

Ruth returned home with food and a story about the generous Boaz, and Naomi realized that he was a relative.[38] Naomi was beginning to see that Ruth was a hard worker who had made an important connection. Naomi's view of God was also beginning to shift. In the first chapter she saw God as the source of calamity, but after she found out about Boaz, she said that God's kindness had "not forsaken the living or the dead" (2:20). Perhaps Naomi was not as empty or forsaken as she thought.

A few months later, when the harvest ended, Naomi made a plan. Boaz had not yet initiated a relationship with Ruth, and Naomi decided to prod him a bit. She told Ruth to dress up, put on some perfume, and go to the threshing floor where Boaz was winnowing barley. The men worked late into the night and slept at the site. Naomi told Ruth that after he went to sleep, Ruth should uncover his feet, lie down next to him, and wait for him to tell her what to do. This plan put Ruth in a vulnerable position. "Feet" was often a euphemism for genitals, so Ruth was probably making a sexual proposition to Boaz.

When Boaz woke up, perhaps feeling a chill, he was surprised to find a woman lying next to him. He asked who she was and she identified herself. Instead of waiting for Boaz to tell her what to do, as Naomi advised, she asked him to marry her! In the previous chapter, Boaz hoped she would be blessed by God, "under whose wings [*kanaph*] you have come for refuge" (2:12). Now Ruth asked Boaz to spread his cloak [*kanaph*] over her, as a symbol of protection (3:9). Boaz had offered her a blessing when they met, and now Ruth is saying, "Put your money where your mouth is. You be the blessing. You take care of me. You serve as God's wing."

Ruth took an enormous risk. Boaz could have ridiculed her or refused to consider her request. He could have taken advantage of her vulnerable state and forced her into sexual activity. Instead, Boaz praised her for choosing him, a member of her dead husband's family, rather than a younger man. Boaz promised to do as she asked, but first, Boaz had to solve the problem of a nearer relative. He sorted out the details the next day so they were free to marry.[39] Readers might wonder if Ruth loved Boaz, or if she entered into marriage because it was the only way to achieve financial security for herself and Naomi.[40]

The community celebrated the marriage of Boaz and Ruth and wished for them a house with many children. God has not been directly active in this story, but now the text reports that God made Ruth conceive (4:13). The women in the community named the child Obed and announced that a son had been born to *Naomi*. God had not left her bereft, but had provided a grandson who would restore her life and care for her in her old age. The women affirmed Ruth's love for Naomi and claimed that Ruth was more to her than seven sons. That was high praise in a patriarchal culture where sons meant everything. Naomi might have considered Ruth a burden at the beginning of the story, but Ruth became the source of new life and hope for the future.

The baby was significant not simply for Ruth, Boaz, and Naomi, but for the future of Israel. Obed was the grandfather of David, Israel's greatest king. Ruth is named as an ancestor of Jesus in Matthew 1. A nation so concerned about ethnic and religious purity had to grapple with the fact that not only David but also Jesus the Messiah had a Moabite woman as an ancestor.

Diving Deeper

Bereft. Naomi was overwhelmed by grief, and she was angry and bitter with God and the people around her.

Grief and loss affect everyone. The most obvious source of grief is the loss of a spouse, parent, child, sibling, or friend. Many other losses can have a similarly devastating effect: divorce, unemployment, illness, moving, the empty nest, and other life transitions. The grief that follows loss can be paralyzing and all-consuming. Grief can make people turn inward and withdraw from their communities. Grief can make it difficult to accept help, companionship, and care. Grief can make it difficult to see the world clearly and to see signs of grace. People who love a grieving person may feel that their offers of care and concern are rejected. It is not easy to care for someone when one's efforts are repeatedly spurned.

Too often we try to move grieving people quickly toward healing, failing to realize that grief is a long, slow process. Grieving people sometimes feel guilty about how much they cry and how angry they are. They wonder why it is taking so long to feel "normal" again, and why they can't bring themselves to take the deceased person's clothes out of the closet. Our best response is simply to acknowledge the depth of anger and pain that people experience in the midst of loss.

"The Almighty has brought calamity upon me." Grief is even more complicated when people feel that God caused their loss, either as punishment for sin or because they believe that God controls everything, including disease and accidents. Grieving parents might initially take comfort in the belief that God allowed their child to die in order to gain an angel in heaven, but that comfort might quickly shift to anger that God took their child. Should God be blamed for tornadoes and cancer and car accidents? Does God bring calamity? Is God a divine chess player who controls every bad event in the world? Or do bad things happen in a fallen world and God suffers alongside people in the midst of their grief and loss?

What we're left with. Naomi thought she had lost everything, but she had more than she realized. She had Ruth. God had not abandoned her. Grief was a long process for Naomi, but eventually she stopped pushing Ruth away and started to appreciate her. The next stage in healing occurred when Naomi had the courage and cleverness to work up a scheme for Ruth and Boaz.

In the face of devastating loss, when it seems that everything is gone, it can be difficult to see what we are left with. A spouse is gone, and that is a terrible loss, but there is a friend or sibling or child who is present. The nest is emptied, but perhaps the lonely parent can mentor another child. What we are left with will not replace what we have lost, but it may help with short-term survival and eventually in the start of healing.

Steadfast love. Ruth is the image of God in this story. She shows *hesed*, or steadfast love, to Naomi, even when Naomi resists. Relationships can be a powerful source of healing and connection and hope. At times we have the resources to provide steadfast love for others.

The greatest good news of this story, though, is the redemption of Naomi. Like her, we are in desperate need of redemption and grace and healing and compassion. Sometimes we are so fiercely stubborn and self-sufficient, even in the midst of grief, that we resist these gifts. We think we can make it on our own, but God provides the persistent presence of Ruth so that we can learn to receive.[41]

Welcoming the stranger. This story is a powerful example of contradiction in the Bible. Israelites were not supposed to marry dangerous Moabite women, but here was a Moabite woman who acted as graciously as God did. The Old Testament often characterized strangers as dangerous or threatening, but this was not the last word. In the future shalom, strangers and refugees will be welcomed into the Israelite community. The refugee will give life not only to the king but also to the Messiah.

Questions for Reflection and Discussion

Have you experienced times of grief and bitterness like Naomi? Were you angry at God? What helped you find your way back to hope and healing?

The author says that Ruth became the presence of God in this story due to the steadfastness of her love for Naomi. Has anyone ever fulfilled that role in your life?

HANNAH
(1 Samuel 1–2)

At first glance, Hannah's story seems relatively simple and straightforward. She was childless, she prayed, and God gave her a baby. We might think that birth was the happy ending, but the real ending includes loss and grief along with joy.

At the end of the book of Judges, the Israelites had hit bottom. The rule of the judges had failed, and many of the Israelites thought they needed a king to govern them. In the midst of this social and political chaos, the author of 1 Samuel tells a story about a family. Elkanah had two wives: Hannah, who had no children, and Peninnah, who had many children.

Hannah desperately wanted children. She felt her failure every year when the family went to offer sacrifices at the temple at Shiloh. At the dinner that followed, Elkanah treated Hannah generously, but she could not help noticing the squirming children on Peninnah's side of the table, while she sat alone as always. One year, when Peninnah joked that it was too bad that dried-up old Hannah couldn't make a baby as adorable as hers, Hannah lost her composure. She tried to ignore her, but finally the tears welled up and she could not stop them. She pushed her food away and cried.

Elkanah was well-meaning but clueless. He responded to her grief with rapid-fire questions, which he did not allow her to answer. Why are you crying? Why aren't you eating? Why are you so sad? And then, "Am I not more to you than ten sons?" (1 Sam. 1:8).

How was she supposed to answer that? Elkanah was steady, loving, and generous. He had never shamed her for her infertility. He was a good husband, but he did not fill her deep need for children. She liked being a wife, but she desperately wanted to be a mother. So her answer was no, he was not more to her than ten sons, but he did not understand that. It might have helped a little if he had said that *she* was more to him than ten sons. But as a childless woman, she was a failure.

When the excruciating dinner was over, Hannah went to the temple to pray. Maybe she did not know where else to go. Hannah did not censor herself or pray in graceful language. She spoke honestly of her pain. She wept bitterly. She cried for all the years that her arms had been empty. She cried about Elkanah's decision to take a second wife and that look of pride in his eyes every time Peninnah had a baby. She cried about her fear of the future. She cried about that ugly word "barren."

She was sad and lonely and desperate, and she did what desperate people often do. She made a vow to God. In this she was a bit like Jephthah (Judg. 11), but her vow did not involve killing. She promised that if God gave her a son, she would give the child back to God.

Hannah did not pray the way people usually did in Israelite religious practice. She did not ask a priest to intercede for her or offer a sacrifice. Instead, she poured out her heart to God. Her lips were moving, but she was praying silently. Eli, the priest on duty, thought she was doing it completely wrong. If he could not hear her voice, then she was not really praying, and he rudely accused her of being drunk. Hannah might have fled in shame at this criticism, but she stood up to him. She was not drunk, she said, but troubled, and she had been pouring out her soul before God. She was not a worthless woman, as Eli had assumed. Hannah had found her voice not only before God but also before this insensitive priest. To his credit, Eli backed off, though he did not apologize. He blessed her and asked that God grant her petition.

Something had happened to Hannah. Perhaps she felt that she had been heard. Perhaps she had finally been able to give voice to all the grief and loss that had built up inside her. Perhaps the crying had been a cleansing and a release for her. Perhaps she let go a little of the dream she had pursued for so long. She went on her way, she ate and drank with her husband, and she did not look so sad anymore. They went back to their home, and Hannah conceived and gave birth to a son, and she named him Samuel.

Though we might be tempted to stop there, with a happy ending, there is more to the story. Several years later, when Samuel was weaned, Hannah brought him to Shiloh and left him to serve the Lord for the rest of his life. Her sacrifice sounds admirable, but consider the raw pain of the phrase, "She left him there for the LORD" (1 Sam. 1:28). What would it be like to leave a five-year-old behind? Many parents find it difficult to leave their eighteen-year-old children at college. How did Samuel feel about being left behind? How could Hannah be content with an annual visit with her only child (2:18–20)? The loss may have been eased a bit when she later had five more children, but she did not know that when she said good-bye to him.

In the midst of this pain and grief, Hannah sang a triumphant song (2:1–10) that parallels Mary's Magnificat in Luke 1:46–55. God had turned the world upside down. The mighty were broken; the feeble found strength. The barren woman had borne children; the mother of many was forlorn. The personal and the political were intertwined. Hannah believed God had given her a great gift, and she believed that God would give Israel a king who would transform the nation into the powerhouse God intended it to be. She did not know the details at the time, but her son would become a prophet and a priest who anointed kings. Hannah's courageous prayer for a child helped bring unity and order to the entire nation.

Diving Deeper

"A woman deeply troubled." Hannah provides a model of honest, raw prayer. She did not hide her distress with elegant language but poured out all her grief, loss, and anger. She trusted that God could handle it and would not be offended. God may have closed her womb (1 Sam. 1:6), but Hannah was not willing to accept that as the last word.

Listen. The story demonstrates the importance of listening and being heard. Elkanah asked Hannah why she was sad, but he did not allow her to answer. He offered platitudes ("am I not more to you than ten sons?"), which gave her no comfort. We can sympathize with Elkanah, because it is not easy to hear the pain of those we love, especially when the pain cannot easily be fixed or healed.

Eli the priest was even less skilled at the art of listening. He intervened in a situation he did not understand and made erroneous assumptions. If he had simply asked Hannah about her situation rather than conclude she was drunk, he would have been a far better priest. People who are in pain and grief need the opportunity to talk without being judged or advised or prematurely consoled. They do not need words as much as they need patient, careful listening. In this story, Hannah found that God was a good listener. In the first chapter she was a silenced, diminished woman, but her prayer helped her to find her voice, which rang out in an articulate, powerful song.

Let's make a deal. Hannah vowed that if God gave her a son, she would give him back to God. This raises a number of questions that deserve further reflection. Are vows to God a sign of faith or a desperate attempt to earn God's blessing?[42] What kind of story was Hannah telling herself about God? Did she believe God was more likely to be gracious if she made a sacrifice? Did she think God must be bribed? Or did she lend Samuel to God out of gratitude rather than debt? Could Samuel have become a great prophet and priest if he had been raised at home rather than at Shiloh?[43]

What happens when people make vows to God that conflict with their family's well-being? One of my colleagues was a missionary kid in the Middle East. At the age of seven, he went to boarding school in India, a thousand miles away. His mother found it so difficult to send the children away to school that his parents eventually left the mission field. They decided that they could fulfill their vows to God in other ways. Ida Scudder was a missionary kid who particularly resented her parents' calling when she had to live with relatives in the United States while attending high school. She later became a doctor in India but never forgot how painful it was to miss her parents. Neither Hannah nor missionary families should be romanticized or spiritualized in a way that diminishes the depth of pain and loss that they felt in letting go of their children.

Not a worthless woman. This is a powerful story with many layers. Before I began reading about Hannah, I assumed that she was boring and predictable. She wanted a child, she prayed, she conceived. I realized instead that she experienced a lot of pain and grief, both before and after she had Samuel. Even the few years she had to raise him must have been marred by the anticipatory grief of intending to give him away.

In spite of this deep pain, Hannah was persistent, courageous, bold, and a little bit sassy. She stood up to an insensitive priest and did not let him bully her. She gave birth to a child who would grow up to help give Israel a new future. She insisted on her value. She found her voice.

Questions for Reflection and Discussion

Some of us find it hard to share our deepest pain with God in prayer, feeling that to do so is to be ungrateful for the blessings God has given us. Has this ever been your experience?

Elkanah and Eli were bad listeners. What makes someone a good listener? What habits and practices can we learn to make us better friends through listening?

4

Women of Israel and Judah

MICHAL
(1 Samuel 18–19; 25; 2 Samuel 3; 6)

If we relied on the Revised Common Lectionary for information about Michal, we would learn only that when David danced joyfully before the ark of the Lord, his wife Michal watched and "despised him in her heart" (2 Sam. 6:16). The portion of the story that shows up in the lectionary portrays her as a mean-spirited woman who did not share David's religious convictions or support him in his time of political and spiritual triumph. No wonder David turned to the beautiful Bathsheba.[1]

Reading the whole story of Michal presents a different picture of her. She might have been a difficult woman who criticized David, but she had reasons for her behavior. Michal was the daughter of Saul, the first Israelite king. After the handsome young David had killed the giant Goliath, Saul was so grateful that he took David into his home. This mentoring relationship failed because as David became more successful, Saul became more jealous.

Michal loved David (1 Sam. 18:20). This is the only time the Old Testament reports that a woman loved a man. Saul approved of her affection for David, because her love could be exploited. Saul offered David the opportunity to marry Michal, but David hesitated, citing his low status. Saul responded that in lieu of a bride-price for Michal,

David could bring Saul one hundred Philistine foreskins (v. 25).[2] Saul was sure that David would be killed in the collection process, since their owners would not give them up willingly, but David managed to preserve his life while gathering the grisly gift. Saul then gave him Michal as a wife. David's motivation is unclear. Did he love Michal? Or did he want to benefit from membership in the king's family?

The tensions between Saul and David increased, and after David won another military battle, Saul sent hit men to David's house. Michal helped David escape by letting him down through the window of their house. David never returned to Michal, which suggests he married her for political gain rather than love. Saul eventually gave Michal to a man named Palti (25:44).

The competition between Saul and David continued until Saul died in battle. David was named king of Judah, the southern part of Israel, but he wanted to gain control over the northern part as well. David decided that he wanted Michal back as his wife, because he hoped that the northern tribes, who were loyal to Saul, would then see David as the rightful heir to the throne.

David commanded one of his henchmen to bring Michal to him. She was not asked her opinion. Her husband Palti(el) did not want to let her go, so he "went with her, weeping as he walked behind her all the way"[3] (2 Sam. 3:16). David's henchman was annoyed with this public display of affection and sent Palti home. Michal was torn away from a man who genuinely loved her, and taken to David, who used her to gain political power.

When David became king of the whole nation, he decided to make Jerusalem the political and religious capital of Israel. He wanted to symbolize God's presence in the city by bringing in the ark of the covenant. The ark was a gold box that contained the Ten Commandments. Several years earlier it had been taken into battle as a good-luck charm and the Philistines had captured it. David thought it was time to return this powerful object to its rightful place in the center of Israelite worship.

Retrieving the ark was more dangerous than David had envisioned,[4] but on the second attempt, David led a procession in front of the ark as it was brought into Jerusalem. A large crowd watched David dance enthusiastically before the ark. He was minimally dressed in an ephod or a loincloth. He was happy, he was celebrating, and he was not worried about propriety. He had achieved his goal of bringing the ark to Jerusalem.

Michal did not participate in the festivities but watched from a window. It might have been inappropriate for a king's wife to be out in public on such an occasion, or she might have refused to participate. She disapproved of David's leaping and dancing and "despised him in her heart" (6:16).

When David arrived home, Michal was furious. She said sarcastically, "How the king of Israel honored himself today, uncovering himself today before the eyes of his servants' maids, as any vulgar fellow might shamelessly uncover himself" (6:20). David had not acted with the restraint and gravitas appropriate for a king. Perhaps she disapproved of the religious abandon he demonstrated in his ecstatic dancing. Perhaps the ephod exposed more of him than she thought proper.

David was equally furious. He was the one God had chosen to be king of Israel, he said, in place of Michal's father and brothers. David danced before the God who had chosen him, he said, and he would dance again. He knew that the people honored him, even if Michal did not. The narrator had the last word on this domestic scene. "Michal the daughter of Saul had no child to the day of her death" (6:23). Did God close her womb in punishment? Did David refuse to have sex with her? Or did Michal refuse to be with him? Whatever the cause, the consequences of childlessness were devastating. She had no children to care for or to care for her.

Many commentators have tried to preserve David's good name by rationalizing that this marital breakdown was Michal's fault. They invented flaws for Michal rather than acknowledge that David might have had flaws. This strategy does neither of them justice. Michal might have been petty and irritable, but she should not simply be dismissed as selfish, stupid, or angry. She knew David and his history well enough to be skeptical about his motives. David was not as purely pious as he postured. He might have been seeking power and adulation even as he claimed to be worshiping God. David had mixed motives and a clear political agenda. He wanted to consolidate the king's power in Jerusalem and he used the ark to do that.

Diving Deeper

The rest of the story. Michal was a complicated woman who did not have an easy time with life and love. Our customary ways of telling her story give a limited and negative picture of her and encourage us to contrast David's exuberant worship with her skepticism. David is the hero, and she is a bad woman who brings him down. A more fruitful approach would be to tell the rest of Michal's story and explore why she might be angry with him.

Killjoys. Michal is often dismissed as a killjoy or a "Debbie Downer." Perhaps she was, but it is also possible that she saw David more clearly than he saw himself. She saw a darker side of David than the one he presented to his constituents. She saw mixed motives, and true devotion to God mingled with a deep need to succeed and be liked.

Killjoys are not popular, and yet we all need people in our lives who can ask hard questions about our motives and seek honest answers. Often it is the people closest to us who see us the most clearly, but it can be difficult to hear the truth about ourselves.

Biblical marriage. The story challenges a romanticized view of biblical marriages and shows instead how complicated they can be. This marriage was not based on mutual love and affection. David used Michal when she had something he needed and disposed of her when she was no longer necessary. Michal's anger at David was not a sign of her anger issues or her lack of faith but the result of years of frustration at being manipulated and ignored.

Flawed humanity. We think we know who David was, but our understanding of him might change were we to tell his story alongside the stories of the women around him. Viewing David through the stories of Michal, Abigail, Rizpah, and Bathsheba offers a more complex perspective and makes it more difficult to assert that David was God's man and God's alone. Recognizing the humanity and the flaws of the biblical characters makes them easier to identify with and learn from. David was not a perfect man without faults, and Michal was not an evil woman without virtue.

Questions for Reflection and Discussion

This story shows us that people are not one-dimensional; heroes have flaws, and villains sometimes get it right. Is there someone in your life whom you consider a bad person? What would it take to come to a deeper understanding of that person?

What do you think Michal was feeling when she saw David dancing before the ark? Was it simply anger and resentment? Was embarrassment or jealousy also involved? Something else?

ABIGAIL
(1 Samuel 25)

Abigail appears only briefly in the story of David, but she influences him at an important transitional point in his life. She is not described as a person in her own right, but her personality is evident from the biblical text. She is outspoken, intelligent, and wise.

When Abigail appeared in his life, David had been anointed to be the next king of Israel, but Saul was still the king. David and six hundred soldiers ran a security force for the local landowners. David and his men had protected a wealthy but mean-spirited farmer named Nabal. He had a "clever and beautiful" wife named Abigail (1 Sam. 25:3). David heard that Nabal was shearing his sheep, a festive occasion that included a large feast. David sent messengers to ask Nabal to share some food, but he refused. He did not know that David and his men had provided security for his property and did not want to share his food with a group of roughnecks.

When David's men reported this rude behavior, David was furious. His men took up their weapons and set off to show Nabal who was boss. Meanwhile, a servant told Abigail about David's request for food. Without telling her husband, she assembled a large quantity of food, loaded it onto donkeys, and went along to supervise the delivery. She met David and his men en route. She bowed on the ground in front of David and began to make excuses for Nabal.[5] She asked David to forgive Nabal rather than kill him. She framed her request for leniency in the context of David's future vocation as a leader. Vengeance was not admirable in a king, she said, and it would not help David's reputation to murder Nabal. She assured David that God would protect him and punish his enemies. When David became the king, his conscience would be clear.

Abigail sounded very subservient in this speech. She referred to David eleven times as *adonai*, or "my lord," a term wives used for their husbands. She referred to herself six times as "your servant." Some feminist commentators criticize her cloying humility, self-effacing speech, and eagerness to win approval. Abigail might have felt that she had to act this way in order to save her husband's life, but she was not a passive doormat of a woman. She was powerful, courageous, and daring. She reframed the situation in a way that allowed David to choose a less violent path. She provided an "out" that allowed him to refrain from killing not out of weakness or fear but because of his strength and integrity. She allowed him to save face in front of his men who might have been eager for a fight.

This was a difficult time in David's life. He spent his time fighting the Philistines and avoiding the jealous wrath of Saul. He might have wondered if he would survive long enough to become king. In the midst of this vocational ambiguity, Abigail expressed her certainty that David would be the next king. She reminded him that he was not destined to spend his life on the run, begging food from the local farmers. He had a larger calling. He should choose his current actions carefully, in light of his future vocation.

David might have wondered what gave this woman the authority and the wisdom to speak to him this way, but he listened and affirmed her. "Blessed be your good sense, and blessed be you, who have kept me today from bloodguilt and from avenging myself by my own hand!" (25:33). He praised her insight and initiative.

When Abigail told Nabal what she had done, he had what might have been a stroke or a heart attack, and ten days later "the LORD struck Nabal, and he died" (25:38). When David heard this, he acknowledged that Abigail had been right. David did not have to punish his enemies, because God would do it for him.

David quickly took advantage of Abigail's widowed state to "woo her." She did not need much encouragement. Marriage to the future king was definitely a step up, although it is not clear whether she acted out of love or the desire for security.[6] Ironically, after her marriage, she does not speak again in the Scripture. The text says nothing about their relationship, or if David benefited again from her good sense.

Abigail had a relatively minimal role consisting of one speech and one scene. Still, her story is worth exploring. She was beautiful, but she was not merely a trophy wife. She was strong and smart, and she took initiative. She possessed emotional intelligence that enabled her to read complex situations and find a solution. She subtly defied her grouchy husband. She saved David from his hot temper and desire for revenge. She was a peacemaker.

Diving Deeper

Saving face? The interpersonal conflict between Nabal and David frequently appears on a larger scale in international relations. One person or group insults or attacks another. An embassy is bombed. A nuclear weapon is developed. A prince is assassinated. The group that is attacked or insulted must save face and defend itself, so it retaliates, but the violence is never exactly proportionate, so the first group retaliates, and war has begun. The violence escalates and harms more innocent people.

After decades of violence and injustice under apartheid in South Africa, Nelson Mandela was elected president in 1994. Thousands of innocent people had been murdered because of their race. Families had been divided because of laws regarding work and housing. When apartheid was finally dismantled and Mandela came into power, some people hoped that white people would have to pay for their crimes. Instead, Mandela and Archbishop Desmond Tutu established the Truth and Reconciliation Commission. Those who had committed horrific acts of violence were required to listen to the victims or their families describe in excruciating detail how they had been hurt by apartheid. The goal was not vengeance, because vengeance could not heal. Both victims and perpetrators were asked to tell the truth, and then to find ways to reconcile. It was a painful and difficult process, but it helped to build a new South Africa based on reconciliation rather than revenge.

The United States has often played the role of policeman in world affairs. It has responded to insults or invasions with a big stick. At other times it has refused to get involved in another country's civil war, no matter how horrific the violence. What if the United States saw its role in international conflict as developing creative solutions for conflict? What if its vocation was not to drop bombs or send soldiers but to send peacemakers who could help others work toward reconciliation and justice? Unfortunately, such an idea is quickly dismissed as naive and unrealistic. There is indeed a risk of hubris and paternalism in such an approach, but it might provide a way to interrupt the cycle of violence that is so easy to start and so difficult to end.

A soft answer. Most people do not deal with violence on an international level, but they experience aggression in smaller ways. A demanding and ungrateful employer, abrupt coworkers, aggressive drivers on the freeway, and rude people on the subway all have the power to raise our hackles and put us in fighting mode. Teenagers who insult their parents, middle schoolers who bully their peers, and church members who make mean-spirited comments under the guise of concern can spark the desire to fight back. In each of these situations it is tempting to react in kind with harsh words or aggressive actions.

David responded to Nabal with harsh words and the threat of

violence. Abigail responded to David with kind words and generous actions. She embodied the proverb "A soft answer turns away wrath" (Prov. 15:1). How might soft answers help to reframe a tense situation? A soft answer need not be weak or passive or afraid of confrontation. A soft answer might be telling a bully to stop picking on a classmate. A soft answer might be a parent who takes a time-out rather than screaming in frustration at the angry teenager. A soft answer might be a gentle refusal to listen to nasty criticism of another person. A soft answer can be strong, courageous, and creative, just as Abigail was.

Soft answers and gracious responses do not come naturally. It was Abigail's grace that ended the story with reconciliation rather than revenge. It is grace that enables a parent to scoop up an out-of-control toddler and make the child laugh. It is grace that inspires a coworker to offer a cup of coffee to a hostile office mate. It is grace that enables a high school student to invite the awkward loner to sit at the lunch table.

"Bound in the bundle of the living." In 1 Samuel 25:29, Abigail says that if David's enemies attack him, "the life of my lord shall be bound in the bundle of the living under the care of the LORD your God." This is a powerful image of God's care and compassion. David was not alone, even if he felt like a fugitive. He was part of a community that supported him. He was one of God's people. Abigail believed that David could be calmer and less aggressive if he knew that God would protect him.

Abigail played a bit part in the drama of David's life. She demonstrated wisdom and independence in a culture where women's brains and voices were not always valued. She was thoughtful, intelligent, and quick-thinking. David was wise enough to receive her advice and change his course of action. He set aside his indignation and listened to an unlikely voice. The encounter with Abigail was one of David's best moments.

Questions for Reflection and Discussion

Think about a time when you were able to give a "soft answer" that made a situation better. What were you thinking at the time? What set that moment apart from others when you were not able to respond that way?

Abigail reminded David that he was not alone, that it mattered to the people in his life that he do the right thing. Who in your life creates the community that makes you a better person? Whom does it help you to think about when you're deciding not to respond in anger?

THE MEDIUM AT ENDOR
(1 Samuel 28)

King Saul was desperate. He was facing a battle with the Philistines, and he was afraid. God seemed to have abandoned him.[7] Everything Saul touched went wrong. He was depressed and anxious and full of self-doubt. Walter Brueggemann perceptively noted that Saul was "dying from the inside out."[8]

Saul's discouragement was so deep that he was unable to formulate a battle plan on his own. He desperately wanted to do the right thing, but he needed advice. In the past, Saul had sought counsel from Samuel the priest, but he was dead. Saul asked God for help, but God did not answer Saul by dreams or prophets. Saul felt abandoned and alone.

Saul was so desperate to talk to someone that he decided to try to contact the spirit of the dead Samuel. Israelite law prohibited the use of mediums to contact dead people (Exod. 22:18; Deut. 18:9–12). Saul had expelled the mediums from Israel in order to help the people avoid temptation,[9] but a few mediums remained. Saul felt he had nowhere else to turn. He asked his servants and learned that there was a medium nearby, at Endor (1 Sam. 28:7).

Saul went to find the medium at night, and he wore a disguise. He asked her to consult a spirit for him, but she resisted, fearing he was trying to trap her. Saul assured her that she would not be punished, and asked her to call up Samuel. She did, but when she saw Samuel's spirit, she also recognized Saul the king. Samuel's spirit appeared in the form of an old man rising up out of the ground. Samuel was angry that he had been disturbed. Saul explained that he did not know how to fight the Philistines, God had not answered, and he needed advice. Samuel was unsympathetic and dismissed Saul abruptly. "Why then do you ask me, since the LORD has turned from you and become your enemy?" (28:16). Samuel explained that God was taking the kingdom away from Saul and giving it to David because Saul had failed to destroy the Amalekites. Samuel had even more bad news. By the next day, Saul and his sons would be dead and the Israelite army would be captured by the Philistines.

Saul was devastated by the news, and he fell to the ground. He was exhausted, he had not eaten, and once again he could not do anything right before God, no matter how hard he tried. Even the dead Samuel was angry with him. And to hear that he would be dead the next day was even more disheartening.

The woman who did not want to attract attention to herself now had the king of Israel in a faint on the floor of her home. She might have been frightened, and she might have been angry with Saul for putting her in an awkward position, but she chose to act with kindness and grace. Clearly Saul was not able to make decisions, so she took charge. She had listened to him, she said, and now Saul should listen to her and allow himself to receive care. He finally agreed to rest while she prepared an elaborate meal for him. It was probably his last, because, as predicted, Saul and his sons died the next day in battle. Saul was wounded, and because he did not want to be humiliated by the enemy, he fell on his own sword (31:4). The Philistines found his body, cut off his head, and displayed it as a war trophy. It was a dismal, degrading death for a man who had started to die on the inside many years before.

The woman at Endor has frequently been dismissed by commentators as either sinful or inconsequential. She is sometimes described as a witch or as an old, stooped fortune-teller. Abraham Kuyper claimed that she obtained the power to communicate with demons by selling herself to Satan.[10]

The text says nothing about demons or Satan. Samuel objected to the conversation not because it was demonic but because he did not want to be bothered. God had taken the kingdom away from Saul, and Saul could not change that reality by seeking answers from the dead.

The story of Saul raises difficult questions about God's favoritism. Saul made an error in judgment, and God abandoned him. David made an error in judgment, and God forgave him. Saul was the problem child who could do nothing right. David was the golden boy who could do nothing wrong in God's eyes (except sleep with Bathsheba and have Uriah killed). Commentators and preachers try to justify God's bias by claiming that Saul was a flawed man who lacked true faith, even though he repeatedly sought God's direction and tried to do the right thing. David, they claimed, had a deep and true relationship with God. David may have sinned with Bathsheba, but he demonstrated genuine repentance.

It is possible that the harsh assessment of Saul reflects the narrator's opinion rather than God's. The narrator believed that God chose David, and therefore David deserved to be king. This required explanation, since God had first chosen Saul to be the king. God's shifting allegiances needed to be justified so that God did not appear fickle. The narrator repeatedly noted that Saul made poor choices and did not deserve to be king.

Diving Deeper

Saul's story is profoundly sad. It raises troubling questions about the nature of God and the advice often given to people who are struggling with God. A man who has lost both his job and his marriage feels that God has abandoned him. His pastor might respond that while the man may feel alone, God will never leave him but will always be present. A woman feels that she has made such a mess of her life that God will never forgive her. Her wise Christian friend might say that nothing can separate her from the love of God. These are compassionate and biblical responses to people in crisis. But in this story, God did abandon Saul when he made a serious error in judgment. God did not offer Saul forgiveness and a fresh start.[11]

The Lord did not answer. One of the most disturbing phrases in the story is, "When Saul inquired of the LORD, the LORD did not answer him" (1 Sam. 28:6). Many people have felt this divine silence. A person who has always felt connected with God suddenly feels that God has stopped listening and responding. There seems to be a wall between them. Some people in the midst of making difficult decisions about health care or relationships or ethical questions say that they begged God for direction and God was silent. They genuinely sought to do the right thing, but God did not answer.

How do we respond in a way that takes seriously the sense of abandonment and avoids platitudes? It is possible that God does not answer definitively because there is no definitive answer. God will be present regardless of which college or job one chooses. God will be present whether or not the cancer patient chooses chemotherapy. We might prefer to be told the right answer, but perhaps God asks us to trust ourselves, make a plan, take a risk, and act.

"Dying from the inside out." This story is not so much about sin as it is about pain, shame, loss, and grief. Saul had done his best, he had

tried to be a good king, but he was never good enough. He struggled with depression. He tried to mentor David, but he was repeatedly humiliated by David's success. This is how we should remember him, rather than focusing on the fact that he visited a medium.

The medium as image of God and source of grace. God seems angry and distant in this story. Surprisingly, the grace comes from the medium. This banished, marginalized woman is the loving and compassionate presence in the story. She is the role model. She is the one who is concerned for Saul's welfare. She is more gracious than either God or Samuel!

She tried to help Saul, even at personal risk, when she saw how desperate he was for answers. He was devastated by the word from Samuel, and she offered him food and a place to rest. She prepared a meal that required some effort and expense. Saul received genuine compassion and hospitality and communion from an unlikely source. The woman saw his exhaustion and confusion and offered understanding, sympathy, and food. She chose to be gracious and caring, not because she was commanded to do so, but because she saw Saul's pain and responded to it. God is mostly absent from the story, even though Saul desperately sought God's advice and approval. But perhaps God was present in this "last supper" between the two of them.[12]

Questions for Reflection and Discussion

Have there been times when you felt that God was abandoning you? Looking back on those times, do you still think that is what happened, or have you come to another understanding of God's presence in those moments?

Who are the people who have embodied God's presence for you when you have been at your lowest?

BATHSHEBA
(2 Samuel 11–12)

Bathsheba is often considered one of the bad girls of the Bible. A common interpretation of her story asserts that she chose to bathe on the roof of her house, knowing she could be seen from King David's palace. David saw her and was drawn to her beauty. He brought her to the palace, and they began a romantic relationship that resulted in a pregnancy. David had to eliminate her husband, Uriah; but because Uriah was a bad husband, David did Bathsheba a favor. David and Bathsheba married and lived happily ever after, although David did have to repent for his crimes of adultery and murder.

This version of the story has inspired numerous artists to paint Bathsheba as wealthy, naked, voluptuous, and seductive. The artists suggest that she was vain, preening, self-absorbed, and desperate for attention from the king.[13]

The biblical story of Bathsheba is far more complicated. King David's troops went to battle but he stayed home. The narrative does not say whether he was shirking his duty or too old to engage in battle.[14] As he walked on the roof of the palace, he saw a beautiful woman bathing. Instead of walking away, he continued to watch. He asked his servants about her, and they reported that her name was Bathsheba, and she was married to Uriah, one of David's soldiers. This should have been enough to discourage him. A man could have multiple wives without committing adultery, but he could not have a woman who belonged to another man.

The text says nothing about Bathsheba's intentions except that she was purifying herself after her period, which meant that she was at the peak of fertility. She might have thought that her rooftop or enclosed courtyard was private. Critics insist she knew she could be seen. If she could look up from her bathing spot and see the king's roof, then obviously he could see her as well.

David saw her, wanted her, and sent for her. So much was left unsaid. Did Bathsheba want to be taken to David? Did she have a choice? Could she have said no when the messengers appeared at her door? The NRSV translates, "David sent messengers to get her, and she came to him" (2 Sam. 11:4). This softens the power of his command and implies that she came willingly, but it is likely that she had no choice. The text provides no hint of a mutual relationship. They do not converse. They express no affection, romance, or intimacy. Nothing is said about what Bathsheba wanted.[15]

When she learned she was pregnant, she sent David a message, and David began a process of damage control. First, David ordered that Uriah be sent home from the front. David told him to go to his house and "wash his feet," which was a euphemism for "sleep with your wife."

Uriah refused to enjoy the comforts of home while his fellow soldiers were sleeping in the fields. The next night David wined and dined Uriah, but Uriah again refused to go home.

When David realized that Uriah's integrity exceeded Uriah's sexual desire, David arranged to have him killed in battle, then married Bathsheba. Did she love Uriah and grieve his loss? Did she despise David for forcing her into a sexual relationship? Did she learn to love David, or was there always tension between them? The text does not say.

David seemed to have successfully engineered a cover-up. Uriah was eliminated. No one else knew the details of the pregnancy. Problem solved. Disaster averted.

Not quite. The narrator reports that David's actions "displeased the LORD" (11:27). The prophet Nathan appeared and accused David of misusing his power and failing to appreciate all that God had given him. To his credit, David did not silence Nathan or make excuses for his bad behavior. He said, "I have sinned against the LORD" (12:13). David's repentance did not avert the punishment that God had promised. David and Bathsheba's son died,[16] and later David's children harmed each other and humiliated their father.[17]

David is considered a heroic figure in the Old Testament. Many commentators and preachers praise him as a deeply spiritual man who had a profound relationship with God. He was Israel's best king and presided over the nation's golden age. Walter Brueggemann refers to him as "utterly Yahweh's man."[18] How could such a fine man commit adultery and murder?

Some preachers and commentators tell the story in ways that make David appear less heinous.[19] One strategy is to blame Bathsheba. David is portrayed as a virile, handsome, desirable man whose only flaw was that women found him irresistible. He committed a sexual sin, but it was understandable in such a manly man. "Boys will be boys," after all. How could poor David resist when the beautiful Bathsheba tried so hard to get his attention?

Bathsheba is regularly made the scapegoat for David's sin. She chose to bathe where she could be seen. She invited David's gaze and his sexual attention. The virtuous David could not have instigated this sinful behavior. Bathsheba must have led him on.

Many of the ways we choose to tell this story make David less offensive while obscuring the narrative's real sin and brokenness. King David did not simply have a naughty moment when he lusted after the bathing Bathsheba. She was not a manipulative woman who tried to seduce David. The two of them did not have an inappropriate affair. The sin in this story is much worse. David misused his power to force Bathsheba to have sex with him. That is not adultery, but rape. David further misused his power to kill Uriah.

Diving Deeper

Choosing the right word. Some Bibles insert a heading in this story such as "David Commits Adultery with Bathsheba." The implication of the phrase is that David made a mistake, but "it takes two to tango." The word "adultery" implies that they mutually agreed to a sexual relationship outside of their own marriages. If Bathsheba did not freely choose the relationship with David, and was in fact coerced, then the relationship should be labeled rape. That is a strong word for such a beloved biblical character, but an accurate one.

We often think of the David and Bathsheba story when a prominent political figure commits a sexual impropriety. Discussions of these situations often focus on the naughty sexual behavior, or they might blame the "other woman" for bringing down a good man. A more accurate analysis of both the biblical and contemporary stories suggests that the sin in these situations is that powerful figures misuse their power and position to get what they want. This is not merely a personal sin but a systemic problem.[20]

Entitled. David had a strong sense of entitlement. He was the king, and he could have what he wanted. No one challenged him when he asked for Bathsheba or arranged for Uriah to be killed. To his credit, after the confrontation with Nathan, David responded with what appeared to be genuine confession and repentance. He took responsibility without rationalizing or scapegoating. He did not say "mistakes were made." He said to God, "Against you, you alone, have I sinned" (Ps. 51:4). He did not, however, acknowledge sinning against Bathsheba.[21]

This story can provide a context for discussion about the meaning of power and consent. When one person has more power in the relationship, it is almost impossible for the other person to freely consent. If a sexual relationship is to be mutual and mature, one person cannot take advantage of or manipulate the other's weakness or vulnerability.[22]

Flawed vision. When Joab reported that other men had died along with Uriah, David told Joab not to let the matter be evil in his eyes, but it *was* evil. David's moral vision had been clouded by his power and position. When Nathan confronted David, he said that David's actions were indeed evil in God's eyes. Most of us have the ability to tell a story in a way that either diverts all the blame to someone else or deposits all the blame onto ourselves. Both can represent a flawed vision of reality that does not lead to genuine repentance and healing.

All's well that ends well? Later in her life, Bathsheba was a powerful woman in the court, first as the queen and then as the queen mother (1 Kgs. 1–2). Her ability to influence those situations suggests to some commentators that she was manipulating David several decades earlier. Had she loved David from the beginning? Had she learned to love him? Or did she make the best of an ugly situation to carve out a place for herself in the palace? Whatever her feelings, she found a voice and learned to use her power and authority.

Questions for Reflection and Discussion

Many presentations of this story portray David and Bathsheba as equally guilty participants in an adulterous relationship, when in fact Bathsheba had little choice in the matter. Why are we so quick to diminish David's responsibility?

The prophet Nathan's part in this story shows the importance of truth telling. Is there someone you can count on to tell you uncomfortable truths about yourself?

TAMAR
(2 Samuel 13)

Amnon was the oldest son of King David and the heir to the throne. Amnon had a secret. He was in love with his beautiful half sister Tamar,[23] but it was not a healthy kind of love. He was so tormented by lust that he made himself sick, and he was angry because "it seemed impossible to Amnon to do anything to her" (2 Sam. 13:2). He wanted sex with Tamar, but he did not want her as a whole person.

Amnon's friend Jonadab suggested a scheme to bring Amnon and Tamar together. Amnon pretended to be sick and told his father, David, that a visit from Tamar would be the perfect cure for what ailed him. David ordered Tamar to serve as nursemaid to her brother. Tamar obediently went to her brother's home and prepared food, but he refused to eat until the servants left the room. Then he grabbed her. She pleaded with him not to force her, because she would be shamed and he would be considered a scoundrel. She suggested that Amnon ask the king to give Tamar to him, in a legitimate, approved marriage, but Amnon would not listen to her. Instead, he raped her.

After the violence was over, Amnon's "love" turned to hatred. He ordered Tamar to get out. Again she protested, and again he refused to listen. He called his servants and told them to put "this" out of his presence. Tamar was devastated. She put ashes on her head, tore her robe, and went away crying.

When her brother Absalom found out what had happened he told her to "be quiet for now" and "do not take this to heart" (13:20). When King David heard what Amnon had done, he was very angry, but he showed no support for Tamar. He would not punish Amnon, because he loved him and because he would be the next king. Jewish law required a rapist to marry the woman he had raped, since theoretically no other man would want her (Deut. 22:28–29). Tamar was willing to marry Amnon, but he sent her away. Tamar was now considered used goods. She had been ruined and shamed. The text reports that she was a "desolate woman" (2 Sam. 13:20). Absalom hated Amnon for what he had done to Tamar, and two years later, Absalom had Amnon killed. The rape and incest affected the entire family.

Diving Deeper

Secrets, violence, abuse, cover-up. Some readers wonder why this ugly story is in the Bible. The painful truth is that these events happened in Israel's royal family, and similar events happen in our families. This text offers insight into a tragic aspect of the human condition. People hurt each other. Even people who are intimately connected by family bonds can misuse their power and sexuality to hurt others. The story is a powerful reminder that abuse can happen in a churchgoing family, a wealthy family, an influential family.

"He forced her." Amnon did not love Tamar; he forced her. He was physically stronger, but he also had power because he was a son of the king. Amnon seems to have emulated his father, David, who valued women for their beauty or their political connections.[24] David did not provide his sons with an example of healthy intimate relationships.

The men in this story all possessed power, but Tamar had none. David commanded Tamar to serve Amnon, and she had to do as she was told. Absalom had the power to silence Tamar. David failed to use his power to prevent the abuse, punish Amnon, or console Tamar. The sin in this story is the misuse of power. The men failed to protect Tamar and then failed to help her move from desolation and shame into a healthy adult life.[25]

Abuse is primarily a misuse of power. Men who batter their wives and parents who beat their children use their greater physical strength to vent their frustration and rage on someone weaker. Parents may also use their size and vocabulary to batter their children emotionally. When parents use their power to hurt children out of anger, frustration, sexual desire, or emotional neediness, it is sinful and abusive.

Why do people abuse others? The reasons are complex. Some were abused as children, so they lack good role models for healthy parenting or intimate relationships. Some abusers have a strong sense of entitlement or privilege, especially if they have a powerful position as a priest or a prince or a president. Abusers believe that they can have what they want, and their sense of entitlement can be further encouraged by "friends" like Jonadab, who enabled Amnon's abusive behavior rather than confront it.

Amnon thought he had the right to possess Tamar. Similarly, some men think they have a right to possess women if they meet them at a party or take them out to dinner. Some men believe they have a right to batter their wives because the Bible instructs wives to submit to their husbands. Some parents believe they have the right to discipline their children, even if such discipline leaves their children black and blue.

It is appropriate to name the problem of abuse, but it is also important to recognize the complexity of treatment and change. Prayer, good intentions, and even a desire to change may not be enough to bring about lasting transformation, because abuse is not a rational act. People know at some level that beating or screaming at their children is wrong, but they do it anyway because they are unable to stop or to change. Most abusers require professional help to make a permanent change in their behavior.

"A desolate woman." Tamar was bruised and broken and ashamed. She had no future. She had done nothing wrong. In fact, her trauma resulted from her obedience to her father and brother. Victims of abuse do nothing wrong, yet they suffer devastating consequences. When Tamar begged Amnon not to rape her, she said, "Where could I carry my shame?" (13:13). The perpetrators of sexual violence ought to feel ashamed of themselves, and yet it is the victims who cannot escape the burning sense of shame.[26]

People who have been abused often find it difficult to trust. If children are afraid of their parents' erratic and volatile behavior, then they learn that people cannot be trusted to care for them. If a husband is afraid of his spouse who screams at him during alcohol-fueled rages, then he will not be able to trust her when she is sober. When people cannot trust those closest to them, they find it hard to trust others.

Abuse exploits the vulnerability and intimacy that are present in a significant relationship, between spouses, siblings, parents and children, teachers and students, or pastors and parishioners. The abusive person ceases to be a mentor, coach, or spiritual guide and instead becomes a predator. The sibling ceases to be a trusted companion and becomes a threat. The abusive spouse is no longer a partner who can be told one's secrets and trusted with one's body.

Sometimes the victims of abuse blame themselves, especially if the abuser says it was their fault. A father may tell his daughter that she is seductive. A husband may tell his wife that she deserved the beating because she provoked him. A man may tell his date that because she consented to kissing, she implicitly agreed to all sexual activity.[27]

People who have experienced abuse often exhibit low self-esteem. They are told repeatedly that they are no good, and they begin to believe it. The words of a drunk or angry parent or spouse have immense power over their identity, more than the affirming words of a friend or a therapist. Low self-esteem among victims can lead to depression, addiction, cutting, and the abuse of others.

Finally, victims of abuse often find it difficult to believe in God, who appears to allow abuse to happen. Abuse makes it difficult to see the world and the family as safe, loving, and reliable. Victims feel desolate, lost, and alone.

"He would not listen to her." Tamar said no to Amnon, but her objections did not matter. She told him the rape would shame her. She suggested a legitimate way she could be given to him, but he did not listen. There was no consent in this relationship. No mutuality. No respect. He took what he wanted and cared nothing about her well-being.

The response to sexual and domestic violence has improved in the last decade, but in the past, religious groups and other sectors of society frequently failed to listen to victims. It is difficult to listen to a child saying, "No, Daddy, no." It is difficult to listen to a church member who says her husband beats her. It is difficult to listen to a boy who says the football coach touches him. It is difficult to listen to the missionary children who speak out about the abuse they experienced in boarding school. It is difficult to listen, because what we might hear is too ugly, too painful, too unbelievable.

The church has talked rather than listened. The church has told battered women to go back to their husbands and try not to make them angry. The church has told women who have been raped that it is their fault for walking alone or dressing inappropriately. The church has told children abused by their parents that they are imagining it. The church has told children and adults who have been abused by ministers and priests that the office of the pastor and the peace and well-being of the church are more important than telling the truth and caring for the victims.[28]

It is difficult to listen, but the church cannot move toward repentance until it listens to the secrets. After listening, the second step is to encourage and empower abused men, women, and children to find a voice, to act, to choose. The church needs to shine the light of the gospel on the dark places in human lives. The church needs to hear the truth, however painful or ugly. The church needs to repent of the sin of denial and admit its need for healing and wholeness.

The story of Tamar ends badly. She is desolate. David is silent. Amnon is dead. This is not an ending to imitate. There is no good news here, but the text invites and encourages us to write a different ending to the story, where the parent takes action, the abuser is confronted, and the victim is heard and cared for. We can write a better ending that chooses to listen rather than ignore, to offer grace and healing rather than shame.[29]

Amnon had a secret, and for centuries the church has helped to keep that secret. Amnon would not listen to Tamar, and for centuries the church would not listen to victims of abuse. But Tamar has not been silenced. She has a story to tell, if only we will listen.

Questions for Reflection and Discussion

Where do you see people who have little or no power being subjected to abuse? What might you be able to do to make their situation better?

When we come across difficult stories like this in Scripture, we are tempted to skip over them. Yet they are in the Bible for a reason. Difficult though it might be to hear, how do you think is God speaking to us through this story?

RIZPAH
(2 Samuel 3; 21)

Rizpah does not speak. She has no words. She is a political pawn without power, status, or significance, but she faced a devastating loss with such courage that even King David took notice.

Rizpah appears briefly in two stories. In 2 Samuel 3:6–11, she is introduced as King Saul's concubine and the mother of two of his sons. When Saul died, the kingdom of Israel was divided. Saul's older son Ishbaal became king over the northern part of Israel, and David became king over the southern part. Ishbaal had been appointed as king by Abner, Saul's powerful general, but Ishbaal no longer trusted Abner's loyalty. Ishbaal accused Abner of sleeping with Rizpah, a sign that Abner was trying to get the throne for himself.[30] Abner resented the accusation and retorted that he was a loyal aide, but the text does not say whether he was indignant about being caught or being falsely accused. Abner implied that Ishbaal was a weak and ineffective king and that David's star was rising while Ishbaal's was falling. Abner wanted to support the king who had the best chance to succeed. The text reports that Ishbaal was silent, which was further evidence of his weakness. The king was cowering before his general.

While the men fought over the woman, the woman was silent. After the death of Saul, Rizpah might have felt vulnerable and alone and hoped a relationship with Abner would protect her. It is equally possible that she had no choice. If a powerful man wanted to "take" her to make a political point, she could not say no. Abner might have cared about her, but it is more likely that he wanted to possess her because she had belonged to Saul.

The Bible does not say whether there was a sexual relationship between Abner and Rizpah, or whether it existed only in the paranoid mind of Ishbaal. Did Ishbaal want Rizpah for himself, to prove his own fitness to reign? Or did he not want Abner to have her? Ishbaal's concern might have been admirable if he was trying to protect Rizpah from unwanted sexual advances, but he simply wanted to limit Abner's access to power. Neither man genuinely cared for her well-being. She was a pawn between two men flaunting their sexual and political power.

The story did not end well for Rizpah. Abner was killed by one of David's men, so if he and Rizpah did have a relationship, she had lost another person who offered her some security.

Rizpah next appears in 2 Samuel 21:1–14. Israel had suffered from a famine for three years. David asked God why this had happened and learned that King Saul had broken an agreement with the foreign Gibeonites and killed them instead of protecting them. The famine was God's punishment. David asked the remaining Gibeonites how he could atone for the sins of Saul. They asked for seven of Saul's descendants whom they could kill in a ritualistic manner. Without any sign of protest, anger, or grief, David agreed to hand them over. Perhaps the reason for this callousness is that David benefited from their deaths. Fewer descendants of Saul meant fewer heirs with a competing claim to the throne.[31]

David gave the Gibeonites the two sons of Rizpah, along with the five sons of Saul's daughter Merab. David did not try to find another way to resolve the issue. He showed no concern for the lives of these boys who had done nothing to deserve a brutal death. He showed no concern for their mothers' grief. The seven young men were brutally killed, and their bodies were left exposed. This was a particularly vile and insulting punishment.

Rizpah could have chosen to withdraw in the midst of this anguish. She had lost her sons, her source of financial support, and her security for the future. She could have decided that there was nothing she could do about the desecration of their bodies.

But there was something she could do. She refused to allow the bodies to be desecrated. She was not permitted to move the bodies or to bury them, but she could try her best to protect them. She went to the place where the bodies were exposed, spread a cloth on a rock, and lived there with the bodies for several months. Picture her yelling and waving her arms to prevent the vultures from tearing the eyes out of the bodies. Picture her waiting for the yellow eyes of the night predators and then driving them away. She would have been in danger herself. She must have been exhausted from keeping this vigil. Did anyone help her? Did anyone bring her food? Did anyone sit with her? What did the bodies look and smell like after two months in the hot sun? No matter how gruesome the task, she honored the bodies and protected them from further humiliation.

After several months of her vigil, David heard about it. He ordered that the bodies of the boys, along with the bodies of King Saul and Jonathan, be given a decent burial. Only then does the text report that God listened and the famine ended. Mere vengeance was not enough to appease God. There had to be mercy as well.

Diving Deeper

Goodness is stronger than evil. Rizpah had no voice or power, but she had courage. She channeled her anger and grief into defiant action. She would not let those bodies be further mutilated. This was the one gift she could still give to her sons. To the Gibeonites and even to David, the bodies rotting in the sun were collateral damage. To Rizpah, the bodies were her children and the children of another woman. By choosing to stay with the bodies and demonstrate her love and compassion, she defied the political powers and forced them to show some respect.

Some commentators say little or nothing about Rizpah, in part because her actions seem insignificant to the conflict between powerful men. Far from being insignificant, however, she is a powerful example of grace and redemption lived out in an ugly tale of revenge. David, the Gibeonites, and even God keep score and return evil for evil. She encounters evil and responds with love and care. Her courageous vigil with the bodies reminded David that although he did not value the lives of these young men, their mothers did. Eugene Peterson summarized her contribution to the story: "Rizpah brought David to his theological senses, demonstrating that it is not sacrifice that God wants, but mercy; it is not by taking life that we expiate sin, but by honoring it, not by inhuman cruelties, but by human compassion."[32]

The power of people with little left to lose. Other women in other times have kept vigils for their children. In Argentina, between 1976 and 1983 a repressive government kidnapped as many as thirty thousand people, many of them young adults, for the "crime" of advocating for labor unions, political reform, and human rights. Many were taken from their homes at night and murdered, and their bodies were never found. They became known as the "Disappeared." The kidnappings and murders were justified as a means of maintaining political and economic control, and the government permitted no questions about its tactics. A group known as the Mothers of the Disappeared began pleading for information and would not be dissuaded or discouraged. They kept insisting until other people paid attention. Finally, the government was replaced by a more democratic one, and the women hoped that their disappeared children would be released from prison. Sadly, most of them had been dead for years. The women did not receive a happy ending. Their children were dead. But they tried. They fought. They persisted. They did not give up. In the end, they helped to bring about social and political change.

A different ending? This story illustrates a profound disregard for human life. The Gibeonites demanded human sacrifices, and David sacrificed seven innocent young men to protect his political agenda. He made no effort to find an alternative strategy for reconciliation.[33]

How might this story have ended differently? What could David have done? Was there a way to respond to the Gibeonites' resentment that did not involve brutal murders of innocent young men? What if David said that there had been enough violence and he would not permit any further murders?

In a time of significant conflict in the world, it is hard to believe that goodness is stronger than evil.[34] Hate seems to repeatedly win out over love, which seems ineffective and powerless. In the face of despair, we are called to write a new story, where we say along with Rizpah, enough violence. There has to be a better way.

Questions for Reflection and Discussion

Not many of us have heard of Rizpah, yet she provides a powerful example of courage and compassion. Is there a Rizpah in your life, someone whom others overlook yet whose life bears quiet witness to the love and care of God?

Violence gets the last word in this story, as it too often does in our own time. Are there stories that have made the news recently where a violent ending might have been avoided? What would it take to get there?

THE QUEEN OF SHEBA
(1 Kings 10; 2 Chronicles 9)

The queen of Sheba plays a minor but intriguing role in the Bible. She is a rare example of a wealthy, powerful, and independent woman in the Old Testament.

The narrator includes few details about her, because her primary function in the story is to provide external confirmation of Solomon's influence and reputation.

King Solomon was a young man when he inherited the throne from his father, David. Solomon asked God to give him wisdom (1 Kgs. 3:9), and God provided not only great wisdom but riches and honor as well. First Kings 3–10 describes several examples of Solomon's wisdom, along with elaborate descriptions of the temple that Solomon built for God and the palace he built for himself. His reputation for wealth and wisdom extended all the way to Sheba.[35]

The queen of Sheba heard glowing reports about the wisdom of Solomon, and she traveled a significant distance to see for herself whether the reports were true. The two leaders talked about strategy and trade. The queen tested his wisdom by asking him difficult questions, and he answered them all. She observed the extravagant details of Solomon's court: the palace, food, officials, servants, and the sacrifices made in the temple. These were so impressive that she was breathless ("there was no more spirit [breath] in her," 1 Kgs. 10:5). She admitted that she had been skeptical, but she saw that his wisdom and prosperity were even greater than she had been told.

She was an outsider to the faith of the Israelites, and yet she acknowledged God's role in Solomon's success. "Blessed be the LORD your God, who has delighted in you and set you on the throne of Israel! Because the LORD loved Israel forever, he has made you king to execute justice and righteousness" (10:9).[36] She recognized that Solomon had not earned the throne by his wisdom. God had placed him there and given him wisdom so he could promote the welfare of the people.

She gave Solomon extravagant gifts of camels, spices, gold, and precious stones, and he returned the favor by giving her "every desire that she expressed" (10:13). Some commentators have suggested that her desire was sexual and that she returned home pregnant with Solomon's child, who eventually became king of Ethiopia. Since Solomon had seven hundred wives and three hundred concubines (11:3), he might have been willing to meet her *every* desire, but there is no evidence to support that claim.

The story of the queen of Sheba provides external confirmation of Solomon's wisdom and wealth, but her comments provide a subtle reminder that the vocation of a king was not to awe people with his extravagance but to execute justice and righteousness. Had he done that? Were the men who built the temple and the palace treated and paid fairly? Could the money spent on expensive materials have been used instead to feed and house the people?[37] Did an excessive display of wealth honor God or Solomon's own ego? Did Solomon use his wisdom and the power of the office to bring about justice or to enhance his own reputation?

Diving Deeper

Breathless. These questions are still important in a culture where the gap between the rich and the poor continues to increase. The queen's visit to Solomon's property might have been a bit like visiting Hearst Castle in California, or the Palace of Versailles outside Paris, or The Breakers in Newport, Rhode Island. No expense was spared to create these beautiful places for the rich and famous, but visiting them elicits some questions. Why can a few people live this extravagantly while so many others have nothing? Was the money to build these homes earned legally and fairly? Did the owners of these places pay living wages to their employees who helped them make their fortunes?

Similar questions can be raised about the American economic system. When corporate executives earn three hundred times more than their employees do, or when they are paid the same for a few hours of work that their employees are paid for an entire year, is that true prosperity? Is it just and righteous when the owners of Walmart are among the richest people in the country, but many of their employees qualify for food stamps?[38]

We are often breathless at ostentatious displays of wealth. What if we were instead breathless, angry, and moved to action by the disparities that exist between the rich and the poor? Or by the ways that corporate executives reap enormous profits while failing to pay their employees a living wage? How might we talk about these questions without simply inducing guilt, railing on the wealthy, or sounding naive?

Recently, the high school youth group from my church spent a week on a mission trip in Brooklyn. One day they worked in a food pantry. That night they went to Times Square. At the end of the evening, Ian, one of the young adults, said, "This morning I was trying to explain to an elderly poor Polish woman why she couldn't have an extra bag of rice and tonight I watched adults throw $30 at souvenir T-shirts in Times Square. How can anyone process this?"[39]

Ian had a firsthand encounter with the realities of poverty and excess, and it made him breathless. What makes us breathless?

Questions for Reflection and Discussion

Solomon's wealth and power brought glory to Solomon, but did it bring glory to God? Why, or why not?

Does material wealth mean that a person is especially close to God, who has therefore rewarded them with wealth? What does our society say about that question? What do you think?

JEZEBEL
(1 Kings 16–21; 2 Kings 9)

When you hear or read the name Jezebel, what images come to mind? A conniving, powerful woman? A seductive woman wearing a lot of makeup?

Jezebel was a devoted wife and mother and deeply committed to her religious faith. That should make her the perfect woman in the Old Testament, but commentators describe her as pitiless, morally loose, heartless, and treacherous or call her a she-devil, dominating wife, idolater, inhuman wretch, witch, and whore. What did she do to deserve such disgust?

Jezebel came from the wrong country and devoted herself to the wrong man and the wrong god. Her husband, Ahab, became king of the northern kingdom (Israel) several generations after King David. Most of the intervening kings had been evil, but Ahab took the bad behavior to a new level. Rather than trust God for protection, he made a political alliance with the king of Sidon, a country north of Israel, then married the king's daughter Jezebel. The text does not mention love. Jezebel might have been given to Ahab as a pawn in a political game.

Jezebel brought her own religious beliefs to the marriage. She worshiped the Canaanite fertility gods Baal and Asherah. Ahab also worshiped these gods and set up worship spaces for them (1 Kgs. 16:32–33), which encouraged the Israelites to look to these gods rather than to the God of Israel for security and well-being.

Jezebel actively supported the Canaanite religion by feeding the prophets of Baal. She despised the prophets of Israel's God, and particularly their leader Elijah. In 1 Kings 18, Elijah and the Israelite people killed the prophets of Baal. Jezebel threatened to kill him, and Elijah fled.

Jezebel next appeared in a domestic scene with her husband (1 Kgs. 21). Ahab wanted a piece of property for a vegetable garden, so he asked Naboth, the owner, if he would sell the property or trade it for another piece of land. Naboth courageously refused, because he had no right to sell the land, which had been in his family for years. Ahab was "resentful and sullen" because he could not have what he wanted, and when he came home he lay on his bed, refused to eat, and pouted like a toddler.

Jezebel asked why he was so depressed, and he told her about Naboth. He omitted some important details about Israelite land ownership, which made it appear that Naboth was simply being stubborn. Jezebel took charge. She reminded him that he was the king, and she told him to get up, cheer up, and eat up.[40] She promised that *she* would obtain Naboth's vineyard. She was a powerful and resourceful woman, and in her country, the king had the right to any land he wanted. She arranged for two men to falsely accuse Naboth of cursing God and the king.

Her plan worked, Naboth was stoned to death, and Jezebel informed Ahab that the land was his. When Ahab went to claim it, the pesky prophet Elijah accused Ahab of murder. Ahab would die, Elijah said, and the dogs would lick up his blood. Jezebel would also die, and the dogs would eat her body.

Ahab's moral sensitivity had not been entirely extinguished, and he repented. God repented also and said Ahab would be spared the worst of the disaster.

Several years later, Ahab wore a disguise while his army engaged in battle. An arrow hit Ahab in one of the few places not covered by armor, and Ahab bled to death in the chariot. When the servants cleaned the chariot, the blood ran out and was lapped up by dogs, as Elijah had predicted (1 Kgs. 22:29–38).

Jezebel survived a few more years. Her son, King Joram, was killed in part because he supported the "many whoredoms and sorceries" (2 Kgs. 9:22) of his mother Jezebel. His killer, Jehu, then went after Jezebel, but she did not go down without a fight. She put on eye makeup and an elegant headdress, and sat in the window.[41] Jehu saw her servants in the window with her and asked for their help. They threw her out of the window, she was trampled by horses, and her blood spattered on the wall. Jehu calmly enjoyed his lunch and then decided that Jezebel ought to have a decent burial since she was royalty. All that remained of her body, however, was her skull, her feet, and the palms of her hands. Elijah's prediction had come true. The dogs had eaten Jezebel's body (vv. 30–37).

Jezebel was not a nice woman. She used violence and murder to eliminate her opponents. She manipulated the legal system and lied about Naboth. There is no evidence, however, that Jezebel was unfaithful to her husband or that she committed any kind of sexual sin. Her crimes, though violent and ugly, were no worse than the sins committed by those labeled "men of God." She killed God's prophets; Elijah killed Baal's prophets. She had Naboth killed because she wanted his land. David had Uriah killed because he wanted his wife. She encouraged the worship of foreign gods, as did Solomon (1 Kgs. 11) and many of his successors. Why do commentators label her not only as a sinful woman but also as a witch and a whore?

The author of the book of Kings was trying to understand how things had gone so horribly wrong for the Israelites. David had been a good king, despite his faults. His son Solomon was wise and prosperous, but most of the kings after him had been evil, and the once unified nation of Israel was now divided into two kingdoms, with two kings. Why did so many kings turn away from God?

Solomon had started the nation's decline, because he "loved many foreign women" who turned him away from God (1 Kgs. 11:1, 4). If a brilliant king like Solomon had such a serious flaw, lesser kings like Ahab were even more susceptible to the dangerous foreign woman. Jezebel did not simply worship another god; she actively opposed the God of Israel and killed the prophets. She was accused of "whoredom" not because she was unfaithful to her husband, but because she was unfaithful to the God of Israel. She became the scapegoat for the sins of the Israelites.

Jezebel certainly deserved the censure of the Israelites, but she has also become a symbol for the frightening power of women. Ever since Adam blamed Eve for giving him the fruit, women have been viewed as dangerous. Women appear to have irresistible sexual appeal, which they use to convince men to do their bidding. Men can be so driven by sexual desire that they will give up their religious, political, and vocational commitments for a woman. Men behave irrationally around women, so women must be controlled because men cannot control themselves.

This view of women leads to an odd paradox. On the one hand, women have been viewed as intellectually deficient and irrational. On the other hand, they are conniving, intelligent, and dangerous. Women are too stupid to realize the flaws in their foreign religions, and yet they are smart enough to entice their husbands into worshiping these gods. Men are supposed to be smart and spiritual enough to recognize true religion, and yet they are easily enticed away from it.

Ahab personifies the stereotypical "henpecked" husband. Several commentators identify Jezebel's dominance of Ahab as one of her major faults. Jezebel was also problematic because she was a *foreign* woman. The belief that outsiders were different and dangerous is understandable in a nation that was anxious to safeguard its boundaries and its identity, but it did not lead to healthy relationships with the neighbors. The Israelites feared that other nations would either dominate them politically or force them to give up their religious identity. They blamed their lack of faith on the foreigner, not themselves. The Israelites were not evil idolaters; the Canaanites were. The Israelites would not have worshiped foreign gods if there had been no dangerous foreign women.[42]

Diving Deeper

Jezebel might not seem to be a very inspirational biblical character, since she is one of the "baddest" girls of the Bible. Jezebel was unrepentant and proud until the bitter end. She was not only bad herself, she corrupted others as well.

Understanding the other. We might find it helpful to shift the perspective on Jezebel for a moment and identify her as a good wife who supported her husband and children. She was devoted to her religion, even though she was harassed for her beliefs. She was an evangelist who encouraged others to adopt her faith. To the Canaanites, she was a hero and a model of religious devotion; but what the Canaanites saw as virtue, the Israelites saw as sin and idolatry.[43]

This conscious shifting of perspective can be a helpful way to approach conflict. People in conflict often assume that the other party operates out of misguided motives and is completely wrong. If they can begin to see the other group has valid motives, they might be a bit less dismissive and more understanding. On an international level, Americans have often denigrated Muslims who fight against the godless West, but failed to see the religious convictions undergirding those actions. Americans may disagree and ultimately condemn those actions, but it is helpful to acknowledge the beliefs. What might happen if we tried to understand how others view the world? If we acknowledged that virtue can lead to evil, both in ourselves and others?

Taking responsibility. The story of Jezebel illustrates the human tendency to blame others for one's own sinfulness. The Israelites blamed foreign women, especially Jezebel, for their own idolatry, and failed to ask themselves the hard questions. Why were the Israelites so susceptible to idolatry? What was so attractive about the other gods? Why was their faith in God not enough?

There are numerous examples of this blaming. Adam said: The woman you gave to me gave me the fruit, and I ate. The rapist said: She was dressed seductively. The white shooter said: The young black man was wearing a hoodie and looked dangerous. The concentration camp guard said: I was just obeying orders. How can we help people take responsibility for their own sinful attitudes and behaviors?

Pedestal or pit? Women, more than men, have been categorized either as pure and worthy of a pedestal, or as sinful, dangerous, and in need of control. Women are not worse sinners than men, but neither are they morally superior and naturally more chaste, pure, and generous. Both women and men can be selfish, greedy, lustful, power hungry, and manipulative. Men should not receive a get-out-of-jail-free card for these sorts of behaviors while women are punished for them. Both are equally sinful and equally responsible for their sin. Both are equally forgiven, equally recipients of grace, and equally capable of love, affection, courage, and leadership.

Other religions? The Israelites tried to suppress or eliminate other religions in order to protect their identity, but in the twenty-first century that is not a viable strategy for human flourishing. People of different faiths must learn to live together without killing each other. We have to find ways to maintain religious identity while also allowing other religious traditions not only to exist but to thrive. Is it possible to find guidance from the Old Testament when it is so profoundly shaped by the fear of idolatry? How can religious people be hospitable to people of other faiths within their community? How do people of different faiths live together without violence, destruction, and fear?

Questions for Reflection and Discussion

The author says that, from one perspective, Jezebel was a devout and patriotic person. Do you have any trouble thinking about her that way? Why, or why not?

The problem of idolatry pops up frequently throughout the Old Testament. We don't often set up idols to Baal in our living rooms, but does that mean we are free of the sin of idolatry?

5

Women and the Prophets

THE WIDOW OF ZAREPHATH
(1 Kings 17)

Elijah the Tishbite was a prophet who regularly confronted the Israelite king Ahab and his wife, Jezebel.[1] Elijah told Ahab that there would be no dew or rain in Israel until Ahab obeyed God (1 Kgs. 17:1). Then, fearing for his life, Elijah left town. The lack of rain created a drought, which made life difficult for the people on the margins of society.

God sent Elijah to Zarephath, a town in Sidon,[2] and told him that a widow in Zarephath would feed him. God neglected to inform the widow of this assignment, and she was taken aback when a stranger asked for water. She consented, but before she could bring it, he asked for bread also. Elijah had a lot of chutzpah to ask a strange woman for food in the midst of a famine. She would have been justified in feeling resentful and irritated.

She responded that she had no food to give him. She had only a handful of flour and a bit of oil, and she planned to make one last meal for herself and her son. Imagine the despair of a woman who has nothing left. Once she and her son ate the last bit of bread, they would die.

An appropriate response to her desperate need would have been charity or sympathy. At the very least, Elijah should have apologized for his presumption, but instead, he made an outrageous and inappropriate request. "First make me a little cake . . . and afterwards make something for yourself and your son" (17:13). What kind of insensitive person would ask a mother who cannot feed her child to share her food with a stranger?

Elijah tried to soften the request by telling her not to be afraid, but she might have responded, "That's easy for you to say!" Of course she was afraid. She had almost nothing. Elijah promised that the God of Israel would sustain her supply of flour and oil until the drought ended. That was a nice promise, but why should she trust a strange man who invoked a strange god? Perhaps she thought she had nothing to lose. Perhaps the promise gave her something to hold on to. Perhaps she felt compassion for Elijah. Whatever the reason, she trusted Elijah enough to share her precious bits of food. She did not hold tightly to the scraps she had left.

Miraculously, there was enough. For that day. For the next day. For a week. The oil and flour never ran out. She found abundance in what looked like scarcity. She found hope and life when she expected despair and death. Her faith might have been only as large as a handful of flour, but it was enough.

This story ended happily, but sometime later, death returned in another form. Her son became seriously ill and died, and she lashed out at Elijah. What had she done to deserve this? Elijah did not try to answer, but stretched himself out over the child's body and prayed to God in words that echoed hers. Why did God treat this hospitable woman so badly? Elijah asked that the child's life be returned to him, God listened, and the child lived. When Elijah returned him to his mother, she made a profound statement of faith. "Now I know that you are a man of God, and that the word of the LORD in your mouth is true" (17:24).

These miracle stories show the power of God at work through Elijah, but the woman is not merely a passive recipient of a miracle. She took an enormous risk when she shared her meager resources with a stranger. She was a foreign woman, like Jezebel, but she was receptive to the God of Israel and willing to care for God's prophet. Jezebel was a negative example of someone outside the Israelite fold; this woman proved that not all outsiders were evil. Some were capable of generosity and faith.

Diving Deeper

Mind or heart? This story makes us think about faith, which is usually understood to be intellectual assent to religious doctrine or a conversion to the God of Israel. The widow of Zarephath does neither. Faith for her is a matter not of the mind but of the heart. She trusted Elijah and a power bigger than Elijah. She shared her food even though it was risky, not only for her but also for her child. She chose generosity rather than hoarding. She let go rather than grasp so tightly. She trusted Elijah with the future even though she had no proof or certainty.[3]

"What have you against me?" When her son died, the woman believed that Elijah, and indirectly God, had let her down. Elijah expressed similar rage and bitterness in his own prayer to God. Why should such a gracious woman experience such a wrenching loss? This story shows that hurting people can be brutally honest with God and God's prophets (clergy). God can handle human anger and despair.

Scarcity and enough. This story might help us consider meaningful ways to address poverty without being paralyzed by guilt or inertia. The conflict between King Ahab and Elijah shows that when powerful people fight their ideological battles it is usually the poor who suffer. Elijah tried to force Ahab to renounce idolatry by sending a drought, but Ahab never lacked food and water, and did not seem to notice that his people were dying. Neither Ahab nor Elijah would back down even though people were suffering.

Similarly, when Congress cannot agree on the federal budget, the government shuts down. The members of Congress continue to receive large paychecks, but poor people may lose food stamps and social services that they cannot live without. When insurance companies, politicians, and medical providers debate the best way to offer health care, none of them live a day without excellent insurance, but some people go without basic health care. The rich and powerful fight their political and economic battles without noticing who is hurt in the process.

The story brings to mind the crushing realities of global poverty. Just as in the biblical text, drought leads to famine, especially in countries with an unstable water supply. Women and children are usually the first and most affected. Churches might consider supporting missionaries and relief agencies that address the causes of poverty by helping people build wells, grow food more efficiently, or find alternative food sources.

The widow of Zarephath was a foreigner who was able both to receive the grace of God and to offer it to Elijah. Her story illustrates that not all foreign women were like Jezebel and that God is gracious not only to the Israelites but also to those deemed outsiders.

Questions for Reflection and Discussion

Have you ever had to let go of your justifiable fears and concerns and trust that God would take care of you?

When you are angry or hurt, do you feel comfortable directing that anger to God? Why, or why not?

THE WIDOW WITH THE OIL
(2 Kings 4)

This story of a desperately poor woman in 2 Kings 4:1–7 is one of a series of incidents in 1 and 2 Kings that demonstrate the miraculous power of the prophets Elijah and Elisha. Elijah had been taken up into heaven (2 Kgs. 2), and now his disciple Elisha was following in his footsteps.

Like the story of the widow of Zarephath, this story illustrates the harsh reality of life as a poor Israelite. The two books of Kings describe leaders, politics, conflict, and corruption, but they also include stories that demonstrate God's concern for marginalized people whose lives were at risk.

In this story, an unnamed woman came to Elisha seeking help. Her husband had been a prophet, like Elisha, and a God-fearing man, but he had accrued a sizable debt. The widow would have to sell her children into slavery in order to pay. Elisha asked what she wanted him to do and what she had in the house.

She had nothing but a small bottle of oil. Elisha saw potential in this inconsequential possession, and he told her to borrow empty jars from her neighbors. He then advised her to shut herself and her children in a room (without Elisha) and fill the jars with oil. She poured and poured, and the small bottle of oil filled multiple large jars. Finally, when she had filled the last available jar, the oil in her small jar ran out. She was able to sell the oil, pay her debts, and live on the rest of the money.

This miracle story celebrates the power of God and the prophet to multiply a bit of oil into a lot of oil.[4] God was wonderfully gracious to this woman and her children. Unfortunately, most desperately poor people do not receive a miraculous supply of oil or any other explicit help from God. Are these people unworthy of God's intervention?

The grim reality of poverty in the world cannot be remediated with a jug of oil. The pressure to sell one's children still exists in the twenty-first century for many parents throughout the world. Some are in deep debt and cannot afford to raise their children. Some choose to sell one child so other children can live. Parents are trapped in horrifying and impossible choices. The new slavery is sex trafficking. Parents are promised that their child or young adult will have a good job as a nanny or a waitress, but then the children find that they are trapped in prostitution and cannot get out.[5]

Elisha did not simply take over and assume he knew the solution to her problem. He asked the woman what she wanted him to do, and he asked what she had. He did not perform a paternalistic act of charity in which he was the hero and she was the passive recipient. The miracle allowed her and her children to work their way out of their debt. "They [the children] kept bringing vessels to her, and she kept pouring" (4:5). This simple statement is a powerful encouragement to those who need to keep trying, keep putting one foot in front of the other, and not lose heart.

Diving Deeper

"*What shall I do for you?*" One response to poverty is to respectfully ask this question. Those who want to help should ask what would be helpful rather than simply assume they know best. The helpers should seek ways to partner and cooperate with those who are being helped. Sometimes offering encouragement and basic resources can have miraculous results. Nicholas Kristof and Sheryl WuDunn point out that small efforts like deworming students and giving them iodized salt can improve the health of third-world children and keep them in school.[6]

It is easy to despair that the problem of global poverty is so large that nothing can be done, but there are ways to help people while preserving their dignity and independence. A store in my town sells products made by people in third-world countries who are assured a fair wage for their work. The Kiva Microfunds program offers small but significant loans to women in third-world countries who are starting small businesses. The Heifer Project allows donors to purchase cows, goats, rabbits, and other livestock to help people produce their own food. People of faith might not be able to provide a miraculous supply of oil, but there are steps they can take to help alleviate poverty.

"*What do you have in the house?*" This story focuses on material poverty, but it also offers insight for those who feel overwhelmed by disease, loss, loneliness, or overwork. A teacher is running low on energy and creativity. A parent of young children is exhausted from the daily grind. A parent of defiant teenagers does not know how to talk to them. An older person is worn down from the struggle to maintain her health and pay the bills. Stressed and exhausted people may feel that their resources are gone and they have nothing left.

Elisha's question is still relevant. "What do you have in the house?" Are there resources available that might have been overlooked? Perhaps a support group might become a source of encouragement and companionship. Perhaps a friend has repeatedly offered to help, but we have been too embarrassed to admit to need. Perhaps we gain new knowledge and abilities by taking a class that helps to develop a skill or an interest we have never fully used. Perhaps our mood can be elevated by exercising or simply spending time outside. Where is the small bottle of oil in our lives that seems insignificant but might be a source of healing, survival, or transformation?

Questions for Reflection and Discussion

Apart from material goods, what resources do you have to help others? What talents and abilities do you possess that, though they seem small to you, might be of much assistance to someone else?

The miracle in this story is that God provided a way out of what seemed no way for this widow and her children. Has God ever done something like that in your life?

THE SHUNAMMITE WOMAN
(2 Kings 4)

This story is the second in a series of miracles that show God's power at work in the prophet Elisha. The woman from Shunem is not poor and needy, but powerful, smart, and independent. She is one of the strongest women to appear in the Old Testament.

The NRSV describes her as wealthy, but the Hebrew word *gadol* suggests a broader meaning of a "great" woman who is competent and respected. She was an observant and generous person who noticed

Elisha passing through her town and invited him for a meal. When she realized that he traveled through frequently, she and her husband made a room where Elisha could stay.

After enjoying this gracious hospitality, Elisha decided he should offer her something in return. He asked if she needed any political favors, but she assured him that she was secure. Then, in a somewhat odd twist,[7] Elisha asked his servant Gehazi what should be done for the woman. Gehazi replied that she had no son and her husband was old. Elisha then promised that she would have a son.[8] She was skeptical and told Elisha not to deceive her; but within a year, she gave birth to a son.

Some years later, the child suddenly became ill and died. The woman took his body to the bed in Elisha's room, and then asked her husband for a servant and a donkey so that she could go to see the prophet. She did not tell him that the boy had died, and the husband did not ask. He wondered why she would visit the prophet when it was not the Sabbath or a feast day. She did not answer directly but said, "It will be all right" (2 Kgs. 4:23). She used the Hebrew word *shalom*, which could also be translated "it will be well." She went quickly to Elijah's home, which was about fifteen miles away.

Elisha saw her coming and sent Gehazi to meet her and ask if she and her husband and child were well. She said only what she had said to her husband: "It is all right" (4:26). She preferred to speak directly with the prophet. She did not tell Elisha that her son was ill, but she implied it with her expression of resentment. "Did I ask my lord for a son? Did I not say, Do not mislead me?" (v. 28). She had not wanted Elisha to toy with her emotions. She had not wanted to have her hopes raised, only to be dashed; but that is exactly what happened.

Elisha sent Gehazi ahead with his staff, a wooden walking stick that was sometimes used in miracles, to try to heal the child. The woman was not satisfied with an intermediary and refused to return home without Elisha. Her suspicions proved correct. Gehazi could not heal her son even using Elisha's staff. Elisha went to his room, prayed, and then lay on the child, mouth to mouth, eyes to eyes, and hands to hands.[9] Finally the child sneezed and opened his eyes.

Diving Deeper

"A small roof chamber." The Shunammite woman provided meals and a room for Elisha. She offered him a place of safety, comfort, and

sustenance when he traveled. Some people have a gift for elegant hospitality. When you are invited to their home for a meal, the table is
beautifully set, the linens are pressed, there are fresh flowers on the
table, and the food is perfectly prepared. These hosts are never frazzled,
and they never fear that the roast will be done twenty minutes before
the potatoes.[10]

Hospitality does not have to meet Martha Stewart's standards in
order to be worthwhile. Everyone is capable of hospitality, because it
is not about filet mignon, roses, and matching table linens. The most
hospitable people welcome and delight in their guests so effectively that
the guests never feel that they are a burden. Some of the most powerful
experiences of being welcomed and cared for have occurred in homes
and situations where the hosts have very little, yet graciously share it
with guests.

The Shunammite woman not only fed Elisha, she provided a comfortable and welcoming space for him. Hospitality is more than dinner
parties. Even those who can't cook can show hospitality by creating
a gracious and welcoming space. Hospitality is inviting friends into
the "man cave" for beer and football. It is offering a listening ear at a
booth in a coffee shop. It is the dorm room where students know they
can speak honestly and will be heard without judgment. Hospitality is
expressed when a trusted teacher or coach conveys support and encouragement. Hospitality occurs when kids welcome the less popular kids
into their games at recess. There are many ways to create space where
others are welcomed and heard and accepted.

It feels gracious to be the hospitable one, but it can often be difficult
to admit our need for care. We can be stubbornly independent, and we
hate to feel "beholden" to another. The Bible doesn't tell us Elisha's age
at this point, but perhaps the years were catching up with him and he
was not capable of making the whole trip in a day. He needed the grace
and humility to admit that he needed a place to stay.

Maturity. The Shunammite woman was a strong, courageous person
who knew her own mind and would not allow herself to be ordered
around. She related to Elisha as an adult. We would do well to recognize the maturity of her relationship with Elisha. She was brutally honest with him. She did not uncritically accept his words. When he told
her about the baby, she was skeptical. "Do not deceive me," she said.
We might translate that, "Don't mess with me! Don't dangle good
news in front of me if it is not going to be true." Later, after her son
died, she expressed her anger and frustration. "Did I not say, Do not

mislead me?" She had begun to hope for a future with her son, and now both her son and her hope were gone.

"It will be all right." How could the Shunammite woman say this when her son was dead? Was she brushing off questions from her husband and Gehazi? Was she saying, "It's fine," through clenched teeth when it clearly was not fine? Perhaps instead it was a profound confession of trust and faith. A similar idea is expressed by Julian of Norwich, a fourteenth-century mystic, who said, "All will be well, and all will be well, and all manner of things will be well." It also evokes the hymn "It Is Well with My Soul."[11] It is significant that she can express both trust and anger in the span of three verses. Trust that all will be well does not preclude asking hard questions and expressing anger and pain.

Here is the powerful pathos and anguish of this story. It is risky to be a person of faith and hope. What if we trust God, and God fails us? What if we hope for a cure for the cancer that eats away at our parent or spouse or child, but there is no cure? We hear so many glib promises about God's love and protection, but the painful reality is that accidents and disease and death happen to everyone. That makes us angry and frustrated and disappointed, and sometimes we want to lash out at God. Didn't I tell you not to get my hopes up?

Life and faith are risky. Trusting in God, loving another person, and having children all demand that we give over our hearts, and those hearts are easily broken. We might wish for a guarantee that God won't give us children who die or spouses who leave or employers who fail us. We would like to say to God, "Don't mess with us! Don't give us false hope." But in the end, we can only put what we love into God's hands, just as the Shunammite put her son into Elisha's hands. And in God's hands, somehow, someday, it will be all right.

Questions for Reflection and Discussion

Do you have difficulty accepting hospitality and help? If so, why do you think that is?

This story shows that our love for one another makes us vulnerable to heartache and loss. Is it worth it? Did the experience of grief and loss ever tempt you to close yourself off from others?

THE MAID OF NAAMAN'S WIFE
(2 Kings 5)

Naaman was the commander of the army of Aram, in what is now Syria. He was a foreigner from an enemy nation, yet he is praised in this story as a great man. He was powerful, but Naaman had a problem, a skin disease, which the NRSV calls leprosy (2 Kgs. 5:1) but is better described as a disfiguring rash or infection.

Naaman received advice about his disease from an unusual source. The Arameans had captured a young Israelite girl, and she served Naaman's wife. The girl was probably about ten years old. She might have been an orphan, or she might have been ripped away from her parents. She was forced to work for a strange family who spoke a different language and had different customs.

She had every right to be sullen and angry about her situation. She certainly did not owe kindness to someone who had enslaved her, yet she chose to offer it. She told Naaman's wife that she knew of a healer, the prophet in Samaria, who would be able to heal Naaman. With this small word she demonstrated compassion for Naaman and trust in the healing powers of Elisha, the prophet. She was a young, inconsequential servant girl, but she knew something that the mighty warrior Naaman did not. She might have kept quiet, thinking that her idea would be ignored, but she spoke up, her mistress reported what she had said, and Naaman listened. Naaman told the king what the Israelite slave girl had said, and the king sent him to Israel to seek healing.

Naaman and his king demonstrate a remarkable sense of entitlement. The army of Aram had raided Israel and taken captives, but the two men believed that Naaman could return to Israel to demand healing!

Naaman set out for Israel with a lot of baggage. He brought large quantities of gold and silver, ten sets of clothes, and servants to carry the bags. He assumed that healing had to be paid for. There was some confusion over who would do the actual healing. The slave girl had named the prophet as the healer, but this detail had been lost in the flurry of activity. The king of Aram sent a letter requesting that the king of Israel heal Naaman, but when Naaman arrived at the palace and delivered the letter, the king of Israel was puzzled and angry. The king knew he had no power to heal and accused the king of Aram of deliberately picking a fight.

Elisha the prophet heard about the king's unfortunate encounter with Naaman and sent a message that Naaman should come to Elisha (5:8).

Naaman and his entourage went to Elisha's house, but Elisha did not meet Naaman directly. Instead he sent a messenger who told Naaman to wash in the Jordan River seven times, and he would be clean. Naaman thought this was foolish. First of all, why didn't the prophet himself come and heal him? Naaman was a very great man, after all, and deserved a dramatic moment of hocus-pocus. Naaman was also insulted by the idea of bathing in the Jordan River. There were better rivers back home in Damascus where he could wash. Naaman left in a huff and prepared to return home. This was not how he expected to be treated.

The servants intervened with the voice of reason. They pointed out that if the prophet had asked him to do something difficult, he would have done it; so why not perform this simple task of washing in a river? To his credit, Naaman listened to the servants. He immersed himself seven times in the Jordan, and he was healed.

Notice the contrast in the story between the powerful men who are arrogant, entitled, and quick-tempered and the powerless servants who are wise and insightful. The powerful men are buffoons who know all the answers and tell other people what to do. The slave girl and the servants are humble and quiet. At the right moment they say politely, "Here is a suggestion about a healer" or "Why don't you try washing in the river?"

Naaman returned to Elisha to thank him and express faith in the one God of Israel. The text makes it clear that healing was not a reward for faith, because Naaman did not express faith until after he was healed. Healing was a divine gift that could not be bought or earned.

Diving Deeper

Use your voice! The servant girl was a minor character who played a major role in this story. She was a stranger in a strange land, far away from her faith, her family, and her home in Israel. She was young, enslaved, nameless, and powerless, and yet she changed the life of a strong, powerful man when she told him about the grace of God. Her courage and spiritual insight offer a positive role model for those who are caught in difficult circumstances and think they have nothing to offer. She used her voice and was a vehicle of God's grace.

Good news from unexpected sources. This story encourages us to pay attention to unlikely sources of insight and advice. The CEO might find that the custodian has insight about employee morale. Those who are comfortably middle class might learn from a first-person story about the realities of poverty. Parents find that their children can be uncomfortable sources of truth, particularly when they are angry. The people with the least status might be the ones with the most accurate insights or solutions.

Similarly, encouragement can sometimes be found in unlikely people. I once heard about a seminary student who works as a bartender to support her family. She went to work one night feeling weary and wondering where she would find the energy to smile and engage her customers. She was further stressed when a customer arrived who had often made embarrassing personal comments about her. On this occasion, though, when he paid his tab, he said, "You are an extraordinary woman. I know you work hard, at school, at work, and on yourself. I am proud of you." He left her a hundred-dollar bill for an eight-dollar drink. "I was leveled," she said.

The slave girl is an example of evangelism at its best. She did not tell Naaman that he was lost or sinful. She did not introduce complicated theological topics. She saw that Naaman had a need and she pointed him to a place where he could be helped. She was compassionate, and she had good news to share.

Questions for Reflection and Discussion

The slave girl belonging to Naaman's wife had little reason to see her powerful captor healed. Why would she have spoken up in this situation?

In which set of characters do you more see yourself: the powerful men who thought they already knew what was best, or the powerless slaves and servants who actually did?

HULDAH
(2 Kings 22; 2 Chronicles 34)

The story of the prophet Huldah is brief and does not provide any detail about her character, personality, or vocation, but it demonstrates that she was respected for her leadership ability.

Around the seventh century BCE, several generations of bad kings ruled the southern kingdom of Judah. The people of Judah then chose an eight-year-old named Josiah as their king (2 Chron. 33:25). Surprisingly, he was devout and honorable. In the eighteenth year of Josiah's reign, a priest found a scroll mislaid in old financial records. The scroll was identified as the book of the covenant, which was another name for the book of Deuteronomy. Josiah ordered the scroll to be read aloud, but when he heard it, he was grief-stricken. The people had not been obeying the rules listed in the scroll.

Josiah wanted to repair the relationship between God and the people, and he assigned five men to discern God's voice and instruction. The men chose to consult the prophet Huldah, who lived in Jerusalem. She was the wife of Shallum, who worked at the temple; no further details about her are provided.

A prophet's role was to convey God's word to the people. At times a prophet predicted the future, and a test of a true prophet was whether the predictions were accurate. Apparently both men and women served God in this way, because the narrator does not suggest that a female prophet was particularly noteworthy.[12] The NRSV calls her a prophetess (2 Kgs. 22:14), because the Hebrew word has a feminine ending, but she was not a lesser, weaker version of a prophet.

The Bible does not specify exactly why the men went to a prophet. They might have wanted to ascertain the validity of the scroll or seek advice about what to do next. They must have seen her as a reliable intermediary for the divine word. When they arrived, they did not explain the problem or ask questions. She spoke and they listened. Huldah used the phrase "thus says the LORD" four times in her speech. She said that disaster would indeed come upon the king and the people, because they had abandoned God, made offerings to other gods, and provoked God to anger. She certainly did not sugarcoat the message, but in the midst of this very bad news for the people of Judah, there was a tiny bit of good news for Josiah himself. Because he had been penitent and had humbled himself before God, his own death would be more peaceful, and he would not see all the disaster that would be brought onto the people.

Josiah took those words to heart and launched a major reform. He destroyed the idols and shrines to other gods. He ordered the people to keep the Passover. Unfortunately, the faith and commitment of one king could not reverse the damage done by all the evil kings who had gone before him.[13]

The story of Huldah provides evidence that women exercised leadership and authority in situations narrated in the Old Testament. Huldah advised the king. She was respected and trusted as a prophet who conveyed the word of God. That sounds like the work of a minister and preacher. Critics of women as ministers and leaders, on the other hand, insist that she was not a role model or a pattern to follow.

Opponents of women as leaders argue that Huldah and the other women prophets had a limited, specific role that was very different from that of a preacher or pastor. They claim that Huldah and the other women prophets interpreted God's word in private, on request, but they lacked the public authority and leadership skills that contemporary preachers must possess. According to this view, the presence of women prophets in the Old Testament does not legitimize women ministers in today's church.

Further, these critics dismiss women in general and Huldah in particular as merely passive conduits of God's word. She spoke only what God told her to say, and had no voice or thoughts of her own. Her advice did not arise out of her education or intellect, because women lack the intelligence and rationality to shape the word they receive.

These commentators draw conclusions about female prophets that they would not make about male prophets. Were male prophets passive transmitters of God's word? On the contrary, Amos, Hosea, Jeremiah, and the other prophets all spoke God's word to the people using language, images, and examples from their personal experience. God was not a ventriloquist whose voice came through the dummy prophets. The prophetic task required all of their intelligence, creativity, and spiritual sensitivity.

Huldah, too, delivered the word of God using her intelligence and savvy. She had earned the respect of the king and his messengers. They knew that she would provide a divine perspective on the words in the scroll. She conveyed hard truths in a compassionate and sensitive manner. The word of the Lord came through her distinctive voice and personality, as it continues to do through many women today.

Diving Deeper

Encountering bad news. Much as we might be tempted to do so, our faith does not allow us to close our eyes to God's hurting world. It is not enough to lament that the world is going to hell in a handbasket.

It is not enough to lament the absence of adequate gun laws. We have to confront the reality that the world's brokenness and our own are one and the same thing. The shooting of church members in Charleston was not simply an isolated ugly event that happened in South Carolina; it is also a reminder of the depth of white privilege, racism, and resentment that occur in varying degrees. The latest crazed shooter is not simply a case of mental illness, but an illustration of the deadly combination of a powerful gun lobby, the reluctance to regulate personal freedoms, a culture of violence, and a pervasive sense of helplessness in the face of repeated violence. How can we remain alert to these persistent social problems of racial and economic inequity in a way that does not lead to despair and disengagement?

Unexpected voices. Huldah's story is a reminder that God's word comes through unexpected channels. God speaks through many different human voices: male and female, old and young. God uses bodies in a rainbow of colors to embody the word. God uses a variety of personality types to enliven the word. God takes a great risk to entrust the word to fragile and flawed human voices. "And the Word became flesh and lived among us, . . . full of grace and truth" (John 1:14).

Questions for Reflection and Discussion

Prior to reading this section, had you known there were women prophets in the Old Testament? Does it surprise you to find them there?

What situations or problems in your community call for the kind of prophetic leadership Huldah displayed in this story?

GOMER
(Hosea 1–3)

The story of Gomer is disturbing, disjointed, and difficult to interpret. She is described as an adulterous woman and compared to the unfaithful nation of Israel. God appears to recommend harsh punishment to force both Gomer and the Israelites to repent and return to faithful behavior.

Hosea was a prophet in the northern kingdom of Israel about 750

BCE. The Israelites had repeatedly turned away from God to seek help from other gods or nations that appeared to be more powerful. Hosea compared their religious infidelity to marital infidelity. God asked Hosea not only to speak the usual prophetic words of judgment, but also to embody God's word in a personal and painful way. God told Hosea to take a "wife of whoredom" who would illustrate Israel's unfaithfulness (Hos. 1:2).

Hosea took a woman named Gomer. Her status was unclear. She might have been a cult prostitute who engaged in sex to ensure fertility and prosperity. She might have been a professional prostitute who sold sex for money. There were other ways to receive the "whore" label, however. She might have had a sexual partner before marriage. She might have been raped, which made her "damaged goods." It is also possible that she was a "good" woman at the time of the marriage but later became unfaithful.

Hosea entered into marriage with the expectation that his wife would be unfaithful to him. He must have been constantly suspicious and on edge, waiting for her to stray. Gomer gave birth to three children,[14] and each was given a name that reflected God's disgust with the Israelites.[15]

Despite all the references to divine anger, the first chapter ends with a hopeful note about restoration. The rejected people of Israel would grow and thrive as God's children. Unfortunately, restoration was short-lived.

The tone of the second chapter shifts abruptly back to condemnation. The text does not say what Gomer did, but Hosea ordered the children to plead with their mother to "put away her whoring from her face" (2:2). Hosea then listed all the ways he would punish his straying wife. He would strip her naked, expose her, and deprive her of water and food. He would forcibly keep her at home so that she could not pursue her lovers. He would publicly shame her. The language is violent and disturbing.

The tone again shifts abruptly in 2:14 from punishment to pursuit. Without giving a reason, Hosea announced that he would speak tenderly to his wife, give her gifts, and try to win her back. She would stop running to other lovers, and he would make a new covenant with her. Their marriage would be rooted in justice and steadfast love.[16] The wondrous and loving Hosea would rehabilitate the badly behaved Gomer and repair their broken marriage.

The sudden shift is difficult to explain. Hosea might have been instructed by God, or realized on his own, that violence would not win his wife back. He needed to use love rather than force. Those who are familiar with patterns of domestic violence, however, note that abusive spouses frequently shift from punishment to pursuit, or anger to love, for no discernible reason. The story is reminiscent of a case of domestic violence where the abusive spouse realizes that he has gone too far and decides to win back the abused spouse with love and affection.

If read literally, this is a terrifying story. Hosea punished and shamed Gomer and involved their children in an unholy example of familial triangulation. If God had commanded him to enact these punishments on his wife, then God appeared to promote domestic violence as a way to compel a wife to be faithful.

This interpretation is so troubling that many commentators suggest that the story did not actually happen but was a hypothetical or metaphorical illustration of the idolatry of the Israelites and the pain it caused to God. If a man was hurt and angry because of his wife's infidelity, then God was even more hurt and angry over the Israelites' infidelity. It seemed that God's only recourse was to punish the Israelites until they returned to God. Punishment would not be effective, however, and God would use love instead. Even though the Israelites repeatedly rejected God, God would continue to pursue and persuade.

This metaphor made sense to the Israelites because they did not view marriage as a mutual relationship between equals. Men had more power, but they were vulnerable to being shamed if a wife was unfaithful. Similarly, God had more power in the covenant with Israel, but the Israelites could shame, embarrass, and hurt God if they trusted in other nations or other gods.

The third chapter repeats the story with a slightly different twist. God told Hosea to love a woman who had a lover, and Hosea then bought an unnamed woman. Was this Gomer? Some commentators speculate that Gomer had left Hosea and sold herself into slavery. She needed rescuing from her errant ways, just as the errant Israelites needed to be rescued from the nation to which they had sold themselves. Again, Hosea is the heroic, long-suffering husband, and Gomer is the weak and sinful woman.

Diving Deeper

The details of the story are so murky and disturbing that it may be wise to read it as a metaphor rather than a literal event.

Through Gomer's eyes. Perhaps we can gain a different perspective on this text by considering what Gomer's experience might have been like. Did she love Hosea, or did she feel that she was damaged goods and had no other option for marriage? Did Hosea genuinely love her, or did he marry her only because God told him to do so? Did she finally simply live down to his expectations? Did she say, "If you are so convinced I'm going to be unfaithful, then I'll be unfaithful"? Gomer might have found it difficult to live with such a self-sacrificing and long-suffering man as Hosea. Maybe she wanted to spend a few minutes with somebody who made her laugh. Maybe she just wanted to be loved by someone who wasn't using her as an extended prophetic object lesson.

Gomer and her children experienced such sadness and shame. Imagine being a child named Reject or Not-pitied. Imagine a father asking a child to confront the mother's adultery. Imagine watching your mother being punished for adultery. Seeing the story through these lenses helps us avoid stereotypes and moralism about the long-suffering Hosea and the naughty Gomer.

A story about God. Given the difficulties involved with a literal reading of the story, we might find it more helpful to focus on what the text says about human failure and divine faithfulness.

Contemporary readers find it easy to mock the Israelites for their idolatries. How foolish to reject the true God for idols of metal and stone. How misguided to trust in another nation's army. How arrogant to assume that they did not need God. But the Israelites were not merely foolish and stubborn; they were terrified. So are we.

Idolatry arises out of vulnerability and fear. We human beings are desperately afraid. We wonder if the next terrorist attack will occur on the plane we just boarded. We wonder how our children will survive the challenges of drugs and alcohol. We wonder who will care for us when we are dying. We wonder if we will run out of money before we run out of life. And then it makes sense to trust in the Department of Homeland Security, a get-tough policy on drugs, and Social Security and the stock market. We may not worship gods of stone, but our various sources of security become idols when we rely on them to save us. They seem more dependable than a vague trust in God. When we are lonely, confused, and frightened, we want something tangible that will give us safety and certainty.

God is often portrayed as angry about this human tendency toward idolatry, but it may be more accurate to say that God experiences deep pain and grief when human beings reject God. God is not a distant, impassible being. God grieves when God's people do not listen, when they dismiss God as irrelevant, when they look to other sources for security or happiness. God is as vulnerable as a teenager in love with someone who never notices. God suffers the pain of rejection. It would be understandable if God finally grew tired of being rejected and said, "I wash my hands of you miserable people! I've had enough." But instead God faithfully, persistently, graciously pulls people back. God can redeem even the most broken relationship.

Does this mean that human beings ought to act the way God does? If God can love the unfaithful Israel, should a husband or wife be able to love an unfaithful spouse? Some interpreters insist that a marriage can always be saved, no matter how damaged it is. An abusive or addicted or absent spouse must be loved the way God loved Israel. No matter how painful the relationship, it must be endured because God also suffered out of love for God's people. These interpretations can be painful and damaging to those who are struggling with a difficult marriage.

The power in the metaphor of Hosea and Gomer is that God's love is so amazing precisely because it transcends the human ability to love. A marriage broken by abuse or addiction is not the same as the relationship between God and Israel. It is certainly possible that some broken marriages may be repaired by an enormous infusion of grace, patience, love, and hard work, but some marriages are damaged beyond repair. A spouse who is being abused should not be told that he must persistently love and forgive as God does. God's love is an ideal to which humans aspire, but there is a profound difference between God's capacity for love and ours.

Saying yes to God. It is not easy to be the recipient of such powerful divine love. Some people think they do not need that love because they are talented, capable, and self-sufficient. Others decide that they are so broken, so hopelessly damaged, so shameful, that God cannot love them. They have given up on themselves and concluded that God has done the same. It is not easy to receive God's love when we think too highly of ourselves or when we think too little of ourselves. And to all of us, God says, stop thinking about yourself! It's not about you! It's about God's incredible, persistent love.

Can we trust in a God like this?

Questions for Reflection and Discussion

The author states that idolatry is often the result of fear. Has fear ever led you to place your trust in something that is less than God?

Have you ever felt unworthy of God's forgiveness? What helped you get beyond that feeling?

6

Other Women in the Old Testament

VASHTI
(Esther 1)

Vashti was a queen whose bad behavior made it possible for Esther, the good Jewish girl, to take Vashti's place.

This story is set in the fourth century BCE in Persia, where a number of Israelites lived in exile. The author of the story had little respect for the Persians and portrayed the king and his men as buffoons who drink too much, party too hard, and overreact. They were arrogant but not too bright, in contrast to the Jewish people who were portrayed as intelligent, subtle, and wise.

The first chapter of Esther is reminiscent of an episode of *Lifestyles of the Rich and Famous*. Ahasuerus, the king of Persia, presided over a party that lasted for 180 days and included all the government officials and the soldiers from the kingdom. When that party ended, Ahasuerus invited all the people who lived in the town of Susa to a party where he displayed his wealth. Alcohol was served in large flagons, and the guests could drink as much as they wanted.

The king thought this stag party needed a beautiful woman. His wife, Queen Vashti, and the women of the city had been celebrating separately at their own banquet. The king decided (probably under the influence of too much alcohol) that he wanted to show off his beautiful wife before all of his guests. He sent seven of his servants to bring

Vashti to this royal equivalent of a fraternity party, and he prepared to receive a little more praise and acclaim. Not only was he wealthy and powerful and generous, the people would say, but look what a smoking-hot babe he married!

Vashti the queen had a mind of her own, and she said no. The text gives no reason. Some commentators assume she was stubborn and disobedient, but perhaps she chose not to display herself before a bunch of drunken men. Perhaps she preferred the company of the women at her party. Or as some rabbis have suggested, perhaps when the king said she should appear wearing the royal crown, he meant *only* the royal crown. She was not about to appear naked for this crowd! Whatever the reason, Vashti said no. The powerful, wealthy king who ruled from India to Ethiopia could not control his own wife.

The king had a royal temper tantrum. He asked his seven advisers what should be done about Vashti. They replied that Vashti's disobedience did not harm just the king but the whole country. Once the Persian women heard what Vashti had done, they would all refuse to obey their husbands, and there would be no end of contempt and wrath! The advisers recommended that Vashti be banished from the king's presence, and that the king order all women to obey their husbands and declare that every man should be master in his own house.[1]

These are anxious men, and their analysis of the situation seems a bit hysterical. Did they really believe they could declare that every man was master in his own house? Or command all women to honor their husbands? This knee-jerk reaction to Vashti's declaration of independence made them look foolish and hypersensitive. They were wealthy and powerful, but they were not very wise.

Vashti must have known how volatile the king was, but she stood up to him. She refused to be an object. She refused to play the part of his trophy wife. She seems more courageous than Esther, who at first glance seems hyperconscious of pleasing the king. Vashti was a strong woman who knew her own mind and preserved her self-respect.

Diving Deeper

We might be tempted to skip Vashti's story and proceed to Esther's, but Vashti is an example of courage and integrity for both men and women.

Vashti said no. In a culture obsessed with women's appearance, young women often learn that their role in life is to please men with their beauty and their bodies. They should not be too smart, which might intimidate the boys or men. They should not be too bossy, which might threaten male authority. They should not be too independent or outspoken or confident. The most important thing women can do is attract male attention and shore up male egos.[2] Vashti refused to do this. She refused to obey a command that would humiliate her. Vashti said no.

Could she have chosen another strategy that did not result in banishment? Given the fact that seven men were waiting to escort her to the party, she did not have many options. Sometimes when people are asked to do something that is emotionally or physically dangerous, the best possible answer is simply no. They need to value themselves enough to preserve their safety and integrity.

How can the church help empower people, especially women and girls, to say no when it is appropriate? Women have often been told in both religious and secular contexts that standing up for themselves is selfish. Saying no is impolite and might make a scene, so it is better to be compliant. The church could provide an alternative message by recognizing that saying no is about setting limits and boundaries. It is being clear about one's identity. It is refusing to be taken advantage of. Saying no often means that a person values herself and will not tolerate being treated badly.

Young adults have often been told to "just say no" to drugs and alcohol and premarital sex. That has been ridiculed as a simplistic and naive approach to moral decisions and it certainly can be, if the "no" is based merely on external authority. How might the church help teens and young adults to make choices that will preserve their health, safety, and integrity? To think about alcohol before they go to the party? To think about drug use before they are offered the joint? To think about sexuality before they begin dating? How can they sort out their limits and decide when they should say no? How can they learn to say no before they are under enormous pressure to say yes?

Adults also encounter situations that compromise their values. Will they manipulate the numbers to make the research look more convincing? Will they use misleading data in an advertising campaign? Will they do something illegal for a good cause? How do they say no when their jobs might be threatened? How might the church help people develop the spiritual and emotional resources they need to say no in these situations?

Overreacting. The story of Vashti, the king, and his advisers provides an example of the human tendency to overreact in the face of conflict or danger. When Vashti said no, the king was shamed. Instead of simply letting the furor die down, his advisers sent a decree commanding women to obey their husbands. This publicized her action to the entire nation, which was exactly what they wanted to avoid. Their fear and anxiety led them to act rashly without thinking through the consequences. The attempt to legislate respect was ridiculous and impossible.

Decision-making bodies sometimes act in similar ways. When government officials, church members, or corporate executives feel threatened or embarrassed, they may be tempted to make a quick but strong response that often turns out to be wrong. When people are driven to act out of fear, anxiety, and a desperate need for clarity and certainty, the results are often disastrous.[3]

Parents are sometimes tempted to make similar hasty but unwise decisions. A teenager fails a course or comes home drunk, and parents might be tempted to ground him in perpetuity. A young woman is unexpectedly pregnant, and her parents belittle her in part because of their own shame, anger, and uncertainty.[4] Parents are most gracious at these moments when they can bracket their own powerful feelings, take a deep breath, and consider the best response to their child.

Commentators have frequently labeled Vashti as a disobedient wife who deserved her punishment, but that is not the only story that can be told. Vashti is a fierce and feisty woman who refused to accept dehumanizing treatment. She is a role model of strength, resistance, and courage.

Questions for Reflection and Discussion

Have you ever heard a sermon or study in which Vashti is held up as a role model? If not, why do you think that is?

This chapter suggests that the church should help young women and girls learn to say no to dangerous or harmful situations. How would you use the story of Vashti to accomplish that goal?

ESTHER
(Esther 2–9)

At first glance, Esther does not seem to be as interesting or admirable as her predecessor. Vashti[5] stood up to the king and refused to compromise her integrity, while risk-averse Esther became queen because she was beautiful and pleased the king.[6] Considering that she was caught between the machinations of three unstable and impulsive men, it is amazing that she took the risks she did.[7]

Sometime after banishing Vashti, King Ahasuerus had second thoughts. He "remembered" Vashti and "what she had done and what had been decreed against her" (Esth. 2:1).[8] Perhaps he regretted his impetuous decision. His servants decided that he needed a woman in the palace and proposed a beauty contest to find a new queen. Virgins from throughout the country were taken to the palace, where they received a year of beauty treatments and one trial night with the king. They did not have a choice about participating, and those who were not chosen by the king probably spent the rest of their lives in a harem, with no possibility for marriage or family.

The narrative abruptly introduces Mordecai, a Jew who had adopted as a daughter a young orphaned Jewish woman named Esther. She was beautiful and therefore taken into the beauty contest, although Mordecai advised Esther not to reveal her Jewish heritage. After twelve months of beauty treatments, Esther had her night with the king. The text does not say if she felt anxious or eager, valued or violated, but she successfully charmed the king, and he chose her to be the new queen.

An odd incident followed Esther's success. Mordecai overheard two men planning to assassinate the king. He told Esther, she told the king, and Mordecai's loyalty was noted in the king's record books (2:21–23).

The text then introduces Haman, the king's chief of staff. The court employees had been ordered to bow down to Haman, but Mordecai refused to do so. He might have had religious reasons, or he might have been jealous or stubborn. Haman, like the king, had a short fuse and a big ego and was easily offended by slights to his authority. He was furious with Mordecai and decided to punish him. He told the king that the Jews were different and disloyal and proposed that "a decree be issued for their destruction" (3:9).[9]

The king was not much of a critical thinker and did not question Haman's proposal. He allowed Haman to order the destruction of the Jews on a day about a year later. The Jews were devastated when they learned about this. They had lived in Persia for many years without conflict, and suddenly they were targeted for destruction. Meanwhile, the king and Haman "sat down to drink" (3:15), oblivious to the chaos and confusion they had caused.

When Mordecai heard about the decree, he asked Esther to use her position to help the Jews escape this death sentence. Esther said that she could not go to the king without an invitation. Mordecai responded with what are probably the most familiar verses in this book. "Do not think that in the king's palace you will escape any more than all the other Jews. . . . Who knows? Perhaps you have come to royal dignity for just such a time as this" (4:13–14).

Esther had reason to be cautious, because Ahasuerus was a volatile man. Once she decided to act, however, she did not hesitate. She told Mordecai to gather the Jews and hold a fast. Esther and her maids would also fast, and then she would go to the king, Then with the combination of bravery, resignation, and recklessness that marks many courageous decisions, she added, "and if I perish, I perish" (4:16).

Esther found an indirect way to get the king's attention without losing her head. First, she dressed the part by putting on her royal robes and her royal authority. She did not slink in wearing old clothes and a self-effacing manner. The king received her even though she came uninvited. He asked what she wanted and said he would give her half of his kingdom, but she asked only that the king and Haman come to a banquet. At the dinner, he again asked what she wanted. She invited the king and Haman to another banquet on the following night.

Some commentators dismiss her strategy as merely a seductive use of her beauty and charm. She teased him with the repeated invitations in order to raise his interest in her. But Esther was not just a bimbo who used her body because she was not smart enough to use her brain. She was a woman with limited power who had to tread carefully. She used her beauty and charm because they were the only resources available.

Haman left the first dinner feeling proud to be in the inner circle with Esther and the king. Then, in another of the book's significant coincidences, Mordecai met Haman outside the palace and again refused to bow before him. The arrogant but insecure Haman felt he was being denied the respect he so richly deserved. Haman complained about Mordecai to his wife and friends, and they recommended that Haman construct an enormous gallows and arrange to have Mordecai killed on it.

Meanwhile, back at the palace, the king could not sleep, and in the absence of Excedrin PM, he asked his servant to read from the book of government records. The reader selected the account of the time when Mordecai saved the king's life. Ahasuerus decided that Mordecai deserved a reward. At that moment, Haman appeared. He was so eager to get Mordecai swinging from the gallows that he had rushed to the palace early in the morning. Before Haman could speak, the king asked what should be done for a man the king wished to honor. Haman (not lacking in ego) thought that could only be him, so he said that the favored one should wear a robe that the king had worn and ride a horse that the king had ridden. The king ordered Haman to implement the plan in honor of Mordecai! Imagine Haman's anger when he not only had to procure the robe and the horse, but also had to walk next to Mordecai in the processional.

The stress of honoring his enemy made Haman cranky, but his day was about to get much worse. At the dinner, Ahasuerus asked Esther a third time what she wanted, and this time, she burst out with a complaint: "We have been sold, I and my people, to be destroyed, to be killed, and to be annihilated." Ahasuerus asked who had done this, and Esther said, "A foe and enemy, this wicked Haman!" (7:4–6).

The king was furious and left the banquet room for the palace garden. Haman threw himself on Esther's couch to beg for a reprieve. At that moment the king came back in the room and assumed Haman was trying to rape the queen! That resulted in an immediate death sentence. One of the king's servants observed that Haman had built a gallows for Mordecai, and the king ordered that Haman be hanged on it.

This was a gruesome and ugly end for Haman, but it did not eliminate the threat to the Jews. The edict ordering genocide was still the law. Once again, Esther went to the king uninvited, and asked him to revoke the decree. The king said he could not revoke it, but he allowed Mordecai (with Esther's help, perhaps?) to develop a counteredict. The Jews were allowed to defend themselves and kill anyone who attacked them.

When the day came for the destruction of the Jews, the Persians were afraid of the Jews and did not try to kill them, but the Jews killed seventy-five thousand of their enemies. They had been threatened, but the actual violence against them appears to have been minimal. Still, they slaughtered those who hated them (9:5).

The book of Esther celebrates a time when the Jewish people triumphed over those who tried to kill them. God was not the obvious rescuer in this story as God was in the exodus. God is not even mentioned in this book. The Jews appeared to deliver themselves from evil through the intelligence and courage of Esther and Mordecai.

Esther had limited power, but she used it to save her people. She took a risk, spoke the truth to power, and confronted injustice. She could not revoke the edict of genocide herself or even confront the king about it. Instead, she used her social and emotional intelligence to read the situation. She used delay, suspense, and secrecy to get what she wanted.[10]

Her strategy was particularly effective with a king prone to impetuous behavior. When other people, and the edicts themselves, were stubborn and rigid, she was flexible. When the men around her tended toward hysteria and overreaction, she remained calm. She found her way out of tough situations with creativity and wisdom.

Diving Deeper

How did this happen? Frequently when a mass killing or genocide occurs, one of the first questions is how it could have happened. The book of Esther provides some insights that are relevant to contemporary situations as well as to her time. Haman was an arrogant, evil, anxious man. He took a personal slight (Mordecai's refusal to bow to him) and punished it with ethnic cleansing. He exaggerated the differences in Jewish laws and concluded that difference could not be tolerated. He offered a bribe to get what he wanted. The king, who could have stopped this, was easily manipulated by Haman. The king did not question Haman's proposal or consult with other advisers to determine whether the threat from the Jews was real.

In the last century, similar patterns of dehumanization occurred in Nazi Germany, African civil wars, and the development of camps for Japanese Americans in World War II. The move to genocide is usually gradual, and there are many points in the process where it might be stopped by someone courageous enough to speak out.

Although King Ahasuerus uncritically acquiesced to Haman's scheme, he would have been equally responsible for the genocide if it occurred, because he approved it without raising any questions. If ordinary people in Persia had destroyed the Jews, then they would have been guilty of genocide, even if they were simply obeying orders. People are often tempted to use the passive voice to excuse their behavior. "It was ordered." "It was decided." "It is the law." "I only did what I was told." Excuses do not absolve us of responsibility.

Indignant. An ancient philosopher was asked, "When will justice come to Athens?" He replied, "Justice will not come to Athens until those who are not injured are as indignant as those who are injured."

Esther could have said that a law was a law and there was nothing she could do. She could have insisted that she had no power with the king and refused to contact him. She could have assumed that the edict would not affect her because of her privileged position. This was not her problem. But even though she might have not been injured, she became indignant. She fought for the lives of the Jews.

Justice will only come to our world when white people are indignant about racism, when men are indignant about sexism, when heterosexuals are indignant about injustice toward LGBTQ persons, and when the middle class and wealthy are indignant about poverty. Some of us are called to be dramatically indignant like Vashti. Some of us are called to be more subtly indignant like Esther. We all are called to find creative ways to speak the truth to power, to fight against injustice, and to make a difference.

There are different ways to confront injustice. The important thing is that we work together. The Vashtis of the world should not dismiss the Esthers as people who have sold out. The Esthers should not accuse the Vashtis of being too radical. Some situations and personalities are more suited for Vashti-like confrontation. Other situations and personalities are more suited for Esther-like cooperation. Both are important.

Religious violence. The story of Esther raises relevant questions about the role of religious violence in the world. The Jews were threatened with genocide and they resisted, even though the threat of violence seemed to be averted. They did not simply defend themselves but took aggressive actions against people who were not harming them. Was this violence justified in order to prevent further violence from occurring? Or was it excessive? What might have been an alternative? This dilemma is still evident in Palestine and other places in the world. How do people appropriately protect themselves without doing violence to others?

The absence of God. God is not mentioned in the entire book of Esther! The Jews were in trouble, and God did not send plagues or intervene with a miracle like parting the Red Sea. The people did not wait around for God to deliver them, but took action themselves. Human initiative, resistance, and courage were essential in this story. Esther and the Jews were not paralyzed by grief and fear but took responsibility for their own safety. They did not wait for God to intervene but acted in the ways available to them. Human lives were at stake.

Questions for Reflection and Discussion

Indignation at injustice often turns to despair when we compare the scope of the world's injustice to the limits of our ability to resist it. What tactics do you use to stay engaged in the work of making the world better without surrendering to despair and disillusionment?

The book of Esther makes no mention of God or divine intervention but instead tells a story of humans struggling to ensure their own safety. Do you see God at work in this story? If so, how?

JOB'S WIFE
(Job 2)

Job and his wife were wealthy people who lost their ten children and most of their livestock in one calamitous day. Job was devout, successful, and involved in his children's lives. He was a blameless man who feared God, and in turn God took pride in Job's exemplary behavior and bragged about him at a meeting of the "heavenly beings." One of those beings was the *satan*, who is best understood in this context as the Accuser rather than the devil.[11]

God asked the Accuser, "Have you considered my servant Job? There is no one like him on the earth, a blameless and upright man who fears God and turns away from evil" (Job 1:8). The Accuser was unimpressed and claimed that Job feared God only because God rewarded him. If Job lost all his possessions, then he would curse God and renounce his faith.

God agreed to place Job's possessions in the power of the Accuser, and in one day Job's life changed. One messenger after another brought bad news. The oxen and donkeys were killed by enemies. The sheep died in a fire. The camels were stolen. The final crushing blow was the report that a violent windstorm had destroyed the house where Job's ten children were gathered. They had all died.

In response, Job tore his robe, shaved his head, and said, "The LORD gave, and the LORD has taken away; blessed be the name of the LORD" (1:21). Job did not sin or accuse God of wrongdoing. Job passed the test. Once again, God bragged about Job's integrity. The Accuser was skeptical: "Stretch out your hand now and touch his bone and his flesh, and he will curse you to your face" (2:5). God permitted the Accuser to test Job by inflicting on him a disease that caused painful, itchy sores all over his body. Job sat on an ash heap and scratched himself with a broken piece of pottery.

Enter Mrs. Job. The text does not introduce her or acknowledge that she was also grieving the loss of her children. She is not developed as a character but serves merely as a foil whose skepticism allows Job to express his piety. She bluntly challenged Job and told him what to do. "Do you still persist in your integrity? Curse God, and die" (2:9). Job responded harshly: "You speak as any foolish woman would speak. Shall we receive the good at the hand of God, and not receive the bad?" (v. 10).

The paucity of information in the text has not stopped commentators from imaginatively reconstructing her emotions and motives. Some critics say that she was a faithless woman who thought belief in God was foolish. Other commentators portray her as an unsupportive, insensitive wife who lacked the patience to comfort him in his misery. Augustine described her as *adiutrix diaboli*, "the assistant of Satan," because she told Job to give up.[12] Some commentators compare her to Eve because they both tempted their pious husbands to do evil.[13]

Does she deserve such criticism? Her words do sound harsh and unsympathetic, but there is not enough information in the text to accurately discern her motives and her actions. It is likely that she was a shell-shocked, grief-stricken woman. Like Job, she had lost everything. Then Job became ill and she had to watch him suffer. She wondered why the God that Job served had not kept him or his children or his animals safe. His scrupulous faith had not protected him from devastating loss.

She raised an honest and important question, and Job would wrestle with it throughout the book. "Do you still persist in your integrity?" Why would Job trust in a God who did not keep him safe? How could Job believe in a God who could not be trusted? Why not curse this God and die?

Her question is complicated by a textual ambiguity. The Hebrew says that she told Job to "*berakah* God and die." *Berakah* usually means "bless," but here it is translated as "curse." Why is the word given an opposite meaning? Did she actually suggest Job should praise God one last time and then give up his struggle?

Most translators translate *berakah* here as "curse," in part because of an old linguistic practice. The Hebrew writers honored the name of God so completely that they refused to place the word "curse" next to God's name, lest someone inadvertently read about cursing God.[14] They replaced the Hebrew word for "curse" with the word for "bless," and assumed that the context would alert the reader that the subject of the verb was actually cursing God out of anger. In Job 1:11 and 2:5, the Accuser predicted that Job would *berakah* God, and it is translated as "curse." In Job 3:1, however, Job cursed the day of his birth, and the Hebrew word for "curse" is the more traditional *qallel.*

If Mrs. Job actually advised Job to curse God and die, what might she have meant by that? Some commentators suggest that Mrs. Job was trying to convince Job to rebel against a God who seemed unfair and certainly did not have Job's back. Perhaps Mrs. Job hoped he would not surrender to this God who acted like a bully. Perhaps she hoped that he would fight back and stand up for himself rather than passively say, "The LORD gave, and the LORD has taken away" (1:21).

Her question about his integrity hints at a tension in the religious logic of the time. A significant part of Jewish tradition (Deuteronomy, Samuel, Kings, Proverbs) insisted that God blessed the obedient people and punished the sinful. In the book of Job, this view was represented by Job's friends, who ostensibly came to comfort him, then tried to convince him that he must have done something wrong.

Job's wife saw the flaw in this logic.[15] She knew that Job was a man of integrity and yet bad things had happened to him. If Job was indeed innocent, and if his suffering came from God, then God was neither good nor reliable. Why believe in such a God? Why not simply curse God and give up on life? Job had built his whole life around his faith in a God who was good and just, and now it appeared that he had been wrong. Perhaps she had the courage to articulate the doubt he could not express. God had not kept up God's end of the bargain.

Diving Deeper

Faith and doubt. A focus on Job's wife offers a different lens for the story of Job. She has often been vilified in order to make Job look more pious, but was she really a shrewish woman who despised her husband and his faith? Or was she, like Job, grappling with difficult questions about the nature of faith, suffering, and the role of God? The question she posed to Job forced him to ask the hard questions of God, which he did repeatedly in the remainder of the book.

The prologue in Job 1–2 portrays Job as trusting, patient, and pious, but in the rest of the book he asks angry questions and defiantly asserts his own goodness. He was not a simplistic example of piety and self-control[16] but an angry and grieving man who vented all his emotions before God. In chapters 3–37 he allowed himself to move beyond the mantra "the LORD gave, and the LORD has taken away; blessed be the name of the LORD." Job learned that he could be honest before God and that God could handle Job's anger. Job was more interesting and human when he spoke honestly about the pain of his tremendous loss.

Job's wife is more interesting and relevant to human experience when she is not quickly dismissed as a bitter, unfaithful woman, but when her question and challenge to Job are taken seriously. She is not simply an unfaithful woman, and Job is not simply a faithful man. There is far more depth and nuance to both of them.

Perhaps that puzzling use of the word *berakah* to mean both "curse" and "bless" says something powerful about human beings and their relationship to God. Perhaps in the end, blessing and cursing are not all that different. When people express their anger with God, they are interacting and engaging with God. They trust that God is present and will listen. They trust that God will not reject them. Perhaps God actually prefers anger, even cursing, to being ignored. Just as people in a committed relationship choose to work through their anger with each other rather than leave, so God invites and encourages people to work through their anger with God, confident that God will not abandon or punish them for asking honest questions.

Questions for Reflection and Discussion

A big question about Job's wife is whether her advice that Job "curse God and die" is authentic or inauthentic, an expression of her belief in God or a rejection of that belief. Which do you think it was? Why?

Job's wife has lost everything that he has lost, with the one exception of personal health. Why, then, are her faith and her questions not also important to the book of Job?

THE WOMAN OF SUBSTANCE IN PROVERBS 31
(Proverbs 31)

The portrait of the woman in Proverbs 31 offers a welcome contrast to the grim stories about Old Testament women who are abused, ignored, or valued primarily for their wombs. She is a strong woman who runs a business and a home. She is not being given or taken. She is not waiting to have a baby. She is talented, busy, active, and independent.

The book of Proverbs reads like a college commencement address, full of good advice and wise counsel. The secret to success, it says, is wisdom, which includes possessing emotional intelligence, making good choices, and avoiding dangerous people. The book concludes with a description of a talented woman and the positive impact she has on her husband, children, and community. It is not clear whether she was a real woman or a man's fantasy of an ideal wife or a mother-in-law's fantasy of the perfect wife for her perfect son. The poem sounds like an idealized portrait that might be found on a Mother's Day card.

The first line of the poem includes the Hebrew phrase *eshet hayil*, which the NRSV translates as "a capable wife" (31:10).[17] Other translations describe her as excellent, competent, virtuous, or worthy. The word suggests physical strength, wealth, property, and bravery. She was not merely capable or well-behaved but strong and valorous. She was a woman of substance. She was the kind of woman men should want to marry.

The poem is divided into twenty-two verses, each of which begins with a different Hebrew letter, in alphabetical order. Each verse highlights an aspect of her character and ability. She rises early and stays up late into the night. She manages the servants. She buys a field and plants a vineyard. She has a business selling clothes. She is a woman of many talents. She not only prepares all the food for the household, she also grows some of it herself. She not only sews all the clothes for her family but also weaves the cloth. She is wise, dignified, and appreciated by her family. Her husband trusts her, and she is an asset to him.

In the patriarchal and agricultural setting of the Old Testament, keeping the household fed and clothed was more than a full-time occupation. Megastores, convenience food, and ready-made clothes did not exist. The ideal woman in this poem made life not only easier but also possible for her husband and children. The text recognizes how much work was required to manage a family.

This text says nothing about the woman's appearance, except that she was strong and well dressed. It does not say she was beautiful. Her value comes from other qualities than appearance. If she had wrinkles, they were a sign of long life and not a problem to be solved by Botox. If she was not a size 0, it was because she needed to be strong and solid to do her work. She was a confident woman who knew what she could do, and she was appreciated for her ability, maturity, and wisdom.

This text still resonates with many contemporary women who demonstrate the same kind of energy and ability. My eighty-year-old mother maintains the yard, keeps a spotless house, serves funeral lunches at church, and fixes Sunday dinners for thirteen. My late friend Margie was a homemaker extraordinaire who built a tepee, a chicken coop, and a house for the family duck. She loved caring for other people and creating a calm, safe space. These women and many others like them have tremendous gifts that ought to be celebrated. Comparing them to the woman in Proverbs 31 is one way to honor them.

The text raises questions for some contemporary readers, however, who notice that the woman seems to do all the work while her husband sits at the city gate dispensing his wisdom. Of course he appreciates her! She works from dawn to dusk to keep her family happy. She channels her prodigious energy and ability into the service of her family. No wonder they rose up and called her blessed! This text may be more affirming to women than others in the Old Testament, but it is hardly an example of liberation.

The text becomes problematic when it is used to set an impossible standard for women and then to shame them when they cannot live up to it. In some religious traditions, the "P31 Woman" is the only model for women's lives. The text is used to create a checklist of virtues. Does a woman support her husband, plant a garden, sew the family's clothes, and earn money from a home business? If not, how can she improve?[18]

This does not feel like good news. It also does not acknowledge that not all women are called to this vocation.

This text may also be difficult to hear if it is the only time a biblical woman is the subject of a sermon. In some traditions, this text is used on Mother's Day to praise women and their work. The message it conveys is that a godly woman sacrifices herself for the good of her family, and contemporary women should go and do likewise. Again, this is not necessarily good news. This woman's virtue and strength can become a crippling expectation for real women who do not possess all her abilities. If this practically perfect woman is the only biblical woman ever mentioned in a sermon, the congregation will have a very narrow picture of what it means to be a woman of God. The reality is that the lives of biblical woman are as complicated and messy as the lives of biblical men.

This daunting expectation that a good woman will completely devote herself to home and family is not confined to religious circles. A quick skim of parenting books and mommy blogs generates a list of expectations that Anna Quindlen labeled "manic mothering."[19] Mothers should "wear" their babies so they can practice attachment parenting. They should use cloth diapers and prepare all baby food from organic fruits and vegetables. Mothers of older children should provide them with music lessons, sports travel teams, and extra tutoring to ensure they are ready for the Ivy League.

There are similar expectations for working mothers. The perfect working mother has an MBA and is vice president of a Fortune 500 company. She runs ten miles a day and lifts weights. Her house looks like Martha Stewart lives there. She has a handsome, talented husband who adores her, and three talented children with whom she spends hours of quality time. She coaches a soccer team, teaches Sunday school, and volunteers once a week at a soup kitchen.

The common theme in these scenarios is that women can never do enough. They can always do more for their children. They can always spend more time at the office. They can always do more housework. Their to-do list is never done. Earning the approval of husband, children, other mothers, and the employer always requires something more. It is exhausting. It is a recipe for failure. This is not good news.

Diving Deeper

How could Proverbs 31 offer good news and a gracious word for women rather than another impossible expectation?

In Hasidic Judaism, men sing a version of Proverbs 31 to their wives every Friday night at the Shabbat dinner. The song expresses affirmation and appreciation. The men do not mentally run through a checklist first to see which of their wife's achievements they could praise. The song does not ask, "What have you done for me lately and what more can you do?" Instead, the song is a blessing upon their wives, whom they view as a great gift to them. The song emphasizes affirmation, not expectation.[20]

Enough already. Can this poem speak a gracious word about the expectations that women experience from their culture and those they put on themselves? It is exhausting to be superwoman and to think that the well-being of one's family or workplace depends entirely on one's efforts. Perhaps the gracious word we need to hear from Proverbs 31 is "enough." Women's worth does not come from perfection or from meeting every need or from being available 24/7. Men and women receive enough pressure to excel from the culture; they do not need to hear that message reinforced by the Bible. They already have enough guilt for not being perfect parents or employees. This passage offers a significant word of grace because it de-emphasizes women's sex appeal, beauty, and thinness.

In the past, the church has often contributed to the weight of expectations that women experience. The church has asked women to be devoted Christians, excellent mothers, and a significant source of unpaid labor in the work of the church. How can we as Christians instead help to free women from the burden of unrealistic expectations? We should affirm women for their strength, intelligence, and a wide range of abilities. We should emphasize that there is diversity and variety in women's roles and that not all women must make the same choices. We can encourage women to affirm each other rather than judge and compete.

We are not called to be superwomen and supermen who can do it all and do it better than everyone else. Instead, we are called to be strong and powerful people with balanced lives. We don't need to prove ourselves. We don't need to be defined by our culture's expectations. We don't need to be beautiful, perfect, the best. We don't always need to do more.

We have been given spiritual gifts, but they are not onerous tasks. They do not give us one more thing to do. Instead, our gifts are a way of celebrating who we are, what we love to do, what we are passionate about, and how God has graced us.

God is the only superwoman. Perhaps the best way to keep this woman's gifts from becoming a to-do list is to see her not as a role model but as an image of God who is the ultimate provider. In Matthew 6, Jesus tells people not to be anxious about food or clothes, because God will provide all that they need. If God decks out the lilies of the field, God will take care of you. No need to worry, because God is in charge.

In Proverbs 31, this extraordinary woman is providing the food and the clothes for her household. Her husband and children do not need to be anxious, because she will provide what they need. No need to worry, because she is in charge. Like God, the woman nurtures and sustains her family, servants, and community. She is a compassionate, caring, powerful presence.

Seeing the woman in Proverbs 31 as an image of God offers a very different way to hear this story. Not as a to-do list. Not as a set of expectations to be lived up to, but as a sign of grace, compassion, and care. The woman is practically perfect in every way, not so much because she is an ordinary woman like us who has done everything right, but because she is a picture of what God is like. She is an example, not of how we can do more if we try, but of the way God creates a household where grace abounds.

Questions for Reflection and Discussion

One way to interpret the woman from Proverbs 31 is as an extended metaphor for God. We're accustomed to comparing God to fathers, but not mothers. If God is like the woman portrayed here, what does that tell us about who God is?

Do you feel intimidated by this woman's levels of energy and accomplishment? Does her story make you feel better or worse about your own story? What would it take for this passage to speak a word of grace to you?

Group Discussion Guide

MARK PRICE

INTRODUCTION

The author of *From Widows to Warriors*, Lynn Japinga, points out in her introduction that the stories of women in the Bible are often misread, misunderstood, or simply missed—for various reasons. Her hope is to present these stories of biblical women for a fresh and perhaps first-time hearing. They are fascinating in their own right, and while these "stories may be strange and difficult . . . they are also surprisingly relevant to contemporary issues of warfare, poverty, and justice."

To begin your study of these stories and Japinga's commentary on them, call attention to what she describes as the "lenses" through which she views the biblical text:

1. Biblical characters "are rarely entirely good or entirely sinful."
2. Sin and grace are "not always where we expect to find them."
3. "Signs of strength and courage . . . are not always immediately obvious."

Encourage the group to make use of those lenses in their own reading. Also during the group's study, spend less time on locating a moral or lesson in the stories and more on finding where and how God is active in the stories. During discussions, make use of some of Japinga's suggested exploratory questions: *How is God being gracious? How is God bringing about shalom? How does God redeem human brokenness? How does God work through human beings to bring about God's purposes?*

One additional way Japinga suggests of approaching these stories is to imagine an alternative ending to them. Consider including in each session a time of imaginative discussion, using these questions: *How might things have been different? Who could have intervened to change the course of action? Where might grace have been found?*

Finally, a general word about these stories. Many of the biblical stories that include women are about sex, violence, or sex *and* violence.

167

They can be off-putting, especially when the text offers no explanation. Japinga provides a helpful perspective worth keeping in mind during your study: *"I believe that all the stories of the Bible, even the ugliest, should be taken seriously. They deserve our attention, our conversation, and our criticism. We can challenge and critique the stories without fear, because we care about the texts and respect them, even if we cannot agree with or affirm them. Wrestling with the texts shows that we trust them and God enough to talk back."*

This discussion guide uses the following format for the six sessions:

Gathering   5 minutes

Welcome and prayer. Begin on time by welcoming the group to the study. To open the first session together, be prepared to summarize as briefly as possible what participants can expect from the study and what is expected of them. Then establish a particular ritual of praying together at the start of the study. Keep in mind that the text of this study, the Bible, is a rich source of meaningful prayers, including prayers by some of the women characters (Hannah, for example) the group will discuss. A suggestion of a Scripture prayer will appear in this section each week.

Engaging the Text (Bible)   10 minutes

This study guide corresponds to the six chapters of the book, each one highlighting women grouped canonically by book (Genesis) or section (Prophets). One or more of the biblical passages covered in each chapter will be listed here. Hear the passage(s) read aloud and then invite group discussion. (Consider reading these passages from an edition of the Tanakh, a Jewish translation of the Hebrew Bible. *The Jewish Study Bible* [Oxford: Oxford University Press, 2005] is a good one.)

Engaging the Commentary (Book)   20 minutes

The author retells and comments on the story of each woman. A series of the author's suggested questions are provided here to guide the group's responses.

Diving Deeper   15 minutes

As part of her commentary about each woman, the author offers several concluding insights. Make use of those insights in these sections and the reflection questions that follow to prompt the group to share and explore its own insights into each woman's story.

Looking Further   5 minutes

Women's Bible Commentary, 3rd edition, edited by Carol A. Newsom, Sharon H. Ringe, and Jacqueline Lapsley (Louisville, KY: Westminster John Knox Press, 2012), is a volume of biblical interpretation written by female scholars whose comments address passages from every book of the Bible that have particular relevance to women. As a way to wrap up discussion, invite the group to hear and briefly respond to an excerpt from that volume printed here.

Closing

Turn to the next chapter and preview the focus of the readings for the week ahead.

SESSION 1

The Matriarchs

Gathering   **5 minutes**

Greet each other. Begin by praying the opening words from Psalm 90:

> Lord, you have been our dwelling place
>   in all generations.
> Before the mountains were brought forth,
>   or ever you had formed the earth and the world,
>   from everlasting to everlasting you are God.

Engaging the Text (Bible)   **10 minutes**

Choose one or more of the following passages to read aloud.

    —Eve (Gen. 3:1–20)
    —Sarah and Hagar (Gen. 16)
    —Tamar (Gen. 38)

Invite discussion using some of these questions: *Where in these passages do you see God being gracious? How does God redeem human brokenness? How does God work through the human beings in these passages to bring about God's purposes?*

Engaging the Commentary (Book)   **20 minutes**

Ask the group to consider the author's comments on the matriarchs from Genesis in light of these two questions: (1) What common assumptions or misconceptions about these women and their stories does the author critique? (2) What new ways of understanding these stories do her comments suggest? Discuss as many of the author's comments as time allows.

Diving Deeper   15 minutes

Call attention to the "Diving Deeper" sections throughout this chapter and invite discussion of the author's insights about each woman, using the reflection questions that appear at the conclusion of each section. Work through as many of the questions as time allows.

Looking Further   5 minutes

"All too often readers come to Genesis weighed down by Augustine's or Milton's interpretation of the story. What if one notices that the snake does not lie to the woman but speaks the truth? . . . The woman believes the snake and, in an important pun . . . , the narrator says that she sees the tree is good to look at / good for making one wise (3:6). She is no easy prey for a seducing demon, as later tradition represents her, but a conscious actor choosing knowledge" (Susan Niditch, *Women's Bible Commentary*, 31).

Closing

Turn to the next chapter and preview the next session's readings.

SESSION 2
Women of the Exodus

Gathering   **5 minutes**

Greet each other. Begin by praying with the dancing Miriam in Exodus
15:21:

> Sing to the LORD, for he has triumphed gloriously;
>   horse and rider he has thrown into the sea.

Engaging the Text (Bible)   **10 minutes**

Choose one or more of the following passages to read aloud.

— The Women Who Kept Moses Alive (Exod. 1:15–22)
— Miriam (Exod. 2:1–10; 15:19–21; Num. 12)
— Zipporah (Exod. 2:21–22; 4:20–31; 18:2–6)

Invite discussion using some of these questions: *Where in these passages
do you see God being gracious? How does God redeem human brokenness?
How does God work through the human beings in these passages to bring
about God's purposes?*

Engaging the Commentary (Book)   **20 minutes**

Ask the group to consider the author's comments on the women of
the exodus in light of these two questions: (1) What common assumptions or misconceptions about these women and their stories does the
author critique? (2) What new ways of understanding these stories do
her comments suggest? Discuss as many of the author's comments as
time allows.

Diving Deeper   **15 minutes**

Call attention to the "Diving Deeper" sections throughout this chapter
and invite discussion of the author's insights about each woman, using

the reflection questions that appear at the conclusion of each section. Work through as many of the questions as time allows.

Looking Further   5 minutes

"The lineage of Miriam is a lineage of generations of women who have been rejected or humiliated for doing exactly the same thing as their male counterparts. But the larger biblical tradition presents us with another face of God, beyond the face of the One who puts Miriam outside the camp. . . . The starkness of Numbers 12 must not be undercut, but Miriam outside the camp may point us not only to the painful arbitrariness of her situation, but also, however indirectly and allusively, . . . to the suffering of God" (Katharine Doob Sakenfeld, *Women's Bible Commentary*, 84).

Closing

Turn to the next chapter and preview the next session's readings.

Women of the Promised Land

Gathering   **5 minutes**

Greet each other. Begin by praying this portion of Deborah's song from Judges 5:3:

> Hear, O kings; give ear, O princes;
>> to the LORD I will sing,
>> I will make melody to the LORD.

Engaging the Text (Bible)   **10 minutes**

Choose one or more of the following passages to read aloud.

—Rahab (Josh. 2:1–21)
—Jephthah's Daughter (Judg. 11:29–40)
—The Levite's Concubine (Judg. 19)
—Hannah (1 Sam. 1:1–2:10)

Invite discussion using some of these questions: *Where in these passages do you see God being gracious? How does God redeem human brokenness? How does God work through the human beings in these passages to bring about God's purposes?*

Engaging the Commentary (Book)   **20 minutes**

Ask the group to consider the author's comments on the women of the promised land in light of these two questions: (1) What common assumptions or misconceptions about these women and their stories does the author critique? (2) What new ways of understanding these stories do her comments suggest? Discuss as many of the author's comments as time allows.

Diving Deeper   15 minutes

Call attention to the "Diving Deeper" sections throughout this chapter
and invite discussion of the author's insights about each woman, using
the reflection questions that appear at the conclusion of each section.
Work through as many of these comment sections as time allows.

Looking Further   5 minutes

"Similar to Gothic literature, which plays with the possible destruction of male dominance, only to reassert its social validity, the biblical
tale [of the Levite's concubine] criticizes, exposes, and challenges the
patriarchal system that simultaneously keeps assertive women, such as
the concubine escaping her husband, in their places" (Susanne Scholz,
Women's Bible Commentary, 124).

Closing

Turn to the next chapter and preview the next session's readings.

SESSION 4

Women of Israel and Judah

Gathering   **5 minutes**

Greet each other. Begin by praying these words from Hannah in 1 Samuel 2:1:

> My heart exults in the LORD;
> my strength is exalted in my God.

Engaging the Text (Bible)   **10 minutes**

Choose one or more of the following passages to read aloud.

—Abigail (1 Sam. 25)
—Tamar (2 Sam. 13:1–33)
—Bathsheba (2 Sam. 11; 1 Kgs. 1:15–31)
—Rizpah (2 Sam. 3:6–11; 21:1–14)

Invite discussion using some of these questions: *Where in these passages do you see God being gracious? How does God redeem human brokenness? How does God work through the human beings in these passages to bring about God's purposes?*

Engaging the Commentary (Book)   **20 minutes**

Ask the group to consider the author's comments on the women of Israel and Judah in light of these two questions: (1) What common assumptions or misconceptions about these women and their stories does the author critique? (2) What new ways of understanding these stories do her comments suggest? Discuss as many of the author's comments as time allows.

Diving Deeper 15 minutes

Call attention to the "Diving Deeper" sections throughout this chapter and invite discussion of the author's insights about each woman, using the reflection questions that appear at the conclusion of each section. Work through as many of the questions as time allows.

Looking Further 5 minutes

"Women play a larger role in the books of Samuel than in most of the rest of the Bible, and they appear in these narratives in the domestic sphere (Hannah, for instance), in the public sphere (the medium of Endor and the two wise women), and in the gray area that is the domestic sphere of a ruling family, where private decisions have public consequences. It has, in fact, been suggested that one of the major themes in the stories of David and his family is precisely the unavoidable link between public and private life within a ruling family" (Jo Ann Hackett, *Women's Bible Commentary*, 162).

Closing

Turn to the next chapter and preview the next session's readings.

SESSION 5

Women and the Prophets

Gathering   **5 minutes**

Greet each other. Begin by praying this from Psalm 43:3–4:

> O send out your light and your truth;
>   let them lead me;
> let them bring me to your holy hill
>   and to your dwelling.
> Then I will go to the altar of God,
>   to God my exceeding joy.

Engaging the Text (Bible)   **10 minutes**

Choose some of the following passages to read aloud.

—The Widow of Zarephath (1 Kgs. 17:8–24)
—The Widow with the Oil (2 Kgs. 4:1–7)
—The Shunammite Woman (2 Kgs. 4:8–37; 8:1–6)

Invite discussion using some of these questions: *Where in these passages do you see God being gracious? How does God redeem human brokenness? How does God work through the human beings in these passages to bring about God's purposes?*

Engaging the Commentary (Book)   **20 minutes**

Ask the group to consider the author's comments on the women and the prophets in light of these two questions: (1) What common assumptions or misconceptions about these women and their stories does the author critique? (2) What new ways of understanding these stories do her comments suggest? Discuss as many of the author's comments as time allows.

Diving Deeper   15 minutes

Call attention to the "Diving Deeper" sections throughout this chapter and invite discussion of the author's insights about each woman, using the reflection questions that appear at the conclusion of each section. Work through as many of the questions as time allows.

Looking Further   5 minutes

"Readers can glimpse a wide variety of social roles among the books' female characters, from servants to women prophets to queens. Kings presents, then, no uniform portrait of women in the monarchic era of Israelite history; the portraits of female characters in Kings are shaped by class, ethnic or national status, and the exigencies of the narrative. At the same time, nearly all of the women in Kings are mothers who are described in some relationship to that part of their identities" (Cameron B. R. Howard, *Women's Bible Commentary*, 166).

Closing

Turn to the next chapter and preview the next session's readings.

Other Women in the Old Testament

Gathering   **5 minutes**

Greet each other. Begin by praying these words of Queen Esther from the Greek version of Esther in the Apocrypha:

> O my Lord, you only are our king;
>   help me, who am alone and have no helper but you.

Engaging the Text (Bible)   **10 minutes**

Choose some of the following passages to read aloud.

—Esther (Esth. 2:12–18; 3:7–4:17; 7)
—Job's Wife (Job 2:9–10; 19:17; 31:9–10)
—The Woman of Substance (Prov. 31:10–31)

Invite discussion using some of these questions: *Where in these passages do you see God being gracious? How does God redeem human brokenness? How does God work through the human beings in these passages to bring about God's purposes?*

Engaging the Commentary (Book)   **20 minutes**

Ask the group to consider the author's comments on the other women of the Old Testament in light of these two questions: (1) What common assumptions or misconceptions about these women and their stories does the author critique? (2) What new ways of understanding these stories do her comments suggest? Discuss as many of the author's comments as time allows.

Diving Deeper   **15 minutes**

Call attention to the "Diving Deeper" sections throughout this chapter and invite discussion of the author's insights about each woman, using the reflection questions that appear at the conclusion of each section. Work through as many of the questions as time allows.

Looking Further   5 minutes

"In the world portrayed by the book of Esther, Esther has no choice but to obey the king's command. Disobedience would mean death for her and her guardian Mordecai. Once made queen, Esther skillfully manipulates the power structure of the Persian court in order to attain her goal, the salvation of her people. This goal takes precedence over any personal considerations, including her fear for her own life. In fact, Esther, precisely because she was a woman and therefore basically powerless within Persian society, was the paradigm of the Diaspora Jew, who was also powerless in Persian society" (Sidnie White Crawford, *Women's Bible Commentary*, 204).

Closing

Reflect together on the biblical women from whom you've learned the most in this study.

Notes

Introduction

1. My thanks to Mackenzie Andreolli for describing this in her journal.

2. My thanks to Katelyn Hacker for this observation.

3. Elizabeth Cady Stanton, *The Woman's Bible*, vol. 2 (1895–98; repr., Seattle, WA: Coalition Task Force on Women and Religion, 1974), 19–20.

4. The preachers included Fred Craddock, Peter Gomes, and Fleming Rutledge.

5. See John Calvin, Commentary on Genesis 16:4 and 16:8, and Phyllis Trible, *Texts of Terror* (Philadelphia: Fortress Press, 1984), 9–35. The easiest way to access Calvin's commentaries is at the Christian Classics Ethereal Library, https://www.ccel.org, or at Bible Hub, https://Biblehub.com. Because there are so many different versions of Calvin's commentaries, I will simply cite the verse on which he was writing.

6. Brené Brown explains how human beings make up stories to explain the mysteries and uncertainties in their lives. See *Rising Strong* (New York: Spiegel & Grau, 2015).

7. The sources I found most helpful include *The New Interpreter's Bible* (Nashville: Abingdon Press, 1994), and commentary series such as Interpretation (Louisville, KY: Westminster John Knox Press, 1982–2005); Anchor Bible (New Haven, CT: Yale University Press, 1964–2009); Westminster Bible Companion (Louisville, KY: Westminster John Knox Press, 1995–2012); and the Abingdon Old Testament Commentaries (Nashville: Abingdon Press, 2001–12). There are a number of excellent online sources, such as John Calvin's Commentaries at the Christian Classics Ethereal Library website, https://www.ccel.org. The Text This Week (www.textweek.com) is a very helpful website organized according to the lectionary. It includes links to sermons, commentaries, art, liturgies, and educational material. Biblehub .com provides easy access to a variety of older commentaries. A Google search of a biblical woman's name leads to a number of sermons or Bible studies, although many of these fall into the category of bad examples. Books on the history of interpretation were particularly helpful; examples include David Gunn, *Judges* (Malden, MA: Blackwell, 2005); John Thompson, *Writing the Wrongs* (New York: Oxford, 2001); and the Ancient Christian Commentary on Scripture series (Downers Grove, IL: InterVarsity Press). See also the

excellent feminist commentaries by Phyllis Trible, *God and the Rhetoric of Sexuality* (Philadelphia: Fortress Press, 1978), and *Texts of Terror*; Danna Nolan Fewell and David Gunn, *Gender, Power, and Promise* (Nashville: Abingdon Press, 1993); Alice Bellis, *Helpmates, Harlots, and Heroes: Women's Stories in the Hebrew Bible*, 2nd ed. (Louisville, KY: Westminster John Knox Press, 2007); and many others cited in the notes. Bellis is particularly helpful because she includes an extensive bibliography and a thorough discussion of various feminist approaches to the texts.

8. My thanks to Mary Bridget McCarthy and the Hope College Theater Department.

Chapter 1: The Matriarchs

1. Gen. 1:1–2:4a describes six days of creation in which humans are created last. Gen. 2:4b–3:24 is a distinctive account with a different order. Some readers assume it is an elaboration of the first story, but the details are quite different. The fact that these two stories coexist can help readers see that they are not eyewitness accounts meant to be read literally.

2. The opening scene of the television show *Desperate Housewives* included images of a man and woman in fig leaves, an apple, a tree, and a serpent, all cues that suggest the presence of seductive or dangerous women.

3. Trible's article can be accessed at http://academic.udayton.edu/michaelbarnes /E-Rel103/RG4-Trible.htm. It was originally published as "Eve and Adam: Genesis 2–3 Reread," *Andover Newton Quarterly* 13, no. 4 (March 1973): 251–58.

4. Unfortunately, this idea of woman as an equal help has been transformed into the demeaning phrase "helpmate." The King James Version translates the Hebrew phrase *ezer kenegdo* (Gen. 2:18, 20) as a help "meet" (appropriate) for the man, but over time the words became blurred together into first "helpmeet," and later "helpmate." This phrase suggests that he is strong, and she is fragile and in need of guidance. One of the most extreme examples of this interpretation can be found in the Christian Domestic Discipline program, in which men are encouraged to exercise their leadership and authority by regularly spanking their wives to correct their sinful attitudes and behaviors. See Linda Schearing and Valarie Ziegler, *Enticed by Eden: How Western Culture Uses, Confuses, (and Sometimes Abuses) Adam and Eve* (Waco, TX: Baylor University Press, 2013), 65–89.

5. Phyllis Trible, *God and the Rhetoric of Sexuality* (Philadelphia: Fortress Press, 1978), 113. Her chapter on Adam and Eve in this book is an expansion of the earlier article.

6. There are hundreds of images of Eve in paintings and contemporary advertising. Artists often make visible the common assumptions about Eve and other biblical characters. For examples of artists' interpretations of many Old Testament women, see http:/japinga.wixsite.com/mysite.

7. For a powerful example of a character who feels life closing in on him, see Jojo Moyes, *Me before You* (New York: Penguin Books, 2013).

8. See a futuristic portrayal of this practice in Margaret Atwood's novel *The Handmaid's Tale* (New York: Anchor Books, 1998). In the book, handmaids are used to provide children for women who are infertile because of age or environmental pollution.

9. This text demonstrates that people who are oppressed will sometimes oppress others rather than stand in solidarity with them. See the odd story in Gen. 12 in which Abraham and Sarah went to Egypt, and Abraham lied that Sarah was his sister, because he feared he would be killed by someone who wanted to marry his wife. Pharaoh himself took Sarah as a wife, but sent her back to Abraham when he learned they were married. Sarah knew what it meant to be given and taken when she was powerless to resist, and yet she was willing to take and give Hagar without her consent.

10. Phyllis Trible, *Texts of Terror* (Philadelphia: Fortress Press, 1984), 12.

11. Some commentators suggest that Sarah might have caught the two of them together after Hagar had conceived, having sex out of desire rather than for conception.

12. The same Hebrew word is used to describe the Egyptians' treatment of the Hebrew slaves in Exod. 1.

13. It is unfortunate that the lectionary passage ends with v. 16, when Abraham's laughter is recorded in v. 17. Is his laughter omitted as a way to preserve his reputation as a man of deep and unquestioned faith? His reaction is so wonderfully human and humorous! It would be more helpful to preach an honest sermon on the complexities of faith than to imply that Abraham and Sarah simply accepted this bizarre news without batting an eye.

14. Abraham was not chastised for laughing, which leads some commentators to treat the laughter of Abraham and Sarah quite differently. John Calvin claimed that Abraham believed God's promise, but he was astonished, so he laughed in joy and amazement. Sarah did not trust in God's power to transcend her biological limitations. She did not laugh out of joy and wonder but out of doubt (Commentary on Genesis 17:17 and 18:12).

15. In 1 Pet. 3:6, Sarah is cited as an example of an obedient wife. "Thus Sarah obeyed Abraham and called him lord. You have become her daughters as long as you do what is good and never let fears alarm you." Twice, though, Sarah has told Abraham what to do! Perhaps women possessed more power in their marriages than is usually recognized.

16. There is an odd contradiction in this story. Ishmael was thirteen when he was circumcised approximately four years prior to this event (17:25), so he should be about seventeen. But 21:14 says that Abraham put the bread and water on Hagar's shoulder, "along with the child." It seems unlikely that an almost adult male would have ridden piggyback on his mother's shoulders. Later, when the water was gone, the text says Hagar "cast the child" under the bushes, as if she had been carrying him.

17. This good news may not feel comforting to those who have prayed, trusted, used reproductive technologies, and still have no baby. Many couples

experience the pain of infertility and miscarriage and most do not have a miraculous birth like Sarah's.

18. Hagar and Ishmael are thought to be the ancestors of Muslims, so some preachers have blamed Sarah for indirectly giving rise to this competing religious tradition.

19. See an example of a positive relationship between the first and second wives in Khaled Hosseini, *A Thousand Splendid Suns* (New York: Riverhead Books, 2007). The first wife was understandably jealous when her husband brought home a teenage girl as a second wife, but the two of them eventually became friends and allies.

20. Phyllis Trible describes Hagar's experience as a rape, because she could not consent freely. She and other feminist commentators compare Hagar to an African American slave woman in the nineteenth century who was raped by the white master and beaten when she tried to flee. *Texts of Terror*, 9–35.

21. See the movie *Twelve Years a Slave* (2013) for an example of the jealousy a white woman felt toward the slave woman her husband had taken as a mistress. See *The Help* (the book published by G. P. Putnam & Sons in 2009 or the 2011 movie) for examples of the complicated relationships between white women and the African American women who worked as their maids or nannies.

22. See the discussion of Hagar and Sarah in Delores Williams, *Sisters in the Wilderness: The Challenge of Womanist God-Talk* (Maryknoll, NY: Orbis Books, 1993), 15–33.

23. For a fascinating exploration of the interactions between Muslims, Christians, and Jews, see Geraldine Brooks, *People of the Book* (New York: Penguin Group USA, 2008).

24. The text does not initially state the nature of the evil in Sodom and Gomorrah. Much later, the prophets described the inhabitants as proud and wealthy people who refused to care for the poor (Isa. 1:10–17; Ezek. 16:49; Amos 4:1–11). Two brief references in the New Testament suggest that the sins of the cities were dissolute habits, fornication, and unnatural lusts (2 Pet. 2:4–10; Jude 6–7).

25. Deut. 23:3–6 insists that no Ammonite or Moabite should be allowed in Israelite worship.

26. Martin Luther, *Luther's Works: Lectures on Genesis, Chapters 15–20*, vol. 3 (St. Louis: Concordia Publishing House, 1961), 308–10.

27. The rape of the daughters seemed less offensive than the rape of the men, because at least the sex was "natural" with the women. Homosexual sex in this cultural context was considered unnatural because it did not produce children and because a man was forced to take on the role of a woman.

28. Some commentators suggest that the story of Lot's wife was told to explain the presence of salt and rock formations that were shaped like a woman.

29. I am indebted to Kyle Dipre for these insights.

30. Compare this story with that of Tamar in Gen. 38. She slept with her father-in-law in order to conceive a child.

31. John Calvin argued that Isaac would have wanted children from the beginning of the marriage and would not have waited until twenty years had passed to offer prayers. He wrote, "Reason dictates that these prayers had continued through many years" (Commentary on Genesis 25:21). Calvin does not read Scripture literally and is willing to make these reasonable adjustments to clarify the story.

32. Gen. 25 describes Esau selling his birthright to Jacob for a bowl of stew. The narrator claimed that Esau "despised his birthright" and did not respect his inheritance (v. 34). Some commentators conclude that Rebekah (and God) preferred Jacob because he was more worthy.

33. Compare the story of Samson's mother below. She received an oracle from God regarding the birth of her son, and her husband Manoah demanded that God speak to him directly.

34. See examples of unusual blessings in Gen. 48:8–22 and 49:2–13.

35. See the chapter on blessing in Barbara Brown Taylor, *An Altar in the World* (New York: HarperOne, 2009), 193–209.

36. The fact that Esau was willing to reconcile with Jacob when he returned two decades later suggests that Esau had not held on to his murderous rage.

37. See the section on Rebekah.

38. A Jewish commentator suggested that Leah and Rachel had collaborated in the deception of Jacob. Rachel was hiding under the bed and talking, so that Jacob heard her voice! Sandy Eisenberg Sasso and Peninnah Schram, *Jewish Stories of Love and Marriage: Folktales, Legends, and Letters* (Lanham, MD: Rowman & Littlefield, 2015), 18.

39. For a more positive fictional view of what the relationships between these women might have been like, see Anita Diamant, *The Red Tent* (New York: St. Martin's Press, 1997).

40. "Hired" is the same word used to describe Jacob's relationship with Laban.

41. Later in their lives both women resented their father for selling them to Jacob (31:15). Perhaps they realized that Laban had put them in a competitive situation for his own benefit. They were eager to leave Laban when Jacob wanted to move back home to his family.

42. I heard a sermon on Jacob in which the preacher said that you can't be in a serious relationship with God and not find yourself on the run. He cited Jacob, Jonah, and Moses as characters who were on the run. Does that mean that biblical women who were pregnant, nursing, or responsible for small children could not have been in a serious relationship with God? They were certainly not free to be "on the run." This illustrates the problem of defining spirituality only in terms of male experience.

43. Par Westling used this phrase in a sermon on the text.

44. For a fictional treatment of this perspective, see Diamant, *Red Tent*.

45. See Lyn Bechtel, "What If Dinah Is Not Raped? (Genesis 34)," *Journal for the Study of the Old Testament* 62 (June 1994): 19–36.

46. Compare the silence and inaction of King David when his daughter Tamar was raped by his son Amnon (2 Sam. 13).

47. Despite the hotheadedness of the brothers, Abraham Kuyper, *Women of the Old Testament*, 2nd ed. (Grand Rapids: Zondervan, 1936), insisted that the tragedy was Dinah's fault. An "avalanche of catastrophes" occurred because of her mistake. She caused her brothers to misuse the rite of circumcision, destroy the city, and take the women and children as spoil (literally, "prey"). Kuyper feared that there were many young women in his time whose desire to see the world could destroy religion in the home and cause the death of the soul (34–36).

48. For examples, see Nicholas Kristof and Sheryl WuDunn, *Half the Sky: Turning Oppression into Opportunity for Women Worldwide* (New York: Alfred A. Knopf, 2009), 81–87.

49. Note the connections between shame, violation, and invasion. The terrorist attacks of 9/11 in the United States and the bombings in Paris in November 2015 felt as invasive to the nations as a rape might feel to an individual.

50. See the television show *Madam Secretary* for examples of creative responses to national conflicts.

51. This unusual biblical custom is called levirate marriage. If a man died without a son, the man's brother married the widow, and the firstborn son was considered the son of the dead man (Deut. 25:5–10). This practice ensured that a childless widow had a son to support her. It was also important because the Israelites did not believe in an afterlife, but that people lived on in their children who preserved their names and kept their memory alive.

52. Martin Luther King Jr., "Letter from a Birmingham Jail," in *Why We Can't Wait* (New York: Harper & Row, 1963), 84.

53. Martin Luther used Tamar's story to advise that if a woman could not get pregnant, then with her husband's permission she could sleep with his brother in an attempt to have a baby.

54. See Prov. 5–7 for warnings about the dangerous woman: "The lips of a loose woman drip honey, and her speech is smoother than oil; but in the end she is bitter as wormwood, sharp as a two-edged sword" (5:3–4).

Chapter 2: Women of the Exodus

1. See the section on Potiphar's wife in chap. 1 for more information about Joseph.

2. Scholars are not certain about the ethnic identity of the midwives. The word "Hebrew" was a synonym for "Israelite" and emphasized their low status. "Hebrew midwives" could mean either Hebrew women who served as midwives to their own people or Egyptian women who cared for the Hebrew women. It seems unlikely that the king would assume that the Hebrew women would kill the children of their own people, but he was an arrogant man who easily commanded others to engage in brutality. If the women were Egyptian, it is even

more striking that they refused to obey because they feared God. Most scholars think that the midwives were Hebrew.

3. The midwives in this story have names (Shiphrah and Puah), while many biblical women do not. Shiphrah and Puah are remembered. The powerful pharaoh is not named, and scholars cannot definitively identify him.

4. This answer might have confirmed his assumption that the Israelite women were less fragile than the Egyptian women. People in power sometimes assume that their slaves are less than human and more like animals. Slave owners in the nineteenth century thought that female slaves could simply squat in a field to deliver their babies, while their more delicate Anglo wives needed a doctor's care and a week to recover.

5. They are unnamed in Exod. 2 but are identified in Exod. 6:20 and Num. 26:59.

6. The Hebrew word for "basket" is the same word used for "ark" in the story of Noah and the flood in Gen. 6–9. Obviously Noah's ark was much larger, but both protected those inside from the dangerous water.

7. Miriam is identified as the sister of Aaron, who is Moses' brother. No other sister is mentioned, so it is assumed that she is the sister who kept watch. See the section on Miriam in this chapter.

8. The author of the book of Hebrews gave equal credit to Amram even though he did not take any action in Exodus. "By faith Moses was hidden by his parents for three months after his birth, because they saw the child was beautiful; and they were not afraid of the king's edict" (Heb. 11:23).

9. Terence Fretheim noted that she "came down" to the river, she "saw" the basket, and she "heard" the baby crying (Exod. 2:5–6). Her actions parallel God's actions in Exod. 3:7–8: "Then the LORD said, 'I have observed the misery of my people who are in Egypt; I have heard their cry . . . , and I have come down to deliver them from the Egyptians.'" Pharaoh's daughter acts like God! In rescuing Moses, she was doing God's work. Fretheim, *Exodus* (Louisville, KY: John Knox Press, 1991), 38.

10. Many other examples could be cited, particularly in the civil rights movement. See the movie *Selma* (2014). No one person could overturn segregation, but a series of small actions, bus boycotts, marches, sit-ins, and voter registration drives eventually brought about change.

11. See references to God as a midwife in Pss. 22:9–10; 71:6; and Isa. 66:9. Virginia Ramey Mollenkott discusses these texts in *The Divine Feminine* (New York: Crossroad Books, 1983). Jennifer Worth's book *Call the Midwife* (New York: Penguin Group USA, 2012) and the PBS television show of the same name also provide powerful examples of the role of the midwife.

12. Fred Rogers, *The Mister Rogers Parenting Book: Helping to Understand Your Young Child* (Philadelphia: Running Press Book Publishers, 2002), 107.

13. See the previous section on the midwives and mothers for a fuller description of these women and their roles.

14. The sister is not identified but commentators assume she was Miriam. A genealogy in Num. 26:59 reports that Amram and Jochebed had three children: Aaron, Moses, and Miriam.

15. The entry into Canaan and defeat of those people had not yet occurred at the time of the song, since the Israelites were still on the banks of the Red Sea. Because of these references to events that happened later, scholars think that this long version of the song was added to the text much later.

16. When scholars analyze the layers of editing that occurred to produce the current version of the Bible, they believe it was more common for something unexpected to be replaced by something expected. Miriam singing the song would be unexpected, so it is more likely that Miriam as the original singer would be changed to Moses than it would be for Miriam to replace Moses. See Phyllis Trible, "Bringing Miriam out of the Shadows," *Bible Review* 5, no. 1 (February 1989): 14–25, 34.

17. See the following section for further discussion of Zipporah and her marriage to Moses.

18. Miriam's name appears first in v. 1, and the form of the verb "complained" is third-person feminine singular ("she complained") rather than third-person plural ("they complained"). This suggests that Aaron's name might have been added later.

19. Her punishment was relatively light compared to what others received when they challenged Moses. In Num. 16 three men and their families were swallowed up by an earthquake. In Num. 11 those who complained were struck down with a plague.

20. Elizabeth Cady Stanton argued that Miriam would have been a better leader than her brothers. "If Miriam had helped plan the journey to Canaan, it would no doubt have been accomplished in forty days instead of forty years." If Miriam had been in charge, the Israelites would have experienced peace and prosperity rather than constant war with other nations. *The Woman's Bible*, vol. 1 (1895–98; repr., Seattle, WA: Coalition Task Force on Women and Religion, 1974), 103.

21. Carol Lakey Hess, "Reclaiming Ourselves: A Spirituality for Women's Empowerment," in *Women, Gender, and Christian Community*, ed. Jane Douglass and James Kay (Louisville, KY: Westminster John Knox Press, 1997), 143–46.

22. Sheryl Sandberg, *Lean In: Women, Work and the Will to Lead* (New York: Alfred A. Knopf, 2013).

23. I am indebted to my student Kelcee Sykes for this insight. She wrote, "I think [Miriam] can handle being the bad guy for one story."

24. The well seems to have been the ancient equivalent of a singles bar. Abraham's servant found Isaac's future wife Rebekah at a well, and Jacob met Rachel at a well.

25. Jonathan Kirsch noted that the phrase "bridegroom of blood" might

have been common in a culture where circumcision was performed immediately before marriage. *The Harlot by the Side of the Road: Forbidden Tales of the Bible* (New York: Ballantine Books, 1997), 159.

26. Fretheim, *Exodus*, 79–81.

27. Zipporah and the children are mentioned briefly in Exod. 18:1–6, when her father brought them to Moses after the Israelites had escaped from Egypt. Did Moses prefer to avoid being encumbered by family while negotiating with Pharaoh? Did he want to spare her the uncertainty? Was she safer at home with her father? Or had she left Moses in anger after this bizarre incident and taken the children back to Midian?

28. Some commentators wonder if the fact that she knew what to do meant that she served in a priestly role in Midian, along with her father, who is identified as a priest. There is a ritual or magical quality to her actions and words.

29. Walter Brueggemann, "Exodus," in *The New Interpreter's Bible*, vol. 1 (Nashville: Abingdon Press, 1998), 718.

30. C. S. Lewis, *The Lion, the Witch and the Wardrobe* (New York: Collier Books, 1950), 64.

31. The Israelites believed that after their death, people lived on and were remembered through their children, their name, and their land. If Zelophehad did not have land, he would be forgotten.

32. The Israelites had been wandering for forty years and had been slaves in Egypt for many years before that. Did they really have such rigid rules about property when they had not owned any for centuries? Perhaps they had spent the forty years of aimless wandering developing the rules for an ideal society! Or perhaps the story was edited much later, and the patrilinear pattern was assumed to be true for this time as well.

33. Religious attitudes about wealth and poverty have shifted dramatically since the time of the Old Testament and its emphasis on equality. Question 27 of the Heidelberg Catechism (1563) asserts that prosperity and poverty are assigned as part of God's providence. No one is rich or poor by chance but by God's direction. The Israelites believed (in theory if not in practice) that radical economic differences were sinful. The Heidelberg Catechism suggests that radical income differences are God's will.

34. Some Jewish rabbis describe themselves as "expanders." They argue that the Torah set some precedents but did not answer every question. Rabbis needed to expand the law to deal with contemporary situations, just as the daughters wanted to expand the law to preserve their father's name. Tal Ilan, "The Daughters of Zelophehad and Women's Inheritance: The Biblical Injunction and Its Outcome," in Athalya Brenner, ed., *Exodus to Deuteronomy*, A Feminist Companion to the Bible, 2nd ser. (Sheffield, UK: Sheffield Academic Press, 2000), 178.

Chapter 3: Women of the Promised Land

1. See the section on Ruth and Naomi in this chapter for a discussion of Boaz, who married Ruth the Moabite.

2. Some commentators note a contrast between Achsah getting off the donkey unassisted, and the dead concubine being placed on a donkey in Judg. 19. The treatment of women grows increasingly dismal in the book of Judges. In the beginning of Judges, where her story is told again, Achsah is a relatively strong and independent woman who is able to ask her father for land. At the end of Judges, the concubine is a passive woman who is completely at the mercy of her husband and father, who both fail to protect her.

3. The Septuagint (Greek) and Vulgate (Latin) versions of the Old Testament both translate the verse to say that Othniel initially urged Achsah to ask for land. They made the two actions (who is urged to ask and who actually asks) more consistent.

4. Nicholas Kristof and Sheryl WuDunn, *Half the Sky: Turning Oppression into Opportunity for Women Worldwide* (New York: Alfred A. Knopf, 2009), 186–87.

5. *Lappidoth* has a feminine ending, which makes it an unusual name for a man. Commentators think that it is possible Deborah was not married, in part because nothing more is said about her husband, and in part because she had an unusual amount of freedom.

6. The celebrative song in Judg. 5 suggests that God sent so much rain that the river flooded and Sisera's chariots were bogged down in the mud.

7. See the following section for a discussion of Jael.

8. Abraham Kuyper, *Women of the Old Testament*, 2nd ed. (Grand Rapids: Zondervan, 1936), 63.

9. Jennell Riddick, sermon preached in a class in the Association of Chicago Theological Schools Doctor of Ministry Program, July 3, 2015.

10. The poetic version in chap. 5 includes some slightly different details. In the poem, she did not invite him into her tent or cover him with a blanket. Instead of milk, she gave him a bowl of curds or yogurt. She did not kill him when he was asleep, but she crushed his head and he fell at her feet.

11. I am indebted to my student research assistant Kelcee Sykes for this insight.

12. See the vignette at the end of the song in Judg. 5. It mocks Sisera's mother, who is waiting for him to come home, not knowing that he is dead. He is late, so she speculates that he and his men are dividing the spoils and distributing two women (literally, a "womb or two") for every man. In warfare, both sides make the other out to be particularly evil and inhumane, while justifying their own violent actions.

13. See the documentary *Pray the Devil Back to Hell* (2008) for more information on this movement. Sirleaf received the Nobel Peace Prize in 2011.

14. Two other judges, Othniel and Samson, also received the spirit of the

Lord (Judg. 3:10; 13:25; 14:19; 15:14). Receiving this spirit did not guarantee success, however, particularly for Samson. See the sections on Samson's mother and Delilah below.

15. The NRSV translates as "whoever," but the Hebrew word could also mean "whatever," which might suggest he was thinking of an animal rather than a person.

16. Phyllis Trible, *Texts of Terror* (Philadelphia: Fortress Press, 1984), 97. Trible wrote, "The making of the vow is an act of unfaithfulness. Jephthah desires to bind God rather than embrace the gift of the Spirit. What comes to him freely, he seeks to earn and manipulate. The meaning of his words is doubt, not faith; it is control, not courage. To such a vow the deity makes no reply."

17. J. Cheryl Exum, *Fragmented Women: Feminist (Sub)versions of Biblical Narratives* (Sheffield, UK: Sheffield Academic Press, 1993), 34.

18. Elizabeth Cady Stanton, *The Woman's Bible*, vol. 2 (1895–98; repr., Seattle: Coalition Task Force on Women and Religion, 1974), 25–26.

19. Jephthah is mentioned in Heb. 11:32 with Gideon, Barak, and Samson, all of whom had somewhat flawed faith. See sections on Deborah and Delilah.

20. God does not approve of human sacrifice, except for the strange story in Gen. 22, when God asked Abraham to sacrifice his son Isaac. Abraham did as God asked, but God intervened just before Abraham killed Isaac and pointed out a ram that Abraham should sacrifice instead. Did God desire this sacrifice or was it purely a test of Abraham's faith? Such a test makes God appear rather manipulative and mean-spirited. Some commentators have wished that God would have provided a similar alternative when Jephthah was sacrificing his daughter. The sacrifice of Isaac seems to have been God's idea, while the sacrifice of his daughter was Jephthah's choice. God usually does not intervene in human activities and impinge on human freedom.

21. Kristof and WuDunn, *Half the Sky*, 14–16.

22. See Num. 6 for a further explanation of the term. Nazirites promised not to drink alcohol, touch dead bodies, or cut their hair.

23. Unlike some other judges, Samson was not very effective, and he did not completely defeat the Philistines.

24. J. Clinton McCann, *Judges* (Louisville, KY: Westminster John Knox Press, 2002), 96.

25. My student Kyle Dipre observed that Manoah is somewhat similar to Peter in the transfiguration story (Mark 9:2–8). He wanted to make dwellings for Moses and Elijah so they could live on the mountain. He wanted to capture the moment of glory and continue it.

26. This is one of Anne Lamott's favorite phrases and appears in many of her books and blog posts.

27. See the previous section on Samson's mother for a description of his birth and young adulthood.

28. See Judg. 13–15 for a description of these episodes.

29. When Samson visited a prostitute in Gaza in Judg. 16:1, the prostitute was clearly labeled as such.

30. This detail hints that he might have been exhausted from a sexual encounter.

31. It is helpful to explore some of the paintings of Samson and Delilah and also the 1949 movie *Samson and Delilah*. Both art and movie tend to romanticize the events into a tragic love story. See J. Cheryl Exum, *Plotted, Shot, and Painted: Cultural Representations of Biblical Women* (Sheffield, UK: Sheffield Academic Press, 1996), 175–237.

32. The details are similar to a story in Gen. 19, where two angels visited Abraham's nephew Lot. The men of Sodom also wanted to rape the visitors, and Lot offered instead his two virgin daughters. The angels then blinded the men at the door, and everyone escaped. In the Judges version of the story, there were no angels. The men at the door were not blinded, and the woman was not spared.

33. See John Thompson, *Writing the Wrongs: Women of the Old Testament among Biblical Commentators from Philo through the Reformation* (New York: Oxford, 2001), 179–221.

34. In the fourth season of *Downton Abbey*, the lady's maid Anna was brutally raped by a visiting manservant. Anna said repeatedly in the following episodes that she felt dirty and ashamed and at fault.

35. Does the narrator write this with a straight face? Or is the narrator satirizing the pretentious piety and misplaced compassion of the Israelites?

36. This would have been a humiliating move, because the Israelites despised the Moabites (Deut. 23:3–6). Their women were considered especially dangerous to Israelite men.

37. She referred to the practice of levirate marriage. If a man died without having children, his brother should marry the wife and have a child with her who would serve as the dead brother's heir. See the story of Tamar in Gen. 38.

38. This exchange raises some questions. If Naomi knew about Boaz, why didn't she ask him for help? If Boaz knew he was a relative, and Naomi was poor, why didn't he offer to help or to marry Ruth? Did he think he was too old for her? Was he reluctant to marry a Moabite woman?

39. The property and the existence of the other relative (Ruth 4:1–4) raise questions. If Naomi owned property, why did she claim to be completely empty? Why didn't this relative offer to help them? The presence of the relative may explain why Boaz did not act sooner.

40. Some commentators argue that the intimate bond in this story is between Ruth and Naomi, not Ruth and Boaz. They cite as evidence the radical nature of the vows Ruth made to Naomi. These words demonstrated not merely friendship but also deep love and commitment. The text also says in 1:14 that Ruth "clung to" Naomi, which is the same word used in Gen. 2 when the man

"clings to" his wife. Did Ruth marry Boaz because he could provide financial stability and the cover of propriety?

41. Kathleen Farmer, "The Book of Ruth," in *The New Interpreter's Bible*, vol. 2 (Nashville: Abingdon Press, 1998), 893. Farmer wrote that the story "encourages us to see not just that we *ought* to be like Ruth but that we *are* like Naomi. And when we see ourselves reflected in the story as we really are (rather than as we think we ought to be), the good news comes to us as revelation rather than application."

42. See the section on Jephthah's daughter for a discussion of Jephthah's vow and the impact it had on his daughter.

43. Danna Nolan Fewell and David Gunn, *Gender, Power, and Promise* (Nashville: Abingdon Press, 1993), 138.

Chapter 4: Women of Israel and Judah

1. See the section on Bathsheba. The story of Bathsheba and David (2 Sam. 11:1–15) appears in the lectionary two weeks after this one about Michal and David. Does the portrayal of Michal as a cold, difficult woman in this passage make it easier to sympathize with David for being attracted to Bathsheba?

2. When David fought the giant Goliath in 1 Sam. 17, David referred to him twice as that "uncircumcised Philistine." Israelite men were circumcised as a mark of being set apart to God. Most other men were not circumcised and this signified both their status as non-Israelites and their worship of foreign gods.

3. "Something had changed for Michal. Someone cared enough for her to weep." Danna Nolan Fewell and David Gunn, *Gender, Power, and Promise* (Nashville: Abingdon Press, 1993), 153.

4. On the first effort to retrieve the ark, the oxen stumbled, the cart tipped, and a man named Uzzah put out his hand to steady the ark. This action made God angry enough to strike Uzzah dead. David was angry and frightened and cautious when he tried again to retrieve the ark. The lectionary omits this strange story, and what remains is an upbeat tale about the enthusiastic celebration of a valued religious object. Everybody is happy and no one gets hurt. The real story is far more complicated.

5. Her speech is the longest by a woman in the Old Testament.

6. She gave birth to a son, Chileab, who was David's second son, born after Amnon. He did not seem to play any role in the later political maneuvering over which son would succeed David.

7. See the section on Saul's daughter Michal for a more detailed discussion of Saul.

8. Walter Brueggemann, *First and Second Samuel* (Louisville, KY: John Knox Press, 1990), 192.

9. Consulting spirits and using other forms of magic were practices often used by other nations. In part the Israelites were told to avoid these practices as a

way to maintain their distinctive identity. These practices also offered an alternative way to find answers and guidance, but the Israelites were supposed to trust in God completely for guidance.

10. Abraham Kuyper, *Women of the Old Testament*, 2nd ed. (Grand Rapids: Zondervan, 1936), 102.

11. Deirdre Levinson, "The Psychopathology of King Saul," in *Out of the Garden: Women Writers on the Bible,* ed. Christina Büchmann and Celina Spiegel (New York: Fawcett Columbine, 1994), 123–41.

12. I am indebted to Kyle Dipre for this insight.

13. See J. Cheryl Exum, *Plotted, Shot, and Painted: Cultural Representations of Biblical Women* (Sheffield, UK: Sheffield Academic Press, 1996), 19–53. The artwork can be found on Google Images or through the link to biblical art at The Text This Week (www.textweek.com). See the 1951 movie *David and Bathsheba* for an example of romanticizing their relationships. Clips can be found on YouTube.

14. Some preachers have used this brief reference to make the homiletical point that idleness leads to sin. Others have suggested that David was too old for battle, which led to a midlife crisis and depression that clouded his judgment.

15. Obviously, the narrator was not in the room at the time, but the clipped tone gives no indication of intimacy. A similar situation appears on the television show *Scandal.* President Fitzgerald Grant has an affair with Olivia Pope. On a couple of occasions, Secret Service agents appear at her door and order her to come with them because the president wants to see her. She protests but does not have the freedom to say no.

16. Bathsheba later gave birth to Solomon, who succeeded David as king. Bathsheba appears in 1 Kgs. 1–2 and possesses power and influence with both David and Solomon.

17. See 2 Sam. 13–16. David's son Amnon raped his sister Tamar (see the following section on Tamar). Her brother Absalom killed Amnon. Absalom staged a coup against his father and raped David's concubines in public view. Neither Bathsheba nor David's wives nor daughter Tamar nor infant son had sinned, but they suffered grief, death, or violation as part of his punishment.

18. Brueggemann, *First and Second Samuel,* 252.

19. Bruce Birch outlines three strategies commentators use to excuse David. "I and II Samuel," in *The New Interpreter's Bible,* vol. 2 (Nashville: Abingdon Press, 1998), 1288–90.

20. Examples of the abuse of political power can be found in recent television shows such as *Scandal, House of Cards,* and *The Good Wife.*

21. A similar sense of entitlement has been particularly pervasive in some universities where athletes accused of sexual assault are protected. Defending the sports program is more important than conducting a fair investigation.

22. Recently a youth pastor wrote an article confessing that he had

committed adultery with a young woman in his youth group. He failed to mention that he was actually guilty of statutory rape because she was underage.

23. Tamar and Amnon had the same father, David, but different mothers. Tamar's brother Absalom, who will be introduced below, was a full brother who shared the same father and mother.

24. See previous sections on Bathsheba, Michal, and Abigail.

25. There is no record that Tamar married and had children. She apparently lived out her life in Absalom's house. Later Absalom had a daughter whom he named Tamar.

26. See Lewis Smedes, *Shame and Grace* (San Francisco: HarperSanFrancisco, 1993). He distinguishes between appropriate—or true—shame, which people ought to feel when they have done something wrong, and false shame, which people feel when they have been violated or told that they are not good enough.

27. See Maya Angelou, *I Know Why the Caged Bird Sings* (New York: Ballantine Books, 2009), 77–88, where she reflects on being sexually assaulted by her stepfather when she was about eight years old. She blamed herself for the assault, because initially she liked being affectionately held.

28. Certainly not all churches and pastors have done these things. In the last decade, religious awareness of and sensitivity to victims of abuse have improved significantly. But in general, the Christian tradition has frequently tolerated abuse.

29. I am indebted to my student Mary Bridget McCarthy for her insight about the importance of writing a new ending to a sad story that ends in despair. She was speaking about her role as Martha in Lillian Hellman's play *The Children's Hour.*

30. Having sex with the king's wife or concubine was the equivalent of sitting on the king's throne, because if a man could "take" the king's sexual partner, he must have the power to "take" the king's role or office as well.

31. The skeptical reader might wonder if the entire exchange was a little too convenient. Was David simply looking for an excuse to eliminate Saul's descendants and fabricated this story as a way to claim divine approval? The story raises some troubling questions about the nature of God and divine wrath. Does God punish innocent young men for the sins a king committed decades earlier? The Israelites might have believed that God acted this way, but do we?

32. Eugene Peterson, *First and Second Samuel* (Louisville, KY: Westminster John Knox Press, 1999), 245–46.

33. For a powerful example of raw evil and disregard for human life, see the movie *Unbroken* (2014) or the book with the same title by Laura Hillenbrand (New York: Random House, 2010).

34. See a hymn by Desmond Tutu, "Goodness Is Stronger than Evil," *Glory to God* (Louisville, KY: Westminster John Knox Press, 2013), 750.

35. Sheba, or Saba, might have been in Ethiopia but was probably in the Arabian Peninsula in what is now Yemen.

36. A few commentators have speculated that these words were a statement of her faith and that she had converted to the Israelite religion. Other commentators say there is no evidence for such a claim. She referred to Solomon's God, not her own.

37. See the detailed description of Solomon's palace and the temple in 1 Kgs. 4–7. "Forced labor" is mentioned in 4:6 and 5:13.

38. See Lawrence Mishel and Alyssa Davis, "Top CEOs Make 300 Times More than Typical Workers," Economic Policy Institute, June 21, 2015, http:// www.epi.org/publication/top-ceos-make-300-times-more-than-workers-pay -growth-surpasses-market-gains-and-the-rest-of-the-0-1-percent/; and Peter Van Buren, "Walmart Wages Are the Main Reason People Depend on Food Stamps," *The Nation*, February 16, 2016, https://www.thenation.com/article/walmart-wages -are-the-main-reason-people-depend-on-food-stamps/.

39. Beth Carroll, "When 'Choice' Is a Name for God," *The Twelve* (blog), August 19, 2015, http://blog.perspectivesjournal.org/2015/08/19/when-choice -is-a-name-for-god/.

40. Frederick Buechner paraphrased her question, "Are you a king or a cup custard?" See "Weekly Sermon Illustration: Ahab, Naboth, and Jezebel," Frederick Buechner Center, June 6, 2016, http://www.frederickbuechner.com/blog /2016/6/6/weekly-sermon-illustration-ahab-naboth-and-jezebel.

41. Some commentators claim that she was trying to seduce Jehu, which would provide evidence of her "whoredom." Jezebel was probably politically astute enough to know that would not work. Other commentaries suggest that she dressed up to preserve her dignity and remind everyone of her status as queen mother.

42. Psychologists refer to this as projection. A more recent example can be found in southern slaveholding culture in the nineteenth century. White male masters or overseers who raped slave women often justified their actions by saying that the women had tempted or seduced them. African American women were characterized as hypersexual tramps who lacked modesty and virtue. The white men claimed to be helpless in the face of such potent sexuality. Their wives at times colluded in this, perhaps because it was easier to excuse the husband for being seduced by a powerful woman than for raping a powerless one.

43. For an excellent discussion of Jezebel, see Phyllis Trible, "The Odd Couple: Elijah and Jezebel," in *Out of the Garden: Women Writers on the Bible*, ed. Christina Büchmann and Celina Spiegel (New York: Fawcett Columbine, 1994), 166–79.

Chapter 5: Women and the Prophets

1. See the preceding section on Jezebel for more information about Elijah.

2. Sidon was north of Israel. Its people worshiped the Canaanite god Baal. The despised Jezebel was a native of Sidon.

3. Some preachers have used this text to proclaim a simple cause-and-effect relationship between faith and survival. The woman believed and her faith was rewarded. If poor people simply trust God, God will miraculously provide for them. At worst, a preacher of the prosperity gospel might say that though the widow had almost nothing, she gave what she had to Elijah the pastor and was rewarded with far greater blessings. If church members give graciously to their pastor, they will be rewarded too.

4. See the story of the widow of Zarephath, in which a woman has only a bit of oil and flour, but it lasts until the end of the famine.

5. See Nicholas Kristof and Sheryl WuDunn, *Half the Sky: Turning Oppression into Opportunity for Women Worldwide* (New York: Alfred A. Knopf, 2009), 3–45, for examples of desperately poor parents selling their children and ways that readers of the book might make a difference.

6. Kristof and WuDunn, *Half the Sky*, 171–72. Ensuring that girls have feminine hygiene products is another small but significant way to help girls get an education.

7. The logistics of this story are confusing. Elisha asked that she come to him, but had his servant Gehazi ask her what she needed. Then, as if she were no longer present, Elisha asked Gehazi what she needed, and then Elisha asked her to come back.

8. The men assumed that she wanted a child although she did not mention it. Her feelings about the conception and birth are not recorded. She might have come to terms with infertility and did not want to get her hopes up.

9. Elijah had performed an almost identical action when he healed the son of the widow of Zarephath.

10. Hospitality is not a gift confined to women. My friend Jack, a ninety-three-year-old widower, was a superb host who set a beautiful table and prepared an elegant meal.

11. Her words also resonate with the first question and answer of the Heidelberg Catechism. "What is your only comfort in life and in death?" "That I am not my own, but belong—body and soul, in life and in death—not to myself but to my faithful Savior Jesus Christ."

12. For examples of female prophets, see the sections about Miriam and Deborah. Neh. 6:14 mentions a female prophet named Noadiah.

13. Josiah died before he turned forty, murdered by the treacherous king of Egypt who had supposedly come for a peaceful meeting. Some commentators concluded that Huldah was a false prophet, because she had told Josiah that he would die in peace.

14. The paternity of the children is not clear. The text says regarding the first child that she "bore him" (Hosea) a son (Hos. 1:3). It says of the next two that she "bore" a child. Was the author saying that the second and third children were

fathered by another man? Or was this economy of language? The story does not explicitly say that she had another relationship.

15. Jezreel was a place of destruction. *Lo-ruhamah* means "not pitied." *Lo-ammi* means "not my people." English equivalents might be naming a child Auschwitz, Columbine, or Rejected.

16. The Revised Common Lectionary avoids the problematic aspects of this passage by using only this positive section in 2:14–22.

Chapter 6: Other Women in the Old Testament

1. If this text is read with the satirical tone the author seems to intend, it may help to convey a sense of humor about human foibles that will make it easier for a congregation to look honestly at their own fears and tendencies to overreact.

2. This is not necessarily what men actually think, but it is what the media portray as male opinion. In reality, men might actually prefer intelligent women who are comfortable with their bodies and have higher goals than simply pleasing men. The media do not always give men credit for having a brain.

3. Many examples could be cited. The Indiana governor (and future vice president) made a hasty statement about religious freedom in the summer of 2015 that he had to retract. Denominations sometimes insist on making a hasty decision about a controversial matter rather than talking through the difficult issues.

4. See the movie *Juno* (2007) for a powerful illustration. Juno tells her parents she is pregnant, and her stepfather says, "I didn't know you were that kind of girl."

5. See the previous section for background information on the book of Esther.

6. I once titled a sermon "Her Royal Hesitance: Queen Esther." I noted that she was deferential and obedient and not a person of radical courage. After doing more reading, I realized that the title did not give her enough credit. There is more to Esther than hesitance.

7. Esther is a complicated book with many nuances and technical details. See the commentaries by Carol Bechtel, *Esther* (Louisville, KY: John Knox Press, 2002), and Linda Day, *Esther* (Nashville: Abingdon Press, 2005), for additional background.

8. The passive voice is used several times in the book as a way to avoid taking responsibility for actions or decisions. Here the king implies that someone else had banished her, instead of him and his advisers.

9. Again the passive voice suggests that no one was responsible for issuing the decree.

10. Samuel Wells and George Sumner, *Esther and Daniel* (Grand Rapids: Brazos Press, 2013), 63.

11. The Hebrew word *satan* always appears in Job with the definite article,

"the"; it is not used as a proper name but as a descriptor. The Satan asked challenging questions but was not a red man with horns, a tail, and a pitchfork.

12. Cited in Robert Gordis, *The Book of God and Man: A Study of Job* (Chicago: University of Chicago Press, 1965), 11.

13. Perhaps it is easier for commentators to criticize her for impiety than it is to discuss the disturbing picture of a God who is willing to allow the death of their ten children in order to prove a point to the Accuser.

14. Carol Bechtel, *Job and the Life of Faith: Wisdom for Today's World* (Pittsburgh: The Kerygma Program, 2004), 18–19.

15. Perhaps Job responded so harshly to her because she named something he thought but did not have the courage to name. In the remainder of the book he repeatedly articulates the arguments she raises here.

16. A church doing a sermon series on the fruits of the Spirit chose Job 1–2 to illustrate self-control, a virtue he definitely does not demonstrate in chaps. 3–37.

17. The word *hayil* is used twice in the book of Ruth. Boaz is called an *ish gibbor hayil*, which the NRSV translates as "prominent rich man" (2:1). Boaz referred to Ruth as *hayil* in 3:11, and the NRSV translates it as "worthy."

18. See Donna Partow, *Becoming the Woman God Wants Me to Be: A 90-Day Guide to Living the Proverbs 31 Life* (Grand Rapids: Revell, 2008). For a realistic and humorous discussion of taking this and other biblical texts too literally, see Rachel Held Evans, *A Year of Biblical Womanhood: How a Liberated Woman Found Herself Sitting on Her Roof, Covering Her Head, and Calling Her Husband "Master"* (Nashville: Thomas Nelson, 2012).

19. Anna Quindlen, *Lots of Candles, Plenty of Cake* (New York: Random House, 2012), 113–14. See Wednesday Martin, *Primates of Park Avenue* (New York: Simon & Schuster, 2015), for a memoir about manic mothers on the Upper East Side of New York City.

20. Lis Harris, *Holy Days: The World of a Hasidic Family* (New York: Simon & Schuster, 1985).

Index of Scriptures

Index of Names

Aaron, 43-45, 47, 48, 51, 189n7, 190n14
Abel, 9
Abigail, 100-102, 104, 176
Abiram, 51
Abner, 117
Abraham, 2, 4, 12-17, 21,185n9, 185nn13-14, 185n16, 190n24, 193n20
Absalom, 113, 114, 196n17, 197n25
Achsah, 60-62, 192nn2-3
Adam, 7-12, 125
Ahab, 123-26, 128, 130
Ahasuerus, 148, 152-55
Ammon, 18
Amnon, 112-16, 188n46, 195n6, 196n17
Amos, 141
Amran, 40, 189n8, 190n14

Barak, 63-68, 76, 193n19
Bathsheba, 3, 35, 100, 106, 108-12, 176, 196nn16-17
Benjamin, 26
Bilhah, 26
Boaz, 34, 57, 89-91, 194n38, 194n40, 201n17

Cain, 9
Caleb, 61
Chileab, 195n6
Chilion, 88

Dathan, 51
Daughters of Zelophehad, 50-54, 62
David, 3, 18, 26, 57, 90, 97-100, 101-4, 105-8, 109-12, 112-14, 116, 117-21, 123, 125, 177, 188n46, 195n2, 195n4, 196nn16-17
Deborah, 1, 63-67, 174, 192n5

Delilah, 3, 4, 57, 75, 78-82
Dinah, 4, 29-32, 35

Eleazar, 51
Eli, 94, 96
Elijah, 123-25, 128-31, 193n25
Elimelech, 88
Elisha, 131-38, 199n7
Elkanah, 93, 95, 96
Er, 33
Esau, 21-27, 187n32, 187n36
Esther, 148, 149, 151-57, 180, 181, 220n6
Eve, 1, 4, 7-12, 125, 170, 184n6

Gehazi, 134, 136, 199n7
Gideon, 193n19
Goliath, 97
Gomer, 5, 142-46, 199n14

Hagar, 3, 4, 12-17, 170, 185n9, 185n11, 185n16
Haman, 152-55
Hamor, 31
Hannah, 92-96, 168, 174, 176-77
Hosea, 5, 141, 142-46, 199n14
Huldah, 139-42, 199n13

Isaac, 6, 21-25, 187n16, 190n24, 193n20
Ishbaal, 117
Ishmael, 13-14, 16, 185n16

Jacob, 6, 21-29, 31-32, 35, 39, 187n32, 187n36, 190n24
Jael, 64, 66-70
Jehu, 124, 198n41
Jephthah, 3, 5, 57, 70-72, 74, 76, 93, 193n16, 193n19
Jephthah's daughter, 3, 70-72, 74, 174

Printed in the USA
CPSIA information can be obtained
at www.ICGtesting.com
LVHW020401300424
778799LV00001B/49